A MEMOIR ON HOW RUNNING KEPT ME MOVING THROUGH HARDSHIP AND TAUGHT ME TO FIND MY INNER STRENGTH

DID ANYONE TELL YOU THIS WAS GOING TO BE EASY?

LAUREL SLYCK

ISBN: 979-8-9857448-1-1 (Paperback)

ISBN: 979-8-9857448-2-8 (Hardcover)

ISBN: 979-8-9857448-0-4 (Ebook)

Contents

Dedication:

To my boys, Zeffrey and Columbus and to my babies who I carried but never got to hold, Phoenix and Orion

Disclaimer

Introduction

"I'm sorry," he said in a playful, but slightly concerned voice. His sturdy two-year-old body splashed in the tub as he looked at what appeared to be a splash of water spreading across my pants. "My water broke," I told him. "I'm sorry your water broke," he parroted back. He didn't know what he apologized for or what had gone wrong, but sensed my tension and high emotion. Since he was in the tub and I was quite obviously very wet, he thought the broken water must be something he should apologize for.

The next morning, I held my new baby in my arms. I glanced at the strong profile of my husband, saw the big-brother excitement in my older son, and I cried. They were tears of joy, maybe it was the first time in my life I had felt this happy. The tears came quietly as I held those boys close. That moment, dirty and distended, my body not quite my own, stinky and sore, I looked happiness in the face and embraced it. Perfection. It was there. Had I really helped create these two lives? Could I really claim that man as my husband? Was this really my family, all here and in my arms? And how many miles had I run getting here? How many hills, falls, triumphs, terrains? How did I find myself here at the end of this thousand-mile pregnancy, new life in my arms? And what would come next? Was I on the precipice, or a plateau? Life, abundant, surrounded me.

…And that's what I thought this book was going to be about. Me, running through my teens and to my mid-twenties and overcoming some hardships along the way. I even had the book titled, The Thousand Mile Pregnancy. I had surmounted obstacles along the way with a relentless drive to run and move forward. Simple. Easy. As it turns out, that was just the start. This book turned into so much more; a missive about growth, about how strength gathers, slowly over time, about love and moving forward, about letting go. Definitely there's the letting go. Letting go when your hands have held on as long as they can, your aching knuckles grip that last little bit of ledge. Moving when your soul tells you to, and when it tells you not to. Ever forward, because backward is back there, and next is up ahead. A 1000-mile pregnancy, yes, thousands and thousands more miles…that too. Life and death, love and pain, a memoir. Secrets are laid bare, shameful parts exposed and, in the mix, the things of which I am proudest are revealed. Some parts of this book are, admittedly dark. Some sections, I wanted to skip over, but it didn't feel true, so it's all in; dirty details and then some. I promise there are light parts too, and it's all mixed together because that's how it all happened. I've packaged it up in a way that I hope, helps. Helps you hope and gather and grow, knowing that someone has been there too. I hope too that even if no part of this feels familiar, that it at least reminds you that no matter what circumstances you're in, you have the power to change them and to get unstuck. Mostly, I hope that I've done well enough to inspire you to "give 'em hell," as my dad says, and don't stop moving. Ever forward, whether in running shoes or not.

Chapter 1
Building Blocks

"The beginning is the most important part of the work."

- Plato

Igraduated from high school on the seventh of June, turned eighteen on the fourteenth, and left home on the twenty-first. I was a soccer player then, thickly muscled and in what I thought was amazing shape. I was 5'6" and weighed one hundred and forty-two pounds. Not fat, but certainly not runner thin. I defined myself as a runner, because I ran, not because I really understood what it meant to "be a runner". I was about to embark, my life like miles of unmapped terrain, stretching and yawning before me. Before I get to graduation though, a little family background will help set the stage.

My mom was from the Finger Lakes in upstate New York, but her dad had been in the Navy, and they'd moved around quite a bit in her early childhood. Her dad was gone a lot and seemed to leave his wife pregnant most of the time when he left for extended periods, or at least that was the assumption. She had six siblings including an identical twin. My mom wasn't entirely convinced that her dad was the sole producer of all the progeny, given the timing of his intermittent presence. Her childhood was abusive and imbued with poverty and she learned exactly how she didn't want to parent and that she wanted to be something other than a continuation of that problematic legacy. She ran away from home, her dad with a gun in his hand, as the story goes, told her to never come back. She was seventeen or eighteen. The couple whom I knew as my grandparents legally adopted her and helped her through college and life. They had been friends of the family, had some inkling of what her youth had been like, and wanted to give her the gift of stability. She went to college to become a teacher and started working with special needs kids. She volunteered at a summer camp for disabled children where she met my father.

My dad. This intro could take pages, but I'll keep it short. My dad had two siblings, a brother twelve months his senior and a sister sixteen months his junior. The summer that the kids were four, three, and almost two, they fell victim to the heartbreak of polio. One night, all three kids went to bed but only their older brother woke up as usual in the morning. When my grandmother went to check on the other two, they were already experiencing the paralysis of polio and were struggling to breathe. An ambulance rushed them away to the hospital where my dad's first memory is of an un-anesthetized tracheotomy. They didn't have time to do anything except open his airway. He doesn't remember anything else of that morning. He and his sister spent almost a year in the hospital, her paralysis impacting an arm and a leg on one side of her body and his impacting his right arm and lung. He was a child who was different, long before differences were accepted. When I think about my paternal grandmother being a young mom with three healthy toddlers, putting them to bed one night, and the next day everything she knew about life that far had changed drastically. She must have been an amazing woman. I'd like to think she passed those traits on to me. That ability to keep going. Visiting your babies in iron lungs while taking care of a four-year-old, seeing them gain back some ability but knowing that they'd never be the same as they were before. And she kept on. Her husband died, she remarried to gain stability. Her second husband turned out to be an alcoholic, but she did what she had to do to keep moving forward.

My dad became the funny guy and the party guy early in life and decided somehow, even though it was a temporal anomaly, to be a normal kid. He built and raced go-karts, was a reckless teenager, and was popular and social. His maternal aunt, whom we considered grandma, contributed a lot to his upbringing when the kids needed to be away from the alcoholism at home. To us, as kids, she was the purest, most joyful version of love we knew, and I imagine she was the same to my dad. He struggled a bit with staying serious enough about college to stick with it and it took a few attempts, with some factory work in between, to be sure that college was the right path. Eventually, though he probably wouldn't put it this way, he decided he wanted to show other kids who were different too, that they could be and do what "normal" kids do. He wanted to teach special education and volunteered at the summer camp where he met my mom.

So, there they were. Both having had their fair shares of painful pasts with an idealistic vision of how to make things better. They got married, ran a group home for special needs adults for a while, and then decided to have kids of their own. Their first baby was stillborn. There were no indications of anything amiss during the pregnancy, yet no baby came home with them. Grieving miscarriages and stillborn babies wasn't really a thing in 1977. My dad internalized it and my mom added one more tragedy to her list. I believe that with all the abuse she'd already suffered, she may have felt that she deserved these egregious kinds of wrongs. I think it felt like par for the course. A year later, I was born. They poured all their ideas for perfect parentage into me and, two years later, to my sister Alycia. My parents built and maintained a loving, healthy, happy home with family dinners and camping and communication and laughter. It was what neither of them had growing up and it was, for much of my childhood at least, idyllic. In 1982, my mom got offered a job teaching Special Education overseas in Okinawa, Japan and had just 48 hours to decide whether she'd take the job. My dad wasn't offered a job and would've had to either be a stay-at-home parent or find a job once they got there. They decided to take this great adventure and move the family to the other side of the world. Our introduction to Okinawa was a shock to the system, we stayed in an Okinawan-style motel for the first several days. The toilets were the type you squat over, instead of the "Western style" ones to which we were accustomed. After the initial shocks though, life resumed its normal cadence and the other side of the world became our home.

Chapter 2
Okinawa

"Over the years, I've given myself a thousand reasons to keep running, but it always comes back to where it started. It comes down to self-satisfaction and a sense of achievement."

- Steve Prefontaine

With that brief but essential background, I can skip ahead to high school. I started running cross country my freshman year when we were still living Okinawa. The move my parents had chosen to make all those years ago had worked out well and our family had been in Okinawa ever since. My brother was born there, at Kuwae hospital, eight years my junior. Because they taught at military schools, when they were stationed overseas, we could live either on or off base. I had run on and off for a couple of years before my freshman year, of my own accord. I'd go out on a hot, humid night and run around the Marine base we lived on. I had a couple of loops, probably between two and four miles, and I'd run them maybe once a week or whenever the mood hit. It wasn't structured, but I always felt a sense of accomplishment when I got home. Truth be told, I was inspired by and envious of the Marines and their cadence calling as they ran around base at five in the morning while I was up teasing my hair. I wanted that team feeling, that strength, the obvious muscles that they had. I didn't consider the masculinity or femininity in it; I wanted the strength they had. I wanted not to look like they did, but to be like they were. If they ran, so could I.

As freshman year approached, I wasn't entirely sure if I wanted to play volleyball with some of my friends or run cross country. My parents, however, dragged me along to a teacher picnic before the school year started. I met the high school cross country coach and he, without any pressure at all, said, yeah, come out for the team and told me when practice started. I think that knowing him in this tiny way was what pushed me to choose cross country. I was a little nervous about being a freshman but having this slight edge of knowing where to go and how to start was all I needed. I showed up on that first sweltering day in Keds. One might be tempted to think that August in a tropical climate paired with ill-fitting, white Keds, and no sports bra, would not have been a combination conducive to a life of running. As that first practice progressed, I fell so far behind the pack that I couldn't even see the person in front of me. My coach, Mr. Dawson, hung back with me and encouraged me to count light poles as milestones. "Just four more light poles and we'll walk two." It seemed like a fair deal. Mr. Dawson kindly but firmly kept me going that first day and with equal kindness and firmness encouraged me to quickly get new shoes. What a gift though; to stay back there with me and make it all seem reasonable. A little urge, a little encouragement, and I could feel myself improving. He was a coach, through and through.

By our first meet, I was running 5k in about twenty-seven minutes without any light pole breaks. People in front of me would stop to walk repeatedly and then take off, galloping away. However, there was something about stopping that just felt wrong to me. I wanted to be able to say at the end that I had "run" 5k. If walk breaks had lured me into their whispering webs of ease, I wouldn't be able to say that. I thought it was better to run a little slower, but to run the whole thing and build speed that I could apply across the whole distance. By the end of the season, I had broken twenty-four minutes and was running into the low twenty-threes occasionally. I felt like I was on my way to the Olympics. In a way, I was. We had a small team and the top four females and males got to compete in the All-Pacific Championships in Seoul, Korea, which were held every two years. I had set my sights on the Championship midway through the season, when the possibility loomed just within my reach and I realized that, even as a freshman, it was looking likely that I could go. I had been running third or fourth, occasionally fifth, on our team and I'd need to run at least fourth in the final meet to realize the goal. And I did it; I was going to Korea. I was fourteen years old and I'd gone from not being able to run a full practice to qualifying for an international championship in less than a year. Mind you, with only two high schools on the island, we had to go off-island for any big competitions. Still, I had worked hard and accomplished something hard. It felt good.

As the season wound down, I thought back on all that had happened. Those first blistering August days that had given me such an intense sock tan line that my legs and feet looked like they belonged to different people. I thought of the mid-season exhibition run we had done at half time of a football game. It was a one mile run under stadium lights. Six males and two females ran, and I had been lapped in front of packed bleachers. But everyone cheered for me as I finished on my own breaking seven minutes. Magic, pure magic. Probably the only time a stadium would ever chant my name, and it felt amazing. And finally, I thought of the end of the season and the trip to the championships, I was running on cloud nine. The championship meet itself in Korea was unremarkable. I ran slowly, cannot even remember my time, and our school placed poorly. While I remember tears and heartache of some of the older runners, there was nothing but bliss on my part. Thank goodness for Mr. Dawson and that pre-school-year teacher picnic. I learned so much from him that season. When I think of him now, I think of wisdom, solidity, and warmth. Outside of coaching, he taught psychology and oceanography and he loved what he did. He talked me through many early teenage issues that I didn't think any adult would want to listen to. He modeled the kind of adult I wanted to be. Learning from season one that he was the kind of person who was a part of the running community, and that runners took care of each other, sold me. That cold November trip to Korea left me glowing. That season left me a runner.

After my freshman year of high school, my family moved to Kaiserslautern, Germany. My parents had put in for a transfer and there were two open positions offered to them. It was a tumultuous move. We had been in Okinawa for eleven years and were all bound to the tiny island more tightly than any of us realized. We had even been absorbed into an Okinawan family and they were what we knew as extended family. Obasan, the grandmother, was our grandmother. Yoshiko was our crazy aunt who'd had a baby out of wedlock. Matsu-ojisan was our uncle who'd been injured by an American truck in the war when he ran into the road to try to grab the candy they were throwing out of it. Sugi was a second mom to my brother Jon. He went through periods of spending more time at her house than at ours. He was fluent in Japanese and English and loved by every Okinawan woman that he encountered. Saying goodbye to it, knowing it wouldn't be easy to see them or visit, was not as simple as just moving. But new adventures have their place too and my parents still wanted to see the world. They wanted us to know more and experience as much as we could as well. So, from tropical Okinawa to the Rheinland-Pfalz we went.

Chapter 3
Germany

"Wir leben alle unter dem gleichen Himmel, aber wir haben nicht alle den gleichen Horizont."
(We all live under the same sky, but we don't all have the same horizon)

-Konrad Adenauer

We got to Germany in August and could see our breath as we stepped off the plane and were ushered quickly inside to the smoky, grayness of Frankfurt International Airport. Already somewhat depressed by leaving behind my friends, those first ten days did not bode well for me. I was fifteen now and since they made me leave my whole life on Okinawa, I wanted my parents to know that I was miserable. The weather seemed to share my sentiment. My mom had gotten to Germany before us to look for a house and begin to get acclimated. When we got to our temporary living facility (TLF), it seemed that the gray confines of the airport had inhospitably followed us outside and all the way home. No, not home. To our temporary living facility. I was feeling resentful because they had made the choice to leave Okinawa for Germany after penciling the option onto their, "dream sheet". As teachers on military bases, they could choose when they transferred by putting a few geographic options down on a form. They had **chosen** to change everything I was comfortable with, and it didn't feel fair. As my dad would opine, "Life isn't fair." I threw my version of a well drawn-out fifteen-year-old tantrum.

As we drove on the Autobahn under that ominous sky, I felt the weight of it pressing down.

Our TLF was tiny. Getting bored seemed an inevitability, especially in a two-bedroom apartment with a family of five. So, I did what I knew and pulled out my running shoes. We were about a mile and half away from the gym on base which had a track. Although very nervous and feeling very foreign, I hopped on my mom's bicycle, rode to the gym, ran a bit on the track, and rode back home to our temporary abode. Although I would never have admitted it, during that first workout, a smile broke out on my face, and it felt like the sun even cast a couple of straggling rays down in my direction. I felt better after that run, but I made sure I didn't show it when I got back to the apartment. Let the tantrum continue! Really, I felt like a boss for figuring out how to get to base, get to the track, get in a killer work out, and get back home in a completely new country. I didn't consciously know that there was some physiology behind why I felt so much better, but some part of me had already figured out what tonic it was for my soul. When you feel bad, run, when you feel good, run. Mr. Dawson, thank you again!

I continued to run, not far and not fast, until school started a few days later. Now one of my favorite things is to figure out a brand-new area by running it inside and out to build my mental map. That August in Germany was my first experience with it and the feeling of success that follows.

On the first day of school, cross country started. I met the rest of the team in the gym that first day as a sophomore. As we stretched before our inaugural run, my new coach, Mr. Kollar, asked me when I had last run. It was a loaded question which he leaned in to ask, his spikey gray hair and deep, tanned, wrinkles looming close. Was I new to the sport? Had I slacked all summer? Had he happened upon the next European champion? When I looked at him levelly and said, "Yesterday", he knew at least that I had done this before. I felt like we had an unspoken understanding, I wasn't a newbie to the sport, but I think he also knew I wouldn't be breaking any records. I was steady. He smiled at me from above his ubiquitous clipboard and I knew I liked him. He wasn't the soft-spoken encourager that Mr. Dawson had been. He had all sorts of tricks up the sleeves of those innumerable running suits which he claimed as tax write-offs. He had been known to talk to himself, was heartily unorthodox, and frankly, a little weird. Mr. Kollar was a marvel, from whom I learned volumes. Sometimes he would mumble quietly to himself, sometimes he'd share vociferous outpourings and sometimes he didn't need to speak a single word for his expression to say everything. He was also as dedicated a smoker as he was a runner, yet another interesting dichotomy. Where Mr. Dawson was soft-sided and steady, Mr. Kollar was sharp-edged and odd. Mr. Kollar holds a special place in my heart to this day and still manages to make me smile when I see his random social media posts. I wonder sometimes if he knows how hungrily I listened to all the phrases, mantras, monologues, and life philosophies that he tossed off so carelessly. He was probably my first example of a truly, original thinker. He possessed no dogma but had a variety of opinions across topics that he'd obtained through critical thinking. Where Mr. Dawson had taught me to run, Mr. Kollar, taught me to think.

About a week and a half into the season, my family moved into a house. Until that point, we had always lived in either base housing or cramped Okinawan houses off base. Our family of five had never had much space. Since my mom was the only one hired from stateside when we moved to Okinawa, the military had only given her the housing allotment. In Germany, however, my parents both received housing allotments and suddenly our cramped quarters were a thing of the past. Our house had an indoor pool on the bottom floor. An indoor pool, for a high school kid. I couldn't believe that change in circumstance. My mom signed the contract and in we moved. From my slanted, skylight bedroom window on the third floor, I could see the ruins of Hohenecken Castle atop a moderate hill. During the day, I could see the castle crowning the green trees, and in the evening, it glowed with soft lights. I put my bed right below the window, feeling a connection to the place which seemed to exude a certain pull on me. Through the unseasonably cool fall, I quickly came to love forest running. All of our running in Okinawa had been on sidewalks or asphalt, so this change was significant. The smells, feels and sights of those beautiful deciduous forests, protected throughout Germany, continued to cement my growing conviction that I was, in fact, a runner.

Although I was still sad about the move, our new house (not yet a home) and my room certainly helped ameliorate the depression. It was too soon to have made any good friends or to have replaced what I had left behind, but slowly the foundations of my new life were being erected. Cross country was going well. I was running in the top five for the team, usually fourth or fifth, and excelling in school. My times continued to hover around the twenty-four-minute range. But once that season, and only once, I ran under twenty-three minutes. As a sophomore, sub twenty-three felt amazingly fast. I was elated and expected to usher in a whole slew of twenty-two-minute 5ks. It didn't happen, of course, and the next week I was back to my twenty-three and twenty-four-minute comfort zone, but ah, I had tasted speed. I think we may have placed third in the European Championships that year. I ran fourth or fifth for the team at my solid, steady pace and have no clear recollection of the outcome. Again, I remember the anguish and heart break of some of the older runners with more ambition, but for me being a middle-of-the-packer in only my second year of running was satisfying enough. I had my own goals, sometimes I broke them, sometimes I didn't, but I was dependable. I didn't stop. I didn't get sick, and I didn't quit.

The very best part of that season though, happened outside of cross country. I had, to my shock, made a friend. Not just any friend, the best friend of my life. Of course, I didn't know it then, but the universe gave me the gift of true friendship that year as I was out there sweating and working steadily on the trails. Jessica was not a runner. She didn't understand the sport. However, our growing and unusually adept teenage minds would debate many other things throughout our adolescence and beyond. Foremost among our discussions that year, though, was whether or not running was even a sport. Was there a point? Not surprisingly, I always asserted that yes, there was a point and yes, it was a sport. But to run so long, three miles felt so long then, just to hear a time at the end? Jessica was not convinced. There were no balls, no goals, no aggressive drive to be the best, just to be better than your yester-self. There was just running, just one foot in front of the other, over and over, from August 'til November, in rain, sun, freezing temperatures, and challenging terrain. Even if it was a sport, did I really think that it was fun? I did, and Mr. Kollar agreed. We even had "Running is fun, and fun is running" printed on the backs of our t-shirts one year.

The following summer, about a week before the start of our junior year, I had worn down Jessica's defenses slightly. She agreed to come out with me and walk the course that our team raced on. Something to note about our course; it was considered the hardest course on the high school circuit. Where other schools tried to cobble together trail and road mixes to make for some challenge, but fast times overall, we went the opposite direction. We had hills. Lots of them. Runners could plan to add a solid two minutes onto their average times on our course. We trained on the hills and knew them all by name and temperament. The one our competitors remembered as they limped away (at least I'd like to remember it that way), was "the wall". It was a quad burning, lung bursting, feat of alpine proportions and just as it appeared you were reaching the top, the trail cut to the left and kept going. The incline dropped off considerably at the turn but for many the spirit and will to keep going dropped off with it. Almost all of our competitors walked the wall; Mr. Kollar didn't want any of us to, though. He pounded into our heads that if we could get a psychological advantage, here, at about half-way in, the opponents would never catch up. I NEVER stopped on the wall; I ran very slowly sometimes, but even the wall couldn't force me to walk. I had warned Jess that it was a hilly course, but my verbalization didn't do justice to The Wall. How could it? It took us about an hour to walk the whole course at a leisurely pace and at the end I noticed Jess was not humming a chorus of "running is fun, and fun is running". Why would anyone run that, train on that, and run to and from it every weekday by choice? Jessica always thought I was a little quirky, this may have cemented it a little further. Maybe out here, treading the soft dirt of the Palatinate forests and the protruding roots of the towering pines, my quirks made a little more sense. A mile and half away from school, and we could be lost in the density of this forest; it felt otherworldly.

Jessica told me after that walk, that she was even further from joining the team than she had been before I took her to the trails. But that didn't turn out to be true. Somehow, after that first traversal, she couldn't turn back. So, Jess ran. It was our junior year, I was selected as the captain of the team for my leadership and honesty if not for speed, and my best friend was on the team. We got to spend two hours a day, every weekday, with the exception of the track workout here and there out on those trails. With our busy high school schedules, to have this chance to make a daily connection with the outdoors, with the forest, was a gift.

In terms of run time, I would not improve at all that season. I had gained a few pounds since our arrival in Germany; pounds that were not forgiving when it came time to check the stopwatch. I think it was winter that did it. A lifetime of tropicality had left me unprepared for four months of desolate, snowy days. Staying active year-round was not even a thought that occurred to me in Okinawa, it was a byproduct of the climate. In Germany, staying active year-round was something that would take an active decision and some learning to layer, that I had never really considered before. There was the occasional winter day that Jessica and I would open the bay windows by the indoor pool and jump out into the snow in our bathing suits to get bone-chilled cold and then jump back in the window and into the warmth of the pool, but overall, I wasn't a fan of this still relatively new cold weather. So, that season, like always, I was steady. Mr. Kollar could give me a six-mile course through the woods and knew there would be no short-cuts, no walk breaks, and no slacking. I was friends with everyone on the team but as captain, people also looked to me as an authority. That season I was also initiated into some of the Coach Kollar secrets of speed. He would call off lap times seconds faster than they actually were (unbeknownst to the other runners) to convince us all that we were "faster than we thought we were". He firmly believed that these little white lies about how fast we were would convince us and then we'd replicate it during races. We'd write our intended one-mile split time on one wrist and two-mile goal on the other, he thought that if we could always look at the times we were supposed to be running, we'd make our bodies do it. We'd jog/walk the courses before we raced on them, being sure to jog past any other meandering schools for psychological intimidation. I don't know if any of the Kollar tactics took even two seconds off the times of the team, but (eureka!) I had been introduced to the role the mind plays in running. With Mr. Dawson, we had all gone out and run our asphalt miles and hills and as the miles increased each week, most of our times decreased, but he would never have considered "enhancing" our times at practice. Mr. Kollar, conversely, was engaged in all-out battle on our "slow" thinking. It was novel to me, this idea that if I believed I could do something, it might actually happen; that I had the power to shape the outcome of a situation. It was equally novel that by being party to the "enhancements", I was helping others believe that they too were fast and getting faster. We felt good, we felt that we were accomplishing big things, and whether or not our speed got markedly faster, I'm guessing that even the esteem boost we got from it was a benefit. We learned to believe.

The season progressed. We boasted the boy's European Champion that year, so most of the attention was focused on the "men" rather than women. Jessica was still learning to run, and it was taking some time to adjust. She had always been on the stockier side and was nearly six feet tall, I had always been thicker too and neither of us were girls you would look at and think, "I bet they run!". This was long before the self-love days that were to come in a couple of decades, when curves and being on the thicker side would be celebrated. Maybe Jessica and I were ahead of our time (maybe we still are!?!), but back then, we were rounder where others were not, and we knew it. I watched her learn to run and somehow experiencing it vicariously was more emotional than my own beginnings. She started out unable to run a mile without stopping and pretty much hating the sport to which she had committed herself. Determination, she had it in spades, and it probably held up a mirror to my own. We ran the Regional Championships that year and the top seven women on our team would go on to the European Championship. I finished fourth or fifth like usual and hung around to cheer on the rest of the team. We were in Bitburg, Germany and the course finished with about three-fourths of a lap around a track. Jessica had usually been running in the twenty-five to twenty-six-minute range, quite an accomplishment considering that she had never run before. This race was different though, it was a battle. I watched her come around the track, jockeying for the seventh position with another girl on our team.

Jessica had given it her all and it was obvious. Pain was written on her reddened face, her lungs heaved, and she had an aura of extreme effort radiating from her. She and Sandy went back and forth, seventh and eighth, seventh and eighth. As they came close to the finish, Jessica reached into some hidden reserve, definitely mental, for she had nothing left physically, and she pushed herself just a hair more. She broke twenty-four minutes, run seventh for the team. Tears coursed down her face, probably instantly turning to steam from the heat she was emanating. My best friend had just achieved something impossible, and I had gotten to share in it. That triumph for me, though not my own, was the height of the season. It was the most beautiful non-runner, running I had ever seen.

We had argued about the purpose of putting one foot in front of another thousands of times, but Jess had proved me correct. I saw purpose stream down her face, and beyond that, I saw that running had an inherently beautiful simplicity that other sports wouldn't and couldn't offer. It didn't require speed or genetic ability or some insider privilege, just the commitment to keep going. The monotony of putting one foot in front of the other and deciding that you would keep going. Might it look different to watch the grace and perfection of an Olympic caliber race? Yes, of course, but do any of those moments really differ from Jessica's traversal of the finish line that day? I would submit that they do not. Scale, may differ, but the essentials are the same.

That season ended shortly thereafter, but the remainder of that year would prove pivotal for everything that was to follow. I wish the challenges that were to come had been as easy to conquer as "the wall". Prior to high school, I'd had periods of feeling like I didn't quite fit in, despite how much I might have wanted to. In fifth grade, people would line up at my desk to request help with math questions. In seventh, I was embarrassed to still have a gifted and talented class. I wanted to feel like I was a part of the group and not apart from them. It wasn't that I wasn't popular or didn't have friends, I just felt like more of a nerd, and I didn't really want others to know that. Also, during my seventh-grade year, I'd been hanging out with some friends after school when they started making fun of my dad's disability without realizing he was my father. One of the kids let the rest of the group know and I acted like it didn't matter. I acted like I didn't care; they could make fun of him if they wanted. It was seventh grade, probably the worst time for having self-assuredness and I certainly didn't have any in that moment. As I'd grown up though, I began to figure it out and I realized, staunchly that I did not want to be a part of the herd anymore.

My junior year, after cross country specifically, I got tired of high school and its fraught social hierarchy. I didn't like the back talk, the backstabbing, and the backwards investment in material attributes and appearance above all else. I just didn't get it. I liked things forward and apparent, just like my time on the trails. I began to intentionally put less time into my physical appearance. I stopped shaving my legs; I thought it was a useless convention. I stopped wearing make-up; it didn't change who I was. I stopped wearing clothing that was flattering to my figure; it was the same body underneath regardless of what I chose to adorn it with. I just didn't want to pretend about anything. I have since changed some of those ideas, but in high school the idea of appearance as a commodity seemed omnipresent and like something I couldn't be a part of. I'd spend evenings in my room looking out that skylight window at the illuminated castle ruins and feeling a sense of peace that I didn't feel walking through the halls of my high school. On the weekends, I'd run up to the top of the hill, fighting my body's urge to stop, and once atop the hill, I'd just sit at the castle ruins and think. Sometimes I'd write. I was probably spending way too much time thinking and writing for a sixteen-year-old. Those runs that brought me up to that castle though, the feeling I got, probably endorphin mediated, definitely increased my bond with running. The important things were the only things that mattered at the castle, and it was running that brought me to that place. I felt connected in a way I'd never experienced at school. I felt open to ideas, to energy, to what was next, and I didn't want to spend any more time among the other high schoolers than I had to. I shared most of these ideas with Jessica and we'd discuss them all. She agreed with me that most of it was useless posturing, but she was always able to see it as a means to an end. Sure, it may have taken a little bit of pretending and game playing, but what doesn't. She was willing to participate at least enough to get where she wanted to go, and I wasn't so sure that I was too.

It was with that frame of mind that I got involved in a relationship in the spring of my junior year. Springtime was soccer season. I'd been playing since I was eight years' old and loved the sport, albeit in a different way than cross country. I'd had a boyfriend during the end of my sophomore year, and he'd joined the Army. We had tried to keep a long-distance relationship going through letters and infrequent communication, but since the relationship had never been at all intimate to begin with, it was more of a pen pal situation. This new relationship was of a wholly different sort. The female assistant soccer coach, let's call her Van, had shown interest in me and although I hadn't considered a same-sex relationship before, I was interested in her too. I didn't realize what that might mean, but I hadn't spent the last year deciding that appearance didn't matter to find myself a hypocrite and suddenly deciding that appearance (or in this case, gender) did. She was six years older than me and female, both of which gave me pause, but I slowly decided that I wasn't going to let that stand in the way. It sounds strange now to think that as a sixteen-year-old, I thought of gender as an attribute that could or could not be a determinant for attraction. I didn't know how to react to how I was feeling, I didn't know what to do with it. Her attraction to me had been clear and she encouraged my reciprocation of that affection. How wrong, or whether or not it was wrong, from her position of relative authority didn't occur to me. The only taboo that I considered was the gender one, and that I was willing to look past. Somehow it eclipsed other questions I might have had about right or wrong. Would I have ever considered dating a male coach without thinking of the authority position and age difference? No, of course not, but somehow the female factor changed my perspective. As the relationship went from flirty and fun to sexual and involved, I began to lie about it. Though, I did tell Jessica and she, being the best friend that she always has been, didn't judge me at all. Even to her though, I know that I downplayed what was really happening. It was exhilarating, but also really difficult to talk about, and a little bit scary. I had gone from not sure and a feeling of butterflies to a full-on sexual relationship in a very short period. My head was spinning, and Jessica was the only person who knew some of what was happening.

To perpetuate the unfortunate head-spinning, towards the end of the year, Jessica and I had a falling out, or really, I pushed her away. I said some hurtful things to her having been urged by Van to see our friendship as lopsided. She pointed out to me how Jessica had never cared about me the way I cared about her and I, infatuated, bought into it. All the way. It wasn't fair to Jessica, and I hurt her badly. I didn't realize then, that this was the beginning of a pattern of isolating me from both family and friends. In the high emotion of a new love though, I fell willingly into a kind of misinformed haze that hurt my best friend deeply. The relationship got more and more serious. Van wanted to spend every evening with me, and we were usually at my house. She wanted all of my weekend plans. We went to soccer tournaments together, with the team, and she'd try to sneak me aside whenever she could. She was making plans for a future together, telling me she'd never loved anyone like she loved me. She said I was her soul mate and her one and only love. What does a sixteen-year-old brain do with such exhortations? Well, believes them, to start with. And the truth was, it felt good to have someone tell me they loved me just the way I was. It just all happened so fast, I went from being a strong, independent thinking teen to having all my spare time, thought and space taken by a relationship. She already wanted more than I could give and though I felt some edge of uneasy, hearing the words to go along with acts of love made me feel good.

Jessica and I had both been accepted into a Summer Science Seminar at the Air Force Academy in Colorado Springs. I think we were the only two people from the same high school who were selected to attend from both the national and international high schools that had applicants. We arrived, still not really talking, and I felt miserable. I turned seventeen there. Jessica, ever the gentlewoman, planned a birthday surprise for me at the group dinner. I didn't attend. I was sick in my room, menstrual cramps, altitude sickness, the universe telling me I was on the wrong track, it was all happening at once. I laid in bed in pain and Jessica's sweet surprise didn't reach me. She overcame her own hurt to plan, though, which says all you need to know about Jessica. I decided during that week away that I was going to tell Van I needed a break. I couldn't do this, it was too much, we were too involved, too soon. As soon as I said those words to myself, I knew they were true. I had this early inkling that the right answer was inside me and there, at the Air Force Academy, I finally felt like I knew what I had to do. I felt some relief at having made the decision. I thought I might still want to be with her, but I knew with certainty that I'd been swept up in her whirlwind only now was I starting to breathe again.

I left the Air Force Academy ready to deliver the news to my soon-to-be-ex-girlfriend. I had called Van from the Academy and tried, unsuccessfully, to tell her that I wanted a little bit of space. She wasn't having it. I was heading from Colorado to New York for summer break and my family had already flown there from Germany. They'd be picking me up at the airport in Rochester. Van was spending the summer in Germany with her family, or so I thought. However, when I got off the plane, she was there in the airport with my family. She had convinced my mom to let her spend the summer with us at our house in New York and that having my "best friend" show up as a surprise would be the best seventeenth birthday present ever. Yeah. That's what a mess it was. So, there she was. She tried to covertly hold my hand and more on the way back from the airport in the backseat of the family van. I tried to tell her that I needed some time, that this was too much for me. She was immediately very hurt, she couldn't understand why I didn't love her anymore, why I would act like this. How could I do this to her? Didn't I love her? Hadn't she shown me how much she loved me? Moreover, she knew that I loved her back and she wasn't going to let me go. Of course she wasn't, she was already there for the whole summer. She'd gone to the source and convinced my parents to let this happen. I was stuck. And my plans to end things didn't work. I had no ability, none, to say no to her line of logic, that loving me and showing me that she loved me was all a relationship needed. I hadn't been equipped to know that sometimes you have to get past the potential reaction someone may have to your actions and you have to do it anyway. This is something that girls especially don't get taught. I was unwittingly taught the opposite. I realized the idea of sex and love coming only with marriage was a romanticized version of reality. But it was still what I had heard as the "best" way throughout my upbringing. No one teaches you how to break up with someone or how to recognize when you're being controlled. Or at least they didn't then. I knew, logically, that you didn't have to stay in love with your first love, but I didn't really get what that might mean. I was a people pleaser and never wanted to hurt people or have them mad at me and breaking up hurts everyone involved. I didn't know how to do it and having her there in my bedroom every night didn't give me an option to anyway.

That summer was crazy. A seventeen-year-old and her twenty-three-year-old "friend" staying together in the same room, across the hall from her parents. I feel so bad that they were involved in this situation; it makes me cringe to remember the deception that was going on. I wish I could apologize for not being the version of myself that I wanted to be. It's tempting to think in hindsight that everyone should have known what was going on. But I had been the perfect kid. I'd never lied. I'd always been responsible. I was a straight-A student and an athlete in all the clubs and activities. I didn't drink (well, except for that one time at Jessica's dad's birthday party.) I didn't use drugs. I didn't do reckless things. I was a kid they could count on, until I wasn't. They wouldn't have known how to wrap their heads around this. I didn't even know how to wrap my head around it. Had I been less trust-worthy, would they have had some inclination? Probably. But there's no reason to look back and guess what might have made it different. There we were, in our summer cabin, and the debauchery continued. Van and I talked and planned our lives, staying up late every night in my room. I was still feeling done with high school; she was ready to leave Germany. So, we planned a life together.

I applied to go to college early at the University of Alaska, told them of my accolades; 4.0 GPA, captain of the sports teams, president elect of my senior class, SAT scores, and all the rest. I was accepted with the contingency that I'd need to pass the GED test within the first couple of months of school. I gathered some courage and asked my dad if I could move to Alaska with my "best friend". He said it was a crazy idea, but that if he hadn't followed some crazy ideas in his life, he wouldn't be who he was. We talked to my mom and convinced her too. They had one requirement though; they had gotten concerned about how close my friendship with Van was and stipulated that we had to spend a couple of weeks apart first.

Okay, I could do that. In early August of 1995, we got on a Greyhound bus in Rochester, New York. We took most of the journey together; spending days on the bus. We talked, we planned, we were starting our lives. We stopped only in the sketchy parts of cities across the country, seeing firsthand what poverty and stuck-ness look like. I felt a little sense of unease, but it was easy to dismiss in the excitement of something so big and so new. She got off in Colorado to head south to Texas to spend two weeks with her brother. I kept going the rest of the way west through Colorado to spend the time with my uncle. The plan after that was for us to meet back up and take another Greyhound the rest of the way to Alaska together. She had a little bit of money saved, I had none. We'd figure out the rest when we got there, or at least that was the plan.

Shortly after we left, my dad got a bad feeling about the situation. He knew something was off, so he chose to go through the bedroom we'd shared in New York and found some letters Van had written me. There was a box of them, and they were sexually explicit. Detailed. He got in the van and tried to chase us down, but we were already out of reach. I called him from a Greyhound station somewhere to check in and discovered that he was livid, and with good cause. He told me that I could get to Colorado, but that from there I was coming back to Germany to finish school and that I wasn't going to see her anymore. There would be other consequences too. I was mortified. Mortified that the letters had been found, that I'd lied, that I'd caused this pain and anger, that I was in this spot. But I was also kind of out of the reach of their control at that very moment. I was on a Greyhound bus.

We parted in Colorado and I was left with hickies all over my neck. She wanted people to know that I was taken. My father had told my uncle the whole story and the updated plan to deport me back to Germany. However, Van and I had another friend in Colorado and she lived just a couple miles away from my uncle. Van came back up to Colorado as soon as she figured it out and stayed with the friend. She would not be away from me. I spent the days until she arrived in the best way. I'd wake up, have a small breakfast, go for a run, workout, and then spend the rest of the day reading and sitting in the sun. When Van arrived at the friend's house, we made a plan. I'd go back to Germany, because I had to, she'd come back too, and we'd sneak around as much as we had to so as not to be separated. It was the way we had to make it work. My heart sighs to write and remember.

My father wasn't the only one who was upset about his discovery. My mother was hurt beyond belief at my betrayal of trust and lapsed into a deep depression which included several suicide attempts over the next few years. My family's Brady Bunch feel fell apart. Medical professionals would tell me that it wasn't my fault. That my mom "got sick", but that what happened with me was the straw that broke the camel's back. I'm sure I had heard the trite straw idiom a hundred times, but never thought should it be applied to a situation like this, what bullshit. To tell a teenager: "it's not your fault, but-" really tells them: "you did this thing, you made the final push." My mother was no camel and there were no straws, just pain, misunderstanding and more pain. But at the time, and for years afterwards, I didn't understand just how much guilt I was shouldering as she was overtaken by this severe depression; I couldn't tease out my push from her pain and the extremity of her reaction didn't seem to make sense.

What I've come to realize is that I was the kid. She was the mom. I was sixteen and seventeen years old, a baby. It wasn't my fault. At all. I was not the straw. Being told that I was the final push probably contributed just as much to my problem as the situation itself. Yes, I lied. Yes, that hurt her. But kids make mistakes. I was acting like an adult and making adult decisions as teenagers do. But it's the job of parents, to deal with that, and to take it in stride. And regardless of whether or not they are equipped to handle that stress, their breaks are not the faults of their babies. For my mom, nothing could or would undo whatever that final "straw" had done. No amount of medicine, shock-therapy, or psychotherapy could fix her. But how does a kid wrap their head around that? I never verbalized or even necessarily thought that it was "my fault" but I know now that I internalized it in a deep and incontrovertible way. Notions of blame and causation are so convoluted that efforts to figure them out are futile at best. But it seems, in retrospect there were some errors made in the way it was addressed. I did behave poorly. I did make bad choices. I did hurt people while in a controlling and abusive relationship with an adult woman. My family's strength couldn't withstand that, and for a time I lost them because of it. It was as if a hurricane entered, swept me up, and wreaked havoc on the normality around it. Messy and painful. It would be the first time in my life that running was crucial for maintaining some semblance of stability, but it was far, far from the last time.

When I arrived back in Germany, I'd missed the first week of school my senior year and cross country had already started when I rejoined the team. My senior year began in a haze. There are still many parts that I don't remember. They were so painful that my brain has just shut them out. At the time, I believed that my parents did not approve of the relationship purely because it involved someone of the same gender. Now, I know that if my seventeen-year-old came home with a coach six years their senior, I too would "disapprove". Gender may have played a role in deepening the disapproval, but their feelings were more parents trying to protect a child being harmed. Ah, the clarity of true adulthood. They saw the manipulation beginning, saw me changing my life plans, and saw that I was not headed in a good direction. And what did I do? I fought them. I dropped out of two AP classes and took electronics and a librarian's assistant elective. I lied to get around their rules, I told my father that I hated him. Hate. I looked my father in the eyes and used that word. I was president of the senior class, captain of the soccer and cross country teams, ambassador to our Model United Nations delegation, National Honor Society member, National German Honor Society member, and the list goes on. I had never smoked a cigarette or tried a single drug. I guess all my rebellion manifested itself at once and with a vengeance. I had fought my way uphill to that castle, I fought my way uphill now, only the stakes were much higher.

Cross country season was an outlet for me, that fall of 1995. I ran because I had to, it was the one thing that stayed normal. My sister was a freshman that year and she ran too. For part of the season, we didn't communicate, and for another part, we were just two lost but loving siblings. Jessica ran again but she was not my friend; we spoke superficially, both hurting. Nobody really knew how to react to my revealed lesbianism, but it was on everyone's tongue and in everyone's mind. I was still team captain and they still respected me, but there was something huge that they didn't understand. Running through all that negativity and anger did nothing for my times. Again, I didn't improve. We went to Europeans again, though. This year we had the girls' European champ on our team. Coach Kollar was a happy man, and he was the same coach to me that he had always been. My sister and I both ran Europeans together that year in about the same time and that was a nice end to my high school running career; A career that I had truly expected to go no further, thinking I would always be a fitness runner, but never fast enough to be competitive.

At home, family drama abounded. My parents initiated an investigation into our relationship. They would have pressed charges if they could have, but in a same sex relationship overseas, there wasn't really much definition for how they might go about it. There was no "statutory rape" so what charges were there? But they were advised to have an investigation done so the Air Force Office of Special Investigations began their work. They questioned us all. They had the letters. They read excerpts and asked me to explain what the sexual language meant. I lied. It was the most lying I've ever done in my entire life. They must have seen right through my lies, but what could they do? It seems like there should have been something. They concluded that Van needed to leave the military community for sexual misconduct. She could not return for a period of five years. Still, she hung around for a little bit longer, she said she couldn't live without me. She was willing to risk everything to be with me. Finally, after more lying and several sightings of her, she decided that she did, indeed, have to go. Her dad was still in the military and her continued presence was a risk to his career too.

I fell into a bit of a depression and started a countdown to the last day of the school year. Months apart seemed an eternity. I walked, zombie-like through the halls of my high school, rarely smiling, rarely paying attention to the judgy people around me. There was a group of boys who would make fun of me for my sexual proclivities. I had lost Jessica didn't really have any other friends, and felt estranged from my family even though I lived in their house. My brother was a bright spot, though. He didn't care about my indiscretions, he loved me through and through and I, him. He got left behind in all the drama the rest of us were going through and is it turned out, never caught back up. I had some teachers who paid attention and cared about me and that made a difference. My German teacher, Frau Kennedy, would see me in the halls, close to tears almost daily, and she'd look at me sternly and say one thing; Die Sonne scheint. She made me say it back: "the sun shines, the sun shines." I wasn't feeling it, there was no warmth in those high school halls, but the act of saying the words, dulled an edge here or there. Die Sonne scheint. My first mantra. Between the Sonne shining and using running as an outlet, I got through a series of very dark days.

It had been February of that year, 1996, when Van had left Germany for Florida with plans of our reunification after my graduation. I had my pick of colleges; I could have gone literally anywhere. But I planned to pick my relationship instead and that's exactly what I did. I turned down all my opportunities and acceptances into great schools and decided to go to Gulf Coast Community College, now Gulf Coast State College, in Panama City, Florida. College, that nebulous treasure chest of my future, for which I had planned my entire scholastic career, suddenly became secondary to that the fact that I'd be living with the woman I thought I loved. I was seventeen and sure. For the first time, I was willing to defy everyone around me. I remember walking across the stage that June evening in the Fruchthalle in downtown Kaiserslautern, Germany. Our senior quotes were read as we tread towards our diplomas. "The only promise of childhood is that it will end and once it is over, it is over," was heard as I stepped across all the jagged broken pieces of my youth. I looked at my fellow students and didn't see friends. I looked out at the sea of the audience and saw my parents whose "unconditional" love had suddenly sprouted conditions that year. I stayed home that night and watched Dirty Dancing with my brother and sister rather than going to the senior party. My brother sat closer to me than he had in a long time as we felt the growing pressure of an approaching end. I wish now that I hugged him tighter and hugged out of him that propensity for self-destruction that he would too-soon discover. He knew how much I loved him, and we had always been close, but I would have liked to have told him a hundred more times that night. High school was done and what did I have to show for it? Probably, most importantly, my running shoes and the desire to keep lacing them up and putting one foot in front of the other. I wanted that night to last forever, but like high school, it ended. The life I had fought for, and thought that I wanted, was about to begin.

I had learned a lot about running and from running those four years. From Mr. Dawson I learned not to quit even if it takes counting light poles. I learned steadiness and consistency and I learned about goodness. His quiet perseverance was a gift to me. Moving to Germany taught me that running through clouds of emotional pain forces the sun to come out, if only for a few minutes. Die Sonne scheint, die Sonne scheint. And Mr. Kollar taught me that running requires mind and heart and heart and mind. That you're "faster than you think you are." He taught me that through surprising victories and painful loss, running would stay faithful and steady. I had run lots of miles those years, running towards, running away and just plain running. I had no idea what roads and mountains were in store for me, but my running shoes were going to come in handy, of that I had some inkling.

I wasn't done learning yet, of course. I hadn't gotten far enough away to look at what I learned from my relationship. What I knew then, or thought I knew, was that I was following my heart. I thought that that was the right choice. It would take many more years to learn and unlearn the things that Van taught me. It's always a question when I tell people about the relationship, how I kind of fell into it, and then got so caught up. I hadn't considered a relationship with another woman before then. I didn't even know how two women had sex, I'd had to ask, and even then, it didn't make sense to my innocent brain. All I can say is that, like everything, it happened by degrees. What we like, love, and accept comes in pieces. Could I accept that a grown woman had a crush on me? I could. Could I accept that when our hands brushed, I felt a little bit of a rush? Sure. And so it goes, by degrees. I got into this relationship the same way you eat an elephant; one bite at a time. But this elephant loved me, it appreciated me for who I was, it recognized the differences in myself that I'd felt from the rest of my high school world. In the infancy of the relationship, I'd felt like I had just developed the ability to choose what others might have been afraid to. I felt like I was heeding the voice of the universe before I even knew how to listen. I should have been hearing the voices of Jessica, my parents, and myself at the Air Force Academy. But I drowned them out and took another bite.

Chapter 4
Panama City

"If you are going through hell, keep going."

— Winston S. Churchill

In the summer of 1996, I moved to Panama City, Florida, knowing no one except Van and expecting our reunion and my return to a sunny climate to be a homecoming of a magnificent scale. She had found an apartment after staying with friends for a few months and was working two jobs. It was the third week in June, so I had two months to get a job, get a car, and get acclimated before school began. Until my arrival, I thought that living with someone would be fun and easy, to my young mind, it would be something like playing house. We'd get to set up the apartment together, go grocery shopping together, and have all the freedom in the world. That had been my fantasy; how fun to be able to go grocery shopping and come home to my own apartment. As if those trivialities were any fraction of what a real life with someone entailed. I didn't realize or at least hadn't given any thought to the fact that paying for electricity can certainly zap the electricity from a fledgling relationship. Although we never fought specifically about finances, having a bank account that emptied itself every two weeks between pay days certainly put a high level of stress on us. Interestingly, we also never really considered the pressure of being a lesbian couple in a small-minded city in Northern Florida. We were definitely the only gay couple living in our apartment complex and we didn't hide that fact. Our lives seemed normal and comfortable to us and so we tried to live as if we were the standard rather than the exception. I was always embarrassed to hold hands or display affection in public which often bothered her and certainly betrayed the idea that I felt totally "comfortable" but at the same time, we never contrived to hide anything. I had tried hiding from my friends and family and caused a sea of pain. Having chosen my living conditions and lifestyle, I aspired not to be ashamed of them. However, at the same time, I didn't want to draw attention. We could go into the one-bedroom apartment we shared together, but I didn't want to hold hands walking through the mall. I didn't like the stares. She really didn't care, and seemed proud of us, but this was all new to me, not something I'd wrestled with for years inside myself. I hadn't thought about "coming out" or being a gay person in a conservative town. I felt bad that I wasn't as ready as she was, and she made sure to let me know my hesitancies bothered her.

That summer sweltered. It was the polar opposite of my introduction to Germany. And it was real life. In Deutschland all of my pain upon being thrust into an environment unfamiliar was cushioned by my parents and the pillow of family life. The routine of high school, the footsteps of cross country, everything combined to ease me through what I had thought to be impossibly difficult. Now that I was transitioning again as an adult, in my own life, with my own choices, the scale of difficulty was entirely new. But I was an eighteen-year-old who thought I was following my heart and my dreams; the cliché of adolescent invincibility was pulsing through my veins. In that golden summer of soaring dreams, empty accounts, and the slap of reality, I got my first job.

Blimpie Subs and Salads was the only spot that would hire me. Another confused assumption of mine had been that getting a minimum wage job would be easy. Apparently though, a 4.0 GPA goes a very short way against diploma-less applicants who know how to work a deep fryer. Finally, after weeks of trying, Blimpie accepted me into their elite staff. I soon became a sandwich-maker extraordinaire. I could slice prosciutto like I'd been butchering for years, no small task for a vegetarian like myself. After a couple week hiatus, I also laced up my Nikes once again. I didn't run far or fast, but I sweat like I did. It took several weeks before I fell into a pattern, and even then, it wasn't regular or defined, but I was running, and it felt good. We also joined a gym that summer. I began to incorporate some free weights and weight machines into my fitness regimen. The results were good. I lost about five pounds and firmed up in areas that I didn't realize were soft. It began to occur to me that sporadic running alone was not enough to maintain the level of fitness that I desired. The weight loss gave me increased confidence. Though at home my confidence was slowly beginning to be sapped by the person who should have been my support structure. The warning signs of a controlling and abusive relationship were cropping up more frequently, but I was too blinded by that summer sun to see that anything was amiss.

I registered for college and started classes in August. Paying out-of-state tuition at Gulf Coast which meant that I was paying more than I would have been at some of the actual private Universities I had been accepted to with grants and aid. My dad had promised to pay the first semester and that I would be on my own after that if I pursued this decision. He stuck to his word, and I paid a very high price for my lackluster education. Classes were not at all demanding, they were far easier than high school, which was good because I had plenty of time for sandwich making, for the gym, and for giving attention to my relationship which was requiring more and more of me. I had a couple of really good teachers, smart people who chose to be there instead of bigger schools, but most of the faculty was mediocre at best. Community college was like high school part two, except that it was even more sophomoric because the top layer and had been skimmed off and sent to real school. Still, I was getting an education and have since come to realize that with only small exception, the school on the degree doesn't determine where you end up in your career. There I was skating along in community college among the established cliques, inundated with the very social patterns that I had tried to evade in high school for the previous couple of years. It was ideal in that I didn't have to study or put forth much effort to be showered with compliments about the quality of my work and to maintain a high GPA. But most of what I was learning were the lessons of real life. And, fittingly, those were the lessons I needed. An Ivy League school would never have taught the lessons that I learned.

I remember a couple of events poignantly from those first six months of cohabitation. I remember wearing some ugly khaki shorts that came maybe an inch above my knee. And I remember being requested, still under the guise of politeness, not to wear them again because they showed too much leg. I also remember wanting contact lenses instead of glasses. I was told that since my eyes were my most beautiful feature, Van should be allowed to enjoy them exclusively and I should keep the glasses so that others couldn't see them as clearly. She attempted to present this in the guise of a compliment and I fell for it a little bit. I recognized the ridiculousness of it, but I didn't resist. I could hear some of the craziness of it, but I didn't know how to catch it. It didn't seem worth arguing, and we didn't really have the money for contacts anyway. Those things seem pretty small when admitting them aloud, but they stand out as a couple of the more obvious flags that I do remember. There were many more, of course.

As I sit here now writing about it, I ask myself just how much of that time should I include? How detailed? If I write the truth, it feels false because it's so far from the person I am today. Yet, it happened; it brought me here and there was no way to get here without it. The shocking thing is how quickly it escalated. In thinking about it, I have to remember that strong women can be weak, independent women, dependent, and that pain can crest and ebb until the tide of it is out forever and entirely new spot of worn-down beach are revealed. And throughout that stormy, wavy time, as more and more of myself washed away, running was the one part of me that stayed true. It was the one thing I had that gave me confidence, strength and which allowed me to maintain some little corner of me, unscathed. Had I not run then, my whole life would certainly be different now. I, as I know myself, would not be here.

So that first half year "on my own," I had been given the hints of things to come in my relationship and hints of things to come running. Having joined the gym and lost a few pounds, I also began to get a little faster. I started participating in local 5ks and taking home age group awards in the sparsely peopled under-25 categories. I hadn't even needed to run to take home many of these awards; participation usually guaranteed me something. I found that I was having fun and that the running community was composed of the same good people that the cross country team was. I hesitate to use the non-descript term "good people", but in this case maybe it's accurate. Of all those various things that runners are and that runners do apart from running, I have met some of the best people and best friends of my life on the trail. When I made my debut at local 5k's, I was running right around twenty-seven minutes and happy with it. But improvement came quickly, and I could measure it from race to race.

My first year of college moved along. Things with Van were getting worse, my running performance was getting better. And school was school, unlike running, my performance was pretty much peak already. Running was becoming more of a habit. Before, I had always fit it in when it was convenient or when I felt a strong urge. It can be difficult to keep up a sport when the structure of high school and a coach has passed, but the ease of running makes it simpler to maintain. I had started the summer with sporadic runs, but I slowly crossed that bridge to the point where I wanted to run every day or fairly close to it and it didn't feel like a chore. I still didn't mind taking a day off now and then, but I started to keep track of how many days in a week I ran. I wasn't calculating miles or attending to speed work, but I would get the itch to get out there even when I had scheduled a rest day. It would be several more years before that itch escalated into a missed running day causing me addict-like twitchy legs and an irritable attitude to top it off.

As equally as I was controlling my running, so too was Van controlling me. I don't clearly remember the sequence or the elevation, just several stark, haunting memories; independent, but cumulatively painting a disturbing image. Most of the abuse was verbal, but not all. What were once gentle pleas to do a certain thing or be a certain way became yelling, became accusing, became ugly. Name calling, empty accusations, all the hurtful things that only a person who knows everything about you can knows how to use against you. And then when yelling wasn't enough, it got physical. Now she had to hold me down to say the things she needed to say. Being threatened with a cigarette held inches away while being completely restrained so I couldn't move at all. Being called horrible names or being pushed into door frames as I tried to escape the room of the mistreatment. One time I got hit in the head with a telephone book after hours of her yelling threats to call a boy whose phone number she had sought because she was sure I wanted to fuck him. I won't write all the things that happened. I don't remember all of them. But there was the constant feeling of unease at home and quite often to avoid the fear or discomfort, I just checked out. The crazy thing was the slide to get there. That lines of what was tolerable and intolerable blurred. The woman who I thought that I was would never have put up with any of that. Yet I did. I didn't have anywhere to go. She literally prevented me from leaving and quite often with physical restraint. I hadn't reconnected with my family. It didn't feel bad enough to seek a shelter for abused women or anything like that and I still believed in some fucked up part of my head that we loved each other and would get through it.

I knew this wasn't me, but I had no idea how to change where I was. As I first learned then and have relearned many times since: it's so much easier than we think to fall into a pattern of taking what is given, thinking wrong things are okay, thinking there isn't a way through or out. I didn't like my job much, but most of the time it was better than being at home. She would meet me between classes to walk me to my next one, so I didn't talk to anyone. She encroached on all sorts of little moments that in the past I had taken for granted as time that was my own, even showering was no longer something I could do alone. My sense of self was being washed down the drain, the gurgle of it louder than my silent scream. Yet still I ran. Still getting faster, still able to get out for my minutes on the road. I remember going to those races, we looked like a happy couple and the running community didn't care about the fact that we were both women. Like many abusive relationships, it wasn't obvious when we were in public. From the outside, we looked like a happy couple. Pictures show us smiling; but inside I was dying.

I took a semester off from college after a year and half to move back to Germany temporarily. I know that it was an attempt to find some sort of protection or sanctuary from the pain I was experiencing, but it wasn't to be. I had talked to her about going by myself, but we'd also talked about going together. In the end, she came with me, and we stayed with my mother and sister. My parents had divorced, and my brother and father were living in a separate apartment. My mom's apartment was small, but Van and I still got enough privacy to continue our fighting almost on par with what had been occurring in Florida. Somehow it didn't feel as bad while I had family nearby, but I still didn't have the courage to get out. I got a job on base which she would drive me to and from. I made my sister lunches for school, I tried to be there for her, and we acted like there was some sort of normality going on. My mom was still desperately ill and in the clutches of her depression, she alternated between being checked out and sad and unreachable. What a strange time. I remember some mornings in that house, I'd wake up after what should have been enough sleep and feel so tired that I just wanted to lay on the couch and go back to sleep. It felt like a pressing tiredness, but I couldn't get any of that rest I craved. I must have been depressed too, on a way smaller scale and I still went through all the motions to look happy and well-adjusted from the outside. And I kept running and working out, my salvation.

Over that semester, I accidently ran my first 20k. It was a total mistake, I had been toying with the notion, but it still just seemed so long. We went to do a local Volksmarch which had 10k and 20k options. I had decided to stick with just the 10k, but out there on the course on a meandering stretch through early gorgeous spring foliage, I missed the sign which notated the separation of the ten and twenty. Needless to say, an extra 6.2 miles later, my quads tired but jubilant, I had completed the longest run of my life. I did not partake of post-Volksmarch bier and bratwurst, though the other marchers seemed to be enjoying them both immensely. I remember such a feeling of accomplishment and surprise that although I was sore, I had completed this behemoth of a run without too much difficulty or forethought. Not all that much earlier, the notion of a 5k required pre-event pasta consumption and led to post-race exhaustion. It was the epitome of serious, distance running and now I was doing 20k by accident. Looking back, I can see that it was inevitable that my brain was moving towards the marathon, even though I wasn't quite there yet.

We went back to Florida in the late spring. Why was it still a "we"? I think I had been partially lulled by the protective influence of my family's presence, but still our "problems" had been bad. I remember laughing at the irony when the stone flew out of the ring she had given me that Christmas when she slammed my hand against the door jamb for trying to get away. I also remember a feeling of surrealism, I was able to recognize the shittiness of what was happening almost from an outsider's perspective, but I still wasn't able to extricate myself. There was always an untouched part of me that felt like it wasn't really happening to me, then too there was the part sitting, sobbing on the bathroom floor not recognizing myself in the mirror. Anyone who has been there will probably recognize the disassociation that happens. It's self-protective and a difficult to describe phenomenon if you haven't experienced it. Older now, wiser maybe, I have thought a lot about what happens to make someone fall and get stuck. It seems that it's especially easy for someone young in an abusive relationship who is isolated from all other relationships to depend on their abuser for comfort. They hurt you, you withdraw, and as soon as you come out of withdrawal, you want to feel better and go to your abuser for comfort and they comfort you because they fear the thought of losing you. This cycle of being hurt and comforted fucks the brain up in a way that it takes many years to undo. And maybe too, there was a part of me that thought all the hurt that was suffered by Jessica, my mom, my brother, my dad, my sister, maybe all of those things had a way of coming back around and I deserved to be where I was. It's easier than you would think to get stuck like that. So "we" went back to Florida. Back to no friends, back to the same patterns of abuse.

I remember going for a speedwork run shortly after we returned to Florida. When we had left, Van and I had moved out of our apartment. So, upon returning, we were starting over. The first week in Florida was spent in a crappy motel while we figured out more permanent living arrangements. I went out for a fast and hard run down the strip in Panama City wanting to do 3 miles in less than 23 minutes. I was stressed, I knew on some level that this wasn't what I wanted and where I wanted to be but there I was, so I tried to run it out. Somehow, I got stopped by the police. I didn't have any identification and I resembled some petty thief who had stolen something from a nearby store. I had a different color hair and was a different age than whomever they were looking for, but I was running hard enough that it looked suspicious. I don't know. As they questioned me; I started to cry. I felt like it was unjust that they had stopped me, but in reality, I was just unable to take one more thing. I cried hard and told them they had interrupted my workout. Finally, they let me continue my run, but the signs of wear had already begun to show. I broke out in horrible acne all over my face, neck, and back which was shocking after having never had more than a few pimples at any point in my life. It was so sudden and so severe, I thought I'd have scarring. My body was giving me all the signs I should have needed; I just wasn't ready to listen. I started school again, took some classes at the local Florida State University campus in Panama City Beach, and finished my Associates Degree at Gulf Coast.

I was still running mostly 5ks, but I would do the occasional longer event too. Nothing changed at home of course, situations like that get worse, not better, but I was focusing more and more on running. Then, sometime that fall, I decided to run the Disney Marathon in Orlando that January, in 1999. I didn't follow a specific plan, nor did I keep track of weekly mileage or speed work, but I did attend to the long run, the magic long run. I ran one long per week, slowly building up my endurance to three hours of solid running. I estimated that to be at least eighteen miles and maybe up to twenty. I also made sure that I ran at least five days a week, though it was usually more than that. It was a laid-back plan without much structure, as pretty much all of my running had been up until then and I was fitting it in around going to school full time and working 32 hours a week.

In November, I participated in one my favorite races of all time, the Sunny Hills Draggin' Tail 18-miler. It was the longest I had ever run and it gave me the most significant feeling of accomplishment I'd experienced since moving out of my parents' house. It had a small turnout, so I placed in my age category and won a hand-painted dragon sculpture. The course is unremarkable, a paved out and back, almost in the outback, with few houses or landmarks and a few good hills. The race is also well known for the chili they serve afterwards. Not having a strong running stomach, I did not venture to try it. The race itself, I highly recommend to anyone in the neighborhood of Sunny Hills, Florida in November; the chili is up to you.

I was working at Walmart in Panama City Beach in the photo lab. I was learning many things about what people like to take pictures of, especially people on Spring Break. School was still easy, running was still my only freedom. I was busy, but not busy enough to distract me from the fear and discomfort going on at home. My increased mileage was still within the realm of my control, as was what foods I was using to fuel my running. Although I was not actually recording and adding up calories, I began to consider the health value of everything I put in my mouth. I had been "controlling" my eating for years, first giving up beef and pork in middle school, then subtracting chicken and turkey mid-high school and finally in college, I gave up fish as well. I didn't eat fast food or fried food or drink soda, and I considered my habits very healthy. I was down to about 135 pounds, ten less than I had been in high school, though I think I had been more content with my body at the heavier weight. In high school, I hadn't thought as much about my body, I played sports most of the year and ran the local trails during the off seasons from sports. I was mostly vegetarian and I ate when I was hungry. After losing some weight though, I started to pay attention more and became more critical of myself. As I was being criticized by my partner and myself and as control over my personal choices and well-being was in the strangling hands of someone else, my eating behaviors began to change. It was always little by little, but in the year leading up to Disney, I became very strict about extraneous calorie ingestion. I still ate three healthy, sizeable meals a day and snacked occasionally, but I began to cut out cheeses, oils, eggs, and all the "high" calorie foods. Some of the pleasure had gone out of eating as so much thinking was going into it. My eating may have still fit into the "normal" category, if you have a flexible definition of the normal category, but it was getting pretty close to the edge of it. Looking back, I see that food and exercise were the two things I could claim as mine, without there being any fight. I clung to that which belonged to me and got more extreme in both cases. I wonder now if hanging onto those pieces of control were what finally let me know that I did have control over whether or not I stayed stuck. Maybe, maybe not, but I clung to those things for dear life.

I was twenty, I had been in this relationship for almost four years. They were the formative years of developing my identity as a woman, as a member of a couple, and as a sexual partner. While my peers had been figuring out how to set boundaries, what things worked and didn't work for them, and finding out what would make them feel happy, loved, and most truly themselves, I was not learning that. Maybe I was, by learning the opposite. I was able to learn what I did want through knowing so deeply what I didn't want. But it came with a cost. I was a different person. I had taken damage. Moreover, I felt damaged. I knew that I should want to be an independent person, I knew that I hated that she had to be with me all the time, but I didn't want to be alone either. Sometimes I would go with her places and not be able to get out of the car, I couldn't force this version of me to have interactions with other people if I didn't have to, it felt too hard. I felt like I was not my own. Maybe it was protective dissociation, I don't know. Most of the time I didn't think about a way out, it wasn't something that occurred to me. She talked about wanting to have a baby with me, she talked about the future, and I couldn't see it, but I also couldn't see anything else. In moments when I did talk about a separation, I never said break up, I was reminded that I couldn't support myself, I was given the litany of "no one will ever love you like I love you", and all the other lines that keep us stuck. These conversations both frustrated and exhausted me and usually left me just wanting to be held. So, I ran. I ran and connected with whatever was left to connect to. I would sweat, I would push, I ran as much out as I could and then I went back home, to her. Running was my scream and my sob, and, though I didn't usually feel it that way, it was my strength.

Finally, that Christmas arrived and with it, the date of my first marathon approached. I remember the mixed-up nature of my emotions. Joy, fear, excitement, anticipation, and the greatest thing of all, my little brother was visiting for his Christmas break from school and would be accompanying us to Disneyland. He was 12 and I still loved him wholly and completely. Home was crazy. The Christmas tree had been knocked over toward me, some might say thrown at me, finances were running thin, and the trip was not a cheap one. However, as I tapered my mileage before the big race, I felt full of energy, strong, and ready to run.

Written then to my brother:

To Jon:

And I see his youthful, surreptitious glance

Enough to make sure I'm watching, but to be
equally sure no one else is

Hoping he'll see pride shining in my eyes

Because he loves and fears attention in the same
precious intensity

And I would give it to him-

All the attention his insecurity could take

Because I know that whatever else changes, he'll
always be my little brother

Desirous of my easy approval- approval he may
never recognize as easy

And because we're just out in an abandoned
parking lot

Me watching him skate,

An afternoon that could possibly be termed
normal

I would tell you, no, for me this day defines special

And

This day defines love

For I could never watch that laugh a second too
long

Disney

At Disney he asked

What my favorite part of the day was

I crinkled my nose and said I didn't know

But I knew-

I knew I was so joyous that I felt the pressure of
tears

Every time I saw him just a kid

Happy and unrestrained

We woke up early and drove to Orlando the day before the run. We settled into whatever cheap motel we had reserved. The motel had an outdoor pool, it was not a warm night, but my brother wanted more than anything to swim. The outside air felt warm to him, he was living in Germany, and it was full blown winter there. He jumped in and let out the highest pitch human squeal I've ever heard. We all dissolved into laughter, it was a disarming, real moment that we all needed. That evening, we walked around the mall, went out to dinner. I actually ate pasta rather than salad for once, in a last-ditch effort to carbo-load before the big event.

Orlando was one time zone east of Panama City Beach and the marathon show time was 5 am. Which meant I was up and getting ready at 4 am and that felt way too early to be up and starting my day. The combination of the seven hour drive the day before, the heavy dinner, and the lack of sleep did not equate to ideal running circumstances, but I just wanted to finish, not necessarily to win.

We got to the start, it was dark and cold, for which I was unprepared. I made one final porta-potty visit and was off to the start. Where I waited and waited and waited. Finally, the actual start came, the multitudes around me began to shuffle forward and it took almost ten minutes to get across the actual start line. I saw lines of people along the sides of the course relieving themselves, both male and female, which shocked my uninitiated mind especially given the normally puritan nature of our bathrooming practices. The crowd stayed thick-for the next several miles. I had a few short conversations, some encouragement on being a first timer, but none were those long, engaged, make time fly, distract you from the fact that you're out there running, conversations that I liked. And I ran, most of the time smiling. The black of the sky was fading and the temperature getting friendlier. At the point where the half-marathoners broke off, the crowd thinned appreciably, and it was finally daytime. My long spandex and sleeveless running jersey now fit the environment more appropriately. I felt strong and kept plodding along. The parts through the park were energizing and motivating, filling me with that bubbly, joyous feeling particular to long run success, but some of the back stretches were enervating with their stretched-out mile markers as my only eye candy. Eventually, I just started to get bored and want it over. By mile twenty, I was sapped but I never stopped, aside from one or two porta-potty stops. I kept plugging, my pace slowed but my smile remained, and that 26-mile marker got closer and closer. I remember some pain and exhaustion over that final three or four miles, but that was tempered by the proximity to the end and the cheers of the onlookers. I was finishing my first marathon with a sense of total accomplishment. The clock said 4 hours 20 minutes or somewhere close to there, but my chip time was several minutes faster.

After receiving my medal and a metallic blanket which I had never seen before, I headed over to the appropriate tent in the runner corral so that my family could find me. I had assumed that they would be there waiting, but I happened to get there at an interval during which they had gone elsewhere to look. It was before cell phones, so we didn't have the easy convenience of a text, nor was I aware before the race how the post-race would be organized. All around me were the sounds and sights of family reunifications. I sat there on the ground huddled in my tarp, my body quaking with calorie-deficit cold, attempting not to cry. I had been on the verge of elated tears at the finish line but in those few lonely moments, the tears quickly transformed from happy to something else. I had done this big thing, I was twenty years old, and I had the weight of all of this stuff pressing down whenever I so much as thought about it. After what felt like an eternity, I was found, and awash with happiness once again. Moments before I had experienced the apex of emptiness, then they were there, filling me to the brim and then some. It was a great feeling, even if there were worse feelings being held at bay. It's funny how mercurial it can be. From empty to full. Even in the depths of knowing that everything wasn't okay, even when I had just felt the veneer peel back, there were good moments, fleeting, that it felt alright. But that's the hardest part, isn't it? There will always be moments when the worst, hardest things feel like they were what you wanted all along. How do you say no to those moments? When the balance tips so extremely the other direction, when it's all toppling, it doesn't take much to hold onto. I was holding. Holding tight. The rope frayed, my hands burned, but I held.

We toured Orlando a bit later in the day. I went to Starbucks for the first time and did something out of my new ordinary, I ordered a hot chocolate and decided not to feel guilty about it. I also asked for a low-fat muffin to go with it. The next day, we went to Disney World and my elation continued. I watched unrestrained joy on my little brother's face. He was a boy with a weighted life too, my parents still experiencing tsunamis of ups and downs back in Germany, but for a time at Disney World, gravity loosened its effects just enough for that pure little boy to float through. My sore muscles needed the interminable walk through the park and my heart needed to see my brother be a child, if only for a blink. That weekend still ranks high among the best moments spent with my brother.

I don't know if it was the way I felt over those two days that left my wanting my own pure happiness more often, or if it was just time. Maybe the physical strength of marathon training and completion strengthened some part me of which I hadn't been aware. But that spring, finally, change was afoot. And corny though it may be, the lyric from the Baz Luhrmann Sunscreen Song was my catalyst: "Do one thing every day that scares you." I had been thinking more seriously about a separation from Van, of getting back to me, but I had never really formed a plan or conceptualized a way out. I didn't want to drop out of college, I didn't have any friends to stay with, and I couldn't afford an apartment on my own, the out roads were not obvious.

I was at work in Walmart, developing pictures in the photo lab. One of my coworkers had changed the schedule to leave me working alone on a busy day. The semester was finishing up in a couple of weeks, I was feeling something unfamiliar, a break, a breakthrough, I don't know. I looked around at all the women working with me at Walmart, they all had plans other than this, and yet they all were here. Most were in their mid-thirties or forties with mediocre or downright unhappy relationships, financial struggles, and hope that their kids won't end up in the same place. Two of the women I worked with were obese and had been sexually abused as girls. One acknowledged she had gotten heavy to protect herself from every feeling that way again. One woman who was black had grown up, not far from where we lived, with signs outside local businesses saying that n-words were not welcome. They had eked out these existences from pain and, as much as I respected them for showing up every day and doing the best they could, I didn't want to be them. I loved these women, I loved that they had shared themselves with me, and we all had our broken parts, though I hadn't shared mine. They took me as I was, but I couldn't stay. I couldn't keep working at Walmart and I couldn't stay in the spot that I was stuck in. I heard that Baz Luhrmann song on the storewide radio tinkling into the background noise and reverberating in my head: "Do one thing every day that scares you." I gave my two-week notice at the end of that shift, went to my house, called my dad, and said that I wanted to come home. The only question he asked was, "When?" He bought my tickets and opened his door. A door which I had seen as shut only because my pride had pushed it closed.

It was horrible when I told her. She begged, she pleaded. When she saw that I was resolute, she tried a different tactic and for the two weeks between when I told her and when I left, she treated me amazingly well. She made promises to never do the bad stuff again. She said she wanted a family with me. She said she knew she'd been wrong, and that forgiveness was part of love. I'd heard the promises before. I knew they didn't stick. Somehow, I stuck to my conviction, but I did assure her that it was just a separation. I couldn't use the term "break up". I had been strong enough to make the decision, but I still wasn't quite ready to use that term.

I went back to Germany that summer of ninety-nine, the summer I turned twenty-one, feeling unfettered but very, very alone. I had been in a monogamous, controlling, and abusive relationship since the end of my sixteenth year. She was everything I knew about adulthood and was a large part of me, we had shared everything. I was a walking (or running) puzzle piece looking for someone who fit my grooves. I was running a lot; my dad and I would travel to Volksmarches at which he would walk the 10k and I ran the 20ks. Those Saturdays with him were some of my favorite times. We found one thing we could do together and began to heal. Drive an hour or so, walk or run separately and then drive home. It was our antidote. It became clearer to me then that he never really stopped loving me like I'd thought. I had left our father-daughter relationship as a kid and come back to it a woman. And he just let me be, giving me space and time. He had to just wait until I came back and that must have been so hard, but he did it. Patience prevailed, Volksmarches healed, and there we were. I went on field trips with his class and filled my days with things so drastically different than what I'd been filling them with the past few years. My sister graduated from high school that summer and was glad to have me back as well. Jessica and I were also repairing our friendship. I'd reached out a couple of times while living in Panama City and slowly, so slowly, we were working back towards what we'd had before. Our connection had always been something special, but we were both a little tentative. She'd grown so much during her time at Duke, and I was so deeply in need of a friend. She was back in Germany that summer too. Between my dad, my sister, and Jessica, I had some much-needed respite from the trauma that had been accruing from my time in Florida.

Chapter 5
The French Boy

"You were standing in the water but only up to your knees
But you know a strong current can always sweep you off your feet"

— Nathaniel Rateliff & The Night Sweats, Face Down in the
Moment

I was beginning to feel the echoes of some chords of normal, and then too soon, I met a boy. Axel was a distraction from what should have been healing time and I was still too tender for a relationship. He knew that, but unfortunately, I didn't. He was also going to college in Florida (returning that fall), intelligent in a bitingly sarcastic way, extremely attractive, trilingual, and just enough of a badass to stop my heart. I lost my budding identity in his presence. He rocked my world and though it was inevitably doomed by my fragile and still-dependent heart, it was probably what I needed to make the final break from Van. If not for him, it would have been easy to fall back into her clutches of familiarity. But that didn't mean that it made sense to me.

One night in particular stands out as a learning lesson to me. We were laying in his bed, post-intimacy, and I asked him how he felt about me. Not a good question to ask most of the time, but I was young. Axel told me clearly and unequivocally that we were friends. I was so shocked and confused. I had some vague notion that some people could have physical relationships and not get emotionally attached, but I didn't really think it was true. In a weird way, I felt doubly heart broken. I was still recovering from years of what I had just been through, and he seemed to be a light at the end of the tunnel. I assumed we both felt the same way, that the timing and fates had collaborated to bring us together. The friend comment shattered that illusion, but I still believed that maybe, if I gave him some space but kept myself physically available, he might just be convinced that I was something special. Shockingly, that's not the way it worked out. I adored him and was infatuated. His aloofness, ah, what sweet intoxication. Was it possible that, it was love? I don't know. Probably not. But he is one of the few men in my life who has ever fully and completely taken my breath away. As I got to know him, there were things that I didn't even know if I liked about him, some of his ideas were antithetical to mine, but I was intrigued. I wanted to be in his presence. He'd tell me on a Wednesday that he'd be calling me that weekend. I'd wait through Friday. And Saturday. Saturday at 8pm, 9pm, almost 10pm. I could call and see what he was doing, right? Nothing wrong with that. I'd call, he'd be out, sure I could come meet him, and all was right with the world again. I needed, then, to define my happiness through another person. Although I felt the waiting by the phone to be somewhat pathetic, I couldn't just go out on my own if I wanted to go out. I would be reading some classic novel, glancing at the phone, trying to convince myself that I was perfectly happy sitting there reading as a 21-year-old on a Saturday night in Germany.

To add to the all the rest of the confusion, this boy was the first *boy* I'd liked. So, I had more stuff to figure out. I had thought about what it would be like to have sex with a man during my time with Van and we'd approximated the act, but this was still different than the facsimile. With Axel, sexuality was there, but sensuality was not. It seemed that it was much more about going through the physical motions than any emotions, despite my attempts to add them in. The "benefits" in this friends-with-benefits situation seemed to only benefit him. I responded as I thought was appropriate but had a very different experience of pleasure than what I'd known before. I enjoyed knowing that it was pleasurable to him, but like the rest of what I was going through, I wasn't willing to express my own needs. I learned a lot, but not the lessons I was expecting. Vulgar though it may be, we fucked. We did not ever, in any sense of the phrase, make love.

My pleasure was not a part of the equation. I can refer to it as intimacy, but it was missing some essential intimate ingredients. We shared things, we really were friends, he was right about that, there just truly wasn't any emotion in the actions on his side. Was my naiveté a beautiful thing or a cringy thing? I think cringy is more likely. I wanted this man to have these feelings, I wanted to feel something and have it back, I wanted not to feel sore after an evening of "fun". How many times, Universe, did you need me to hear that what I wanted wasn't really what I wanted?

The summer passed and I decided to transfer to Florida State University's main campus in Tallahassee where my sister had decided to attend too. Van was going to be moving there also, though we'd be living separately. After a couple of puzzling months in Germany, I flew back to our family cottage in Honeoye, New York. My dad had spent most of the summer in Germany and had flown back to New York for a short stay a little bit before my sister and I got there. Alycia and I took the ol' '85 Dodge Caravan down to Tallahassee. It did not, unfortunately, boast the classic fake-wood side paneling but it was a nice, warm, woodsy shade of brown. We had a sticker made for the back window. "Zwei Zicken fahren dieses Auto" or "Two Bitches drive this Car". We felt like we'd been through enough that that sentiment captured who we were and where we were going. She slept in between finding country music stations we could blast, a task which became easier and easier as we traversed the east coast in a southerly direction. It was a fun trip; there was something so carefree about it. She was almost 19, I was 21, we were on a road trip. It was just us, no A/C, and a case of water. We used that trip to reconnect and mend any severed ties that remained. As the trip went on, the feeling of sisterhood grew.

Three days after leaving New York, we arrived in Tallahassee. Our open windows and the blast of the super-heated air that blew through the caravan did nothing to cool us in the Floridian mid-August. Though soaked in sweat, our desires to get her settled in on campus and me in my new apartment were not at all dampened. I was in contact with, and not completely detached from Van, though I was attempting to make the break final. It was difficult not to fall back into the pattern that I had known up until then, and I had a couple of lapses. It was too easy to let her put her arms around me and feel the good things I'd felt before. The back and forth, as it always is, was much harder than just making a hard choice. I knew I didn't want this, that was definite, but I also really liked the feeling of being wanted. I kept my head as straight as I could, no pun intended, and I think, for the most part, did pretty good. She still kind of felt like family, but I forced myself to keep the space. It was probably aided by the fact that I was still feeling a little head-over-heels for Axel who was now also back in Florida about four hours away working on his graduate degree.

The biggest surprise of those first couple weeks in Tally was that I ran into one of my old friends from Okinawa who was also attending FSU. We happened to recognize each other walking around the mall even though it had been probably six years since we had seen each other. It looked like Virginia, but I didn't believe it could actually be her. It felt uncomfortable because it was so unlikely but I asked her if it was really her…and it was! Virginia put me in touch with a whole network of the Okinawa crowd, some old friends and some new. I had a net of friends to fall into, delivered by the universe, and I regained a little bit of comfort in my life. They were all great people. One friend from my freshman year of high school, Celine, also became my new running partner. We ran about six miles three times a week, got reacquainted, and both got fitter and faster. That running-fueled friendship was pivotal for me in that I continued to get faster and faster and seek more for myself with a friend along for the ride. It was fun. I was 21 and having fun. This was new and it revved up my drive for running success. We would meet sometime "early", like 9am. We were surrounded by an element of the college population to whom nine in the morning was unheard of and six miles was an impossibility. People who could have been at the peak of their physical ability and prowess who chose to bury that potential and capability under pizza boxes and in puddles of vomit. Overindulgence was becoming the standard for our peers as Celine and I hammered the pavement, humid morning after humid morning. It wasn't that we were exempt from the fun or the experience of college, just that we were making decisions based on our established hobbies rather than embracing the college stereotypes. It was at that time that I remember really, deeply realizing the power of choice. I'd chosen to leave an abusive relationship, jump into a non-relationship with an emotionally unavailable hottie, and to get up and run. Just fucking run. We looped, we talked, we grew. My goodness, how I needed it.

I remember doing the loop alone one morning and seeing a fit looking guy giving me the stare down. "Whatever you're doing, girl, it is definitely working," he said through his ogle. As pleased as I was at the random compliment, I began automatically questioning myself. Was he saying that I still had a lot of work to do, but I was on the right track? Did I look like I had just begun a fitness program and my body was just beginning to curve to its mandates? I was already a full fifteen pounds lighter and far fitter than I had ever been in high school but far less satisfied with my body and my speed. A phrase meant as a compliment derailed me into thinking I still wasn't doing enough. From a stranger, no less! This is the definition of two steps forward, one step back. I didn't have any confidence, which was something that would take a very long time to figure out. I'd had confidence in abundance before the Van years, but not only did what I had evaporate during the relationship, it left a hole that filled with doubt at the slightest provocation. I continued to set personal records regularly, which led me to believe I was on the right track. But interspersed with those brief rays of self-satisfaction were vague and nagging feelings of doubt and dissatisfaction. It was a drive to do more and be more, both positive and negative. Even the purest desire for betterment was couched with the desire to be in a state other than my current one. Time wasn't healing as fast as I'd wanted it to. I was keeping my head above water, it probably looked like a comfortable tread, but, oh boy, there was some churning under the surface.

Sometime over that first year in Tallahassee, running to and from so many things, I got the notion that it might be possible to run cross country for the University. I had probably come out of high school as a good enough soccer player to walk onto a D2 and maybe even a D1 soccer team, but cross country had been a far more remote possibility. Okay, it had been an impossibility. But that year at FSU, I saw my 5k times getting closer and closer to the twenty-minute mark. Although I have already chronicled my progress up until that point, I have to say that it was with complete disbelief that I approached that number. The twenty-minute barrier was this mythical and surreal thing; a mark I had set for myself that I needed to break before I even tried to walk onto the team. Earlier in my life, the idea of breaking twenty, walking onto a D1 team, and successfully running cross country was just as much a reality as running for president would have been. But somehow it was happening. And I had trained myself to get there. Years of early runs, late runs, running around all the other commitments, around school and work and through an abusive relationship. It was the thing that was mine and I had done it well despite a few pieces of emotional baggage that I was still most definitely carrying around.

I trained for and ran my second marathon that spring. It was the Pensacola Blue Angels Marathon. I did a lot of the training and rode to Pensacola with my good friend Jack McDermott, still a Tallahassee running Phenom. We didn't plan as well as we could have, I guess, for our arrival in Pensacola on the evening before the race. We got onto the Naval Air Station with just minutes to spare before the close of the race number and packet pick up so we did what any non-military minded latecomers would do and exceeded the exceptionally slow base speed limit. I remember sitting in Jack's car looking at my watch the seconds ticking like hammers on a gong. I listened to Jack's incredulity as the MP demanded his registration and insurance information. Apparently, Jack, who worked for the Department of Insurance had never heard before that carrying proof of insurance was good insurance in case one plans to break the law. Somehow, they let us go, un-ticketed, Jack slowed down for the final half mile to the packet pick-up, and we were next to last, if not completely last in line to pick up our stuff. We ran the next day, and it was decent event; highlighted by a Blue Angels flyover at the start. It was, of course, much smaller than Disney, which to me was a huge advantage. I used a mental trick which I have since come to love and depend on for much more than just marathoning: divide and conquer. I thought of the race as four distinct seven-milers (with the final leg shorter than the first three). I slogged through but didn't hit any walls or walk nor did I run particularly fast. I felt pretty good up through mile fourteen and told myself that if I still felt that way at eighteen, I'd pick up the pace. I knew finishing would be no problem, but I certainly didn't have enough gas for picking up the pace at mile eighteen. I drank water or diluted Gatorade at every stop without stopping but didn't experiment with any other consumption. I finished in 3 hours and 56 minutes. Jack was ahead of me somewhere. He has since gone on to much more marathon success than I ever have. I knew I had trained better and smarter because my muscle soreness and recovery time was a fraction of what it had been at Disney. I did, however, experience some big-time inner thigh chafing. I had rubbed, open raw spots of several inches on the insides of both thighs, very painful. I had started to feel the burn and the skin of my thighs slowly rubbing away by eight miles in. I knew I wouldn't let it stop me, but the discomfort was very real from miles eight to twenty-six. Anyone that saw us at rest stops on the way home along the Florida Panhandle that afternoon with my spread leg shuffle probably did not assume that Jack and I had spent the weekend marathoning. Although it can happen to any runner, I assumed that it had happened because I had gained some weight or size in my thighs and that was a symbol of some failure. I decided to restrict my eating even more because that would solve it. Oh, that I could have been in a better place then.

I was feeling at home in the running community that spring, meeting good people and building healthy friendships. I ran with Celine, with Jack, with a speed work group, and with a Sunday long run group. I could feel myself growing as a person and preparing to embrace new challenges. I would be going back to Germany that summer and was running one last 5k before the trip home. It was some sort of Manatee protection event and my sister decided to run it too. It was my final chance to break twenty minutes which was my ultimate running goal. It was the time that I needed to feel that I could compete with the speedsters of the FSU CC team. Jack was going to pace me for this flat, out-and-back course. We started strong, right on pace, and I held the pace as well as I could. I knew I was ready, and I knew there was no better place or time to hit my goal of running a time in the teens. But I didn't. I came close, but I missed my goal. And it wasn't just any goal, but a culmination of a hell of a lot of work and an achievement I wanted so that I could feel my CC aspirations were worthwhile. I had racked up a second or two in each of the third and fourth kilometers and though I stayed on pace for the fifth, I didn't have enough of a kick to make up for the seconds I had added. My time was 20:04. Four full seconds longer than what I was striving for. I was sorely disappointed, but things quickly fell into perspective. I knew that it wasn't really the make-or-break event which would determine whether or not I could run for FSU. I was still in phenomenal shape, and I had achieved it with my own determination and work ethic. There was a lot that just felt right even though the numbers weren't stacked in my favor. Running is always a chain of events, I couldn't isolate one thing I should have done differently. If I had gone faster earlier, it might have helped, or it might have made me more tired at the end. If I had gone out slower and been able to run negative splits, that might have done it. If I had stayed with that guy wearing green shorts when he passed me, maybe I could have hung. There is never any surefire solution to running, just seconds off a banner goal. Even though running is an independent sport, it is incredibly dependent on so many factors that it is ridiculous to inventory them. Eat, sleep, temp, humidity, precipitation, toenail length, muscle fatigue, the how much you taper. It's not amazing to me that goals are so frequently missed; it's amazing to me that they are ever met. I missed my goal, but was I a different runner because of it, was my ability any different? No. So, I got a massage, got my age group award, and got ready to spend the summer training in Germany.

I had a printed version of the summer training program designed by the coach of the FSU CC team. Most of it seemed reasonable, but some of it just seemed plain impossible, mostly just parts related to the pace. The distance runs, the tempo runs, the total mileage was all doable, but those speed sessions left me fatigued just reading them. I was supposed to be doing mile repeats at a six-minute pace and I had never run below a six-thirty pace. If four to five seconds in a 5k is a big deal, then thirty seconds in a mile is huge! So, I did what I could. I ran the workouts and modified them a little. After all, I had been devising my own workout schedules for the past three years and they had worked out well for me. So I switched days up a bit, trimmed distance in some places and added it in others. I was working at a golf course, spending time with friends and family, and still attempting to pursue the ever-elusive Axel, who I still thought of as the boy of my dreams. My running, while still being a primary focus, had to fit around a busy 22-year-old life. I'd guess, now, as an adult, that I probably got a heck of lot closer to following that summer schedule that most other CC runners training on their own. I suspect it was an overly optimistic plan that the coach anticipated we'd do about 75% of. I hit much more than that. Some days that summer I ran twice a day, which I still do occasionally, and it was like an epiphany for me. I had never before considered getting my daily mileage from two separate sessions. It felt like a lot of running but I lost a couple more pounds over the three-month period and don't remember any muscle fatigue, so I think the divided sessions must have worked for me. It was a great way to get in mileage without needing a huge chunk of time all at once.

Then as suddenly as summer had come, it drew to a close. My summer running plan, once white and crisp, was dull and well-used. I would soon put its results and myself to the test. As much energy and time as I had put into this lofty goal, it still seemed just as out of my reach as before.

I had learned so much about life and running over the four years leading up to that fall. I had gone from ten to fifteen miles a week and 145 pounds when I first moved to Florida, to forty or fifty a week and 125 pounds. I had gone from an average of twenty-five minutes for a 5k, to twenty minutes on my own training plan and my own initiative. I had endured a relationship which pared me down emotionally as the increased mileage had pared me down physically. And although I thought I had done all the healing I needed to do from that, I would find that the damage would creep back up intermittently for quite some time. At the end of high school, I had identified myself as a runner, but by the end of that summer, "runner" was not just a superficial label but who I was through and through. Through pain, loss of self, loss of pride, through school and work, I had run. The two marathons were not the hard part of getting where I was. Everything else was. Yet there I stood, ready to race. Ready to run D1 cross country at FSU. Strong (ish). Strength gathering, ever slowly.

Chapter 6
College Cross

"The brick walls are there for a reason. The brick walls are not there to keep us out. The brick walls are there to give us a chance to show how badly we want something. Because the brick walls are there to stop the people who don't want it badly enough. They're there to stop the other people."

— *Randy Pausch, The Last Lecture*

I remember the first day of cross country practice very well. We had to be back at school a week earlier than the other students to try-out, which was more of a thing for the boys than the girls. There just weren't as many girls wanting to be on the team so anyone who could hang, made it. The boys' competition was fierce, though. Several seconds could separate those who made it from those who didn't. And those who didn't were given a printed training plan and told to come back the following year. Those coveted spots were battled for and held onto in a way that the girls' team just didn't experience. We had between 15 and 18 try out, most already knew that they were guaranteed a spot and were on partial scholarships. Although any financial assistance is, of course, a blessing for most college students, those partial scholarships were certainly a very small part. Cross country, as it turns out, is not as well funded in Florida as football. As a walk-on, I was not privy to a scholarship, but most of the girls had at least their books covered, and many had books and board. Funds poured into football (it seemed to be deified) and barely trickled into the rest of the sports. D1 sports are hard. I think that anyone who has ever participated in sport at that level, can probably convincingly argue that their sport is the hardest. Until of course a participant of another sport joins the discussion. I would say, cross country is a valid contender for the most difficult sport. It might be difficult in a different way than other sports, but that doesn't diminish the level of difficulty. Runners don't deal with spotlight pressure or endless drills to perfect a particular skill. We just run. Yet we spend as much time at practice as the other sports. We have (or at least had) the highest percentage of girls with amenorrhea. It was difficult to have enough time in the day to get to two practices, get to all our classes, get sleep, and have time to eat enough calories to fuel the sixty to seventy weekly miles we were covering; our bodies couldn't always keep up. There are some other sports which take a comparable toll on women and their bodies, but it continues to be more obvious in women's running. Most of the girls were on birth control pills just so that they would still have a "period," not because there was any risk of any of us getting pregnant. No one had extra energy for sex. In calorie deficit, when your period is already gone, your sex drive has likely left sometime before. Only one teammate had a boyfriend and he was a runner too. For the rest of us, there was no time or energy for something so extra.

The challenge of running is different. We get stress fractures, sprains, strains, shin splints, and a whole host of injuries that we acquire simply from our bodies not getting rest and recovery between bouts of contact, repeated relentless contact, of our feet on the ground. We put in sixty to one hundred a week with the goal to take a few seconds off last season's best times. College runners can't have off-days and hope that a teammate picks up the slack. Everything counts. We can't come to practice, miss a few more goals than usual or make some bad passes, and chalk it up to a "bad" day. A little bit of time off the overall plan, can add up to peaking at the wrong time and not being able to contribute to your own best and the team's performance the way you're expected to. Through fatigue, GI issues, soreness, and whatever else might be afflicting us, we push, we get through, and we hope we're on the side of the fine line that doesn't leave us injured and it's a close call every time.

The extremity to which we push our bodies can be summarized in this quick aside memory of running through GI issues. One of the girls who ran close to me time-wise most of the season had had an uncomfortable stomach during a particularly intense speed-work session of mile repeats with quarter mile recovery jogs in between. She'd made it through the workout despite intense abdominal pain but, but had to stop on the cool down jog back to campus to relieve herself in someone's front yard. She couldn't wait another minute, but she made it through the workout. I'll say at the beginning of this section that the major lesson I learned that season was just how psychological hunger and exhaustion were. Over and over again, as I fashioned myself into a D1 college runner, I had to make the decision not to feel hunger, exhaustion or discomfort. It had to be set aside. I realized how easy it is to be deluded into thinking that with basic drives like that, we have to respond because we're human, but running college cross country taught me that there's a choice element in everything. I chose to keep going. One foot in front of the other, faster and faster.

The first day of practice was in late August in the Florida panhandle so it's a given that the weather would fall into the category of what most people would consider unpleasant and would likely keep them inside. It was three in the afternoon, and we met first in an older classroom for an inaugural meeting and our first introduction to the school's new coach. It was as humid as possible outside, in the high 80's, but cooled down slightly by the extreme deluge which was basically flooding campus. Our coach attempted to prolong the meeting as much as he could, just hoping that Mother Nature would choose to be slightly kinder. It didn't happen, of course, and he wasn't going to modify practice on her account. Out we tromped. We did a warm-up jog in preparation for a speed session with time trials around a baseball field. It would be our first opportunity to show the coach, the team, and ourselves how our solo summer training had gone. Either we had done it, or we hadn't, and everyone else was about to know. The grass was about three inches long with random patches of bare, red dirt. We were doing three one-mile repeats, the staple speed workout from our summer training guides.

Our warm-up was about two miles, and it didn't just serve to warm-up our muscles for the upcoming workout, but to give us a chance to evaluate the preparedness of our fellow runners. Many of the female runners were returnees, and they all seemed comfortable with each other, they had known each other for years. Outside of that group, we had one new girl recruited from up north who was very hyped up. She was rumored to be the fastest and she lived up to that. There were two or three Floridian freshman who were not heavily recruited, one transfer student from Mississippi, and me. Don't forget me. I was twenty-two, about to be coached, seriously coached, for the first time ever. This felt so different already from the experience I'd had up until that point with being coached and being on a team in high school. And I was a senior walk-on, certainly not the typical new runner; I kind of kept that atypical feeling all season. Obviously, I would be no record breaker. I was the oddball, but just like in high school, I was going to be steady and strong. That was nothing new. But I was in a totally different mental spot than anyone out there and I was ready to run.

Our adrenaline and inherent competitiveness were definitely coursing as the rain and sweat made rivulets down our faces. Some of those girls seemed so smooth and carefree that first day but everyone was a fighter. It had become obvious after our warm up that there would be no solid time evidence of how fast we had the potential to be, because of the horrendous weather. The weather was so bad that our coach suggested we run with our shoes off if we felt that their heaviness was slowing us down significantly. It seems almost unreal to me now that the torrents were so strong, the mud so sticky, and that baseball field was so nasty that it was actually beneficial to run barefoot. I don't think I had ever done shoeless speed work apart from some backyard sprints when I was eight. Well, I was a long way from my backyard, and an even longer way from eight, but I took my shoes off and ran with all that I had. My miles were each over seven minutes, but our coach must have decided to use the run only as a position establisher as everyone was way off their potential times. I ran that first day about the same as I would run most of the season: twelfth out of fifteen. Twelfth out of fifteen, it was spectacular to me. I could hang, I wasn't lapped or laughed at. I was on the cross country team at Florida State University.

The rain broke but the heat didn't. We trained every weekday at three and either two or three mornings a week. I won't go into the specifics of our workouts, but it was a pretty standard D1 cross country training regimen. One good speed work session per week, and one or two tempo runs with longer recovery days in between. One or two light conditioning workouts with warm up jogs on the double workout days. Log as many miles as you can without destruction and push your body to the very edge of the stress-injury abyss without falling in. Negotiate that balance, try to pay attention when you have pain that's more than soreness, but don't be hypochondriacal, because you'll miss your shot. Just how hard, how fast, and how much can you do before that joint fails, that ligament stretches too far, and that bone develops the tiniest of hairline fractures which will sideline you for the season and leave some other eager athlete in your spot, running your race? These were questions we all had to ask ourselves. There are so many personal struggles going on, so many levels of competition. It is amazing that so many athletes can maintain performance successfully for years of college cross country.

For me that season was the expression of everything I'd learned from high school cross country magnified by a power of ten. Light poles were no more, but I used the same strategy. We'd go out for a six-mile trail run at a 7:10 pace. I'd tell myself that I just needed to hang for the first two miles. I could do fourteen minutes of anything. I'd make it through the first fourteen minutes, glance at my watch and tell myself I could make it through the next fourteen. When I passed that barrier, I'd ask myself if I could do that one more time. The answer was a resounding yes. And then forty-three minutes after I started, I'd finish the workout with the team. I used the Dawson lesson to break the run into chunks and the Kollar lesson to convince myself I was faster than I thought I was. Workout after workout, I looked like I belonged, even if I didn't always feel like I did.

I remember one girl on my team who was also a senior, faster than me, but not the best. She said at practice one day that she was so looking forward to graduating that spring so that she could wake up in the morning, wake up late in the morning (maybe 8 or 9) and have slow cup of coffee and read the newspaper. How small of a thing does that sound like? But there she was, twenty-two, having spent every waking morning since middle school either working out, going for a jog to loosen up, or having to consider how everything she did that morning, including consume a cup of coffee, would affect her running performance later that day. There were no arbitrary cups of coffee and down-time mornings for any of the girls on that team. Ever. She had been seriously schooling and seriously training since her early teenage years and at twenty-two, all she wanted was to experience a carefree morning and not have running guide every decision that she made from wakening to bedtime. It was a whole different world.

I'd had my mornings. My two cup of tea mornings, starting slowly with a book. Mornings that, if I was lucky, Van would have slept in a little past me and I might have had thirty non-running, non-working, non-schooling minutes to myself. The way I had gotten myself to the same physical spot that she was in, was so different. I wanted these mornings, the team mornings, centered on the physical challenge of my running-based exertion. I wanted to be right there thinking about everything I put into my body, every action I took, and how it impacted my running. And it turned out, I was good at that. In fact, I was a little too good at it, to the point that controlling everything around running became a compulsion. The season of college cross country marked a turning point in my dietary extremism. Until that point, I had been vegetarian progressively getting a little stricter and a little stricter. But that season, restriction became an ever-tightening noose strangling my normal body fat, my intramuscular fat and even my menstrual cycle ceased its monthly rounds. I had toyed with the idea of becoming vegan in the past but could never totally eliminate dairy. I still liked the splash of milk in my tea and the occasional yogurt or cottage cheese. Clearly NCAA Division 1 CC is not the ideal time to limit diet so severely. That fact is not lost on me now, but that season, I was getting faster, running successfully and injury free and it seemed like the switch to vegan should come then. Like I wanted to physically push my body to as many extremes as possible. Maybe I was trying to purge out of me all the hell that I had been through, the hardship, the pain, stare it back in the face by pushing myself as hard as I fucking could. Who knows? And then there were the visual cues I was getting.

I had noticed on the first day of practice, in the first few minutes of the first day of practice, that I was big for a college runner. At that time, in August, I was 5'6" and between 125 and 130lbs. A very healthy weight, especially considering that I had a lot of muscle mass. But on the team, my size was about inversely proportional to how I performed. I was running about twelfth out of fifteen and I was about the third biggest in terms of body size. If you lined up the team from smallest to largest, you pretty much had the finishing order. This fact was not lost on me. Most of the girls had tiny frames, were born small and had always been small. There were one or two girls on the team who could fit their fingers around their ankles. There may have been a couple who were in the range of 115-120lbs but most of them were less than 100 pounds. I had weighed 110 in the sixth grade. It would probably have taken five to six years of seriously committed eating and couch potato-ing to turn their fairy frames into anything resembling curvy. I had always subscribed to the notion that there were those who would never be "skinny", we had our genetic paths and that was that. Heredity provided a framework that was molded and sculpted with permanence and was not to be outdone by factors such as physical activity and diet. I thought, of course, that one's form could be moderated within a certain range by personal choices, but the range was kind of a preset and for some it would always be bigger than others. I would soon learn that given the proper levels of extremism, even *I* could, in fact, get "skinny".

I paid attention to the way they ate in group situations and to the way they talked about food, and I never got the impression that anyone else had disordered eating patterns or behaviors, although I'm sure some did and just hid it. I think that almost everyone who runs that kind of mileage, with that much intensity, for that many years, can eat a varied and expansive diet without ever having to even think about weight. The other girls carried calorie rich trail mix with them on trips, their moms sent them homemade, dense granola that they ate. One girl woke up an hour or two before practice, ate and went back to sleep so she could be both fueled and rested before morning workout. For most college runners, it is probably more important to make sure they are eating enough and opting for the proper kinds of foods than to be restrictive about anything. But I was certainly not there. I was far, far away from making sure that I got enough. I never overtly made the decision that I wanted to be small like them or thought that if I lost weight I would be as fast as they were, but I also knew that from my starting point, losing a few pounds would likely help my running. So, I got smaller. I made the choice to eat vegan and I began to eat many of my meals as just vegetables. On a typical day I would run, or run and workout, first thing in the morning, and once home would eat a banana and maybe a bag of frozen vegetables cooked on the stove. For lunch, I would have a cup of oatmeal with soymilk and a side of carrot sticks if it was a speed work day, or a big salad if it was a regular day. I'd go to practice in the afternoon for a couple of hours and have a dinner of baked or boiled veggies. I ate very little protein and almost no refined carbohydrates or sugars. Occasionally, I would splurge on some fat-free, sugar-free hot chocolate with a healthy scoop of Cool Whip Free. That was my treat. So, I was still ingesting a few non-plant-based products, but they were the exception rather than the rule. I would bake and cook for others without sampling, taking some form of vicarious pleasure in the foods I categorically denied myself. When the girls would talk about snacking on granola or having peanut butter, I stood idly by listening with alarm signals sounding wildly in my head: "Do you know how many calories you just put in your body!?!" Just as I was establishing the habit of strenuous running, I was nailing myself to the wall of strict denial-based consumption. It was all about patterns of behavior, once I'd established my routine, I could stick to it. But it was not healthy, and I was definitely getting stuck. I may have been free of the relationship-based control to which I had been subjected, but this self-imposed control snuck right in and took its place. I had cleaned out this spot in my soul, but didn't fix what was broken, leaving an opportunity for something else to flood right back in.

I was barely consuming enough calories to walk to my classes each day or fuel basic body function. But I never missed a single day of practice, never showed up late, never caught a cold, never even had a runny nose that season. Shit, I don't even think I got a blister. Certainly, I was consuming high levels of vitamins and minerals in the form that nature intended, but there was nothing else in my diet that should have fueled me to perform at that level. I continued to get stronger, fitter, faster, every day that I showed up, which was every day. I decided to run, and I ran. That was it. And it happened far away from physiology or biology, it was because I decided to do it. I did well in classes that semester too and breaking twenty was a distant memory; I had come so far past that goal. Decide and do. And I did.

Unfortunately, as absolutely all of my physical force and energy went into running, other normal things began to fall away from me. The relationships with my friends being chief among them. Celine, Virginia and the rest of the friends from Okinawa who I had become reacquainted with and who had helped me start a life apart from Van fell into the chasm of my pre-cross country life. I didn't return phone calls, didn't follow through with plans, I was basically just a bad friend to the people who had been so good to me and whom I loved. I formulated excuses to myself such as "no one else on the team has friends outside of running either" or "I was just too tired" or some similar version of the same delusion. But it wasn't as if I was making friends on the team, I was keeping to myself there too. It became difficult to even see my friend group because I felt the wrongs I was committing. How easy would it have been to let them know that I didn't have as much time to hang out, but that I could manage an evening or two, or a lunch or something? Or even just have explained the why a little more. But I didn't. I let the distance grow and I lost them. The beauty of looking back allows me to realize that, in fact, I probably was too tired to hang out. I had no extra energy whatsoever. Quite bluntly, I was starving myself and my decision to run was the only thing I could get my body to do. Emotions and connections take energy, basic body drives and human needs fall away. I had no idea then that's what was happening. My eating had gotten weird enough that being by myself just felt so much easier and like it was the "right" thing to do.

Now that I know the rarity of friendship even more acutely, I would be sure not to do anything so capricious as to allow myself to hurt those who love me by disappearing. I had spent a little bit of time getting back to myself, but somehow that semester, I was backing myself into a very a lonely corner. Life was becoming solitary and idiosyncratic. I interacted with other people all the time, but I maintained space, ever more and more. I guess I was probably keeping myself safe, in addition to not wasting psychological energy that I didn't have. Like my ex-coworker at Walmart, who had built herself a safety net of weight after abuse, I built myself a little cave. I can still remember the name of my first-grade teacher, but I don't remember the names of any of my team members or even the assistant coaches from FSU. Looking back, it all seems ridiculous. It was one of the most important and intensive things I had done in my life and my energy so totally focused on self-preservation and continuance that absolutely everything else fell into a fog. Singleness of mind and purpose was taken way too far and too extreme that semester. The same way that the final ten miles of a 50 miler or 100k feels like a focused, slog forward, that semester was all about pushing, single-mindedly toward the goal of succeeding at D1 cross. I ignored hunger and pain, carved out a rhythm that worked only to get me through, and followed it, step after step. Maybe I was healing some parts of me, but I was doing harm to others. I was trying to figure out who I was and where I fit, all of the things that most people do when they first get to college and there was something so safe about routine and rigidity. Where others might go to a YOLO mentality to figure out their middle ground, I went the other direction. Full hermit. Safe yes, healthy no.

I got faster, of course, but so did everyone else. I pretty much stayed eleventh or twelfth out of fifteen. A couple of girls fell out due to injury or illness and at times I was as fast as ninth. I participated in one meet in Gainesville early in the season. The coach just sent the "B" team to preserve his better runners for more important things. It was against other local Floridian schools and on a golf course. I remember getting ready for that run, going through our entire hour of warm-up activities, and sitting under our little tent as we all got numbered and got our shoes on. This event was something I had never conceptualized as a possible reality. The other girls were all nervous and cagey, but I was calm. Looking around at the trees, the rolling brilliant green nubs of the golf course hills and thinking: "This is it. Here I am at a college cross country meet." I could do no wrong, even if I had an off-day and ran a twenty-minute race, I was still at exactly the place I wanted to be. It was cool day for Florida, and I felt so good to be a part of this thing; I still could not believe that I was there. I ran, we ran, our B team came in second up against the other A teams and I don't remember my time or place. I remember the spit and snot on our faces, I remember the intensity of the effort, being cheered for, and pushed, squeezing every last drop of speed out of my legs. I remember satisfaction. I only ran two more meets that season. One at the University of Alabama and one at the University of South Florida. Two more golf course runs, two more experiences with all out physical exertion. Even though I wasn't friendship-close to anyone on the team, I loved it. I was a part of something which for so long had seemed to be a physical impossibility. I was on the team, maybe not a part of the team the same way a lot of the girls were, but I was there. I did that.

As the season wound down, I had dropped from my opening weight in that 125-130lbs range to 114lbs on a heavy day. I'd weigh myself on the lifting days on one of those old balance scales in the gym, watching the numbers get closer and closer to where the other girls always were. My bones showed, the striations in my muscles stood out as well as the veins all over my body. One could look at me and see exactly how I was put together, muscles, bones, and veins all standing out as separate things. My medium to large frame belied the fact that my clothing tags all had little tiny numbers or non-numbers like 0's or 2's and snakey little "S's". Even my D-cup boobs had shrunken down a cup or two. I didn't look healthy. The assistant coach pulled me over at the end of the season and suggested that I attempt to gain a little back. When does that ever happen in women's collegiate cross country? He told me it would be a good idea to take a week off and eat well. Honestly though, and this reveals the extent of my fucked-up thinking, I took pleasure in the fact that he had pulled me over among all those skinny, skinny girls to tell me that I was too skinny. That felt like just as much success as my fast times.

We did a last exhibition run with the members of the track team to start figuring out who was going to run what, come spring. It was on the track doing the 2-miler along with many of my cross country teammates. My old friend Jessica was there to watch, visiting. She told me she didn't like looking at my elbows, they looked like the elbows of a skeleton. Even now, she checks my elbows as a marker to make sure I'm not getting skinny like that again. I laced up and headed out, this time a bundle of nerves. It was a test of just what I had been able to accomplish that season. Most of our timed speed work had been on golf courses and dirt roads, we hadn't done a lot of track time trials, so this was going to be a surprise to me. So far, my mile times had been around 6:10 on the golf courses but I had never broken 6. Well, I nailed that two-mile time trial. I ran it in 11:45 and was incredulous. I truly could not believe that I had run not one but two consecutive sub six-minute miles. I was happy, I was too skinny, and virtually friendless but that late fall afternoon on the track at FSU, but I was happy. I was impossible dreams made manifest. I was sacrifice and I was perseverance. The world was small in the palm of my bony hand.

I had deliberated about what to do the following semester. I'd had one lab that was required to graduate, the now infamous Sensation and Perception Lab. It interfered with Monday's speed work, the one non-negotiable workout of the week. Some other workouts we could do on our own if we absolutely had to, but not speed work. So, what did I do? I did was any dream-weaving runner would do, skipped the lab and figured I'd work it out later, and then figure out how to graduate later too. It sounds stupid to write it now, but at the time, I wasn't overly concerned. When I chose to skip it, I thought that I would probably just stay one more semester, run track, take the lab, and double major in Psych and Lit. I was loosely thinking about grad school after that, wanting to work on a college campus and either do research or write. It felt like a toss-up and was a very fuzzy image of what might be to be. As the semester wound down though, my mother's continued illness in Germany, and Jess's own return to Germany after having graduated from Duke the previous May, became a strong pull. Also, my maternal grandmother had passed away and although I hadn't met her, getting together with my mom's side of the family had made me feel this deep ache for the person my mom used to be. Her depression was so deep, that the connections she had with my siblings and I, were undependable and seriously painful. Losing the grandmother, whom I had never known, grew this ache in me for closeness for family and probably just the human connections that I had severed as I whittled my body down throughout the semester. I wouldn't say that I was depressed, but I was detached and trying to make some decision toward reattachment. I decided to return to Deutschland one credit short of graduating and honestly thought it wouldn't be all that difficult to make up later. (Spoiler alert: I WAS WRONG)

So August, September, October, and November I had run for Florida State University's Division I Cross Country team. Me. Me, of the 24:00 minute high school average. I had been successful. I didn't miss a practice, didn't sit out a single warm-up, cool down, or lap of a single workout. I did it. I learned a lot that semester. I learned that the body is capable of amazing things, or far beyond amazing things. I learned that hunger and exhaustion are subjective. And I learned that no matter the size of the dream you're chasing or how good it feels to hold it in your arms, you shouldn't be reckless with the hearts of your friends and loved ones because you may never get a chance to hold them in your arms again.

Chapter 7
Breaking 40 and Broken Down

"Don't go looking for the reasons
Don't go asking Jesus why
We're not meant to know the answers
They belong to the by and by"

-Chris Stapleton, Broken Halos

So, I was back in Germany. Jess was back. Axel was also back and I was still entertaining some fallacious notion that maybe, just maybe I could still win his distant heart. I had been single for some time (at least it seemed like a long time at 22) and had regained some pieces of myself in my time away from Van. To be cliché, I had lost lots of emotional baggage with my physical baggage. I was living with my mother who was surrendering herself, or so it seemed to me, to the throes of the deepest, craziest depression possible. By then, she had been heavily medicated for five years, had had countless electric shock treatments, had been in and out of care facilities in Germany, England, and America, and was still ostensibly caring for my beautiful brother and holding down her teaching job. It was ludicrous, but I thought that maybe I could help right this precarious situation.

And I was fit. At least physically. Psychologically, my eating behavior was getting even further into the overly controlled range and was far from normal. Since what I put in my body was so closely related to the performance I was able to get out of my body, I could only maintain this delicate balance for so long, before a slip could bring me toppling down from the peak. But as I had already ascertained, my body was a fighter. For some reason, it didn't take as much calorie-dense fuel to keep me going as one would expect. I began to grow into the attributes of the skinny girl. My image of myself, which had always been hefty, was finally switching to that of littleness. And it is truly a whole different world to change your concept of how you look. I would love to think that this has changed some, but I would guess that although it might be more "okay" to be any size, you are still received differently when tiny than when not-so-tiny. I was petite. I could walk into a clothing store without worrying about how something would fit or how it would look. It all fit, it all looked good, and quite often I was buying the smallest size. And I was getting more male attention than I had ever gotten in my entire life. In high school, with some small exception, guys hadn't really looked my way, in college, it was mostly the same, and now, everywhere I looked, there was a man looking back. I didn't know how to fit this into my self-image. My mom had never imbued me with a sense of being pretty or cute as a little girl. She wanted the compliments she gave to be about who I was, I was smart, I was good, I never heard that I was pretty and didn't think of myself that way. In high school, I hadn't wanted to be pretty, quite the opposite, I'd done as little possible to make my appearance meet the standard. I wanted people to figure out who I was, not how I looked, or how I might look with the right amount of prep. This was different and it felt strange to me. I was a slender, fit, moderately attractive, educated, quirky, single female on a military base in a foreign country. I had my pick of attractive and eligible men. Based on how much male attention I was getting, it seemed like it was impossible to be too skinny. My experience then was probably what the cultural norm was for a lot of people, that's just what it felt like to be an ultra-skinny 22-year-old in 2000. When I had been curvy and fit, I hadn't felt like I had gotten much attention at all. Now I was anorexic-looking, and I was swimming in attention. This was new. It wasn't that I had the energy for any kind of relationship, but it sure was nice to be the hot chick for once in my life. I will add into this part, that this is my skewed impression of this time. The reality of it was that Jessica, who was curvy and beautiful and Alycia, my sister, who was thin, but not anorexic-looking and beautiful, were also the hot chicks, so I know it didn't really have to do with body size. However, my personal experience was that the smaller I got, the more looks I got, and that was reinforcing. Thank goodness for Jessica and Alycia, though. They got the reinforcement of knowing that they were beautiful and that they could still eat some food that wasn't a vegetable.

Meanwhile, my running and eating habits had pretty much carved out a routine which had the flexibility of a statue. Okay, at this point, my eating was ridiculous. I had even given up bananas for the most part. I ate veggies for three meals a day most days and sometimes I'd roll out a thin dough of wheat flour, a pinch of salt and water and make a thin tortilla if I felt like "splurging". I had a job as a cashier at an eatery on base. I worked from 10am to 2pm five days a week. I'd drop my mom off at school a little after seven, then go to the gym until work, and pick her up again after my shift. The schedule was ideal for my fitness habit, and I was a great cashier. Efficient, accurate, friendly, and superficially polite while truly being viscously sarcastic to those who deserved it. Although I knew I wouldn't be cashiering forever, it was nice to be wholly good at something and have it fit into my life in a way that I enjoyed. I loved interacting with so many people but most of the time across the counter conversation was the extent of my interaction. I dated a little, but my life was so rigid, I was beginning to feel that there would never be anyway to truly let someone in. Further, although I liked the people I'd dated, I never really experienced that spark of harmony or heart-beating-out-of-the-chest attraction. My heart was fairly incapable of beating quickly during any activity other than intervals. I still wasn't menstruating; it had been a couple of years and I really wasn't feeling any hormonally based urges or desires. I was shut off.

Writings from the time:

Close

I remember it with a fondness

Albeit superficial-

A body, disrobed and warm

Hands/arms that hold, caring, affection, the way it
exudes and is absorbed

To be that close-again

Has become so distant,

So foreign

So that even the recollection seems only
theoretical

A far away remembrance, rather than a possibility

Crash

It would take a tsunami

To drown my compulsions

To send me crashing from the ever-moving band—
faster, faster—of the taunting treadmill

To outsound the nagging of the calories counting
themselves in my ears

I recognize my sub-ideal health

I cite changes that would giftwrap my well-being

But really, what cataclysmic, tectonic shift

will cause the tsunami to disrupt this world?

I just hope I am not embarrassed by the collapse.

The second writing sample above I wrote worried that someday I would literally run to collapse on the treadmill and go flying off the back. Some part of my brain knew my behavior wasn't sustainable. Still, I ran and ran and ran. I felt detached from everything. I was cold all of the time. Calorie-deficit cold was deep, un-warmable cold pumping out of my heart and through each artery and capillary. My body was conserving what it could and I'm guessing my resting metabolism had probably reduced by at least a third. I would run around base or on the treadmill or through the woods by my house feeling that each day I was approaching a precipice, but it never came. To others, I was the picture of fitness and health, I remember people saying that I was probably "the fittest girl on base." I thought two things simultaneously: One: Damn Right! Two: If only they knew. Non-runners asked me all the time how I stayed so skinny and runners would ask how I got so fast. I answered them all with one truncated refrain. It was all about decisions. I chose every single day to work out between one and two hours and eat restrictedly. I made that choice every minute of my life. I got tired of people asking me, like I had some secret or there was a magic elixir, or like they just wanted me to tell them that I was just lucky, that I ate crap and drank a six-pack every day and no matter what it didn't affect my six-pack. Difficult choices and a lifestyle that didn't seem to match the people around me, that was what had gotten me where I was. They were choices anyone had the ability to make but they weren't comfortable, and they didn't involve three hours of screen time every evening on the couch. It was beyond practical for most people. But what I really didn't understand was that even if people couldn't commit to two hours of exercise a day, why couldn't they do 30 minutes or 20 or 10? Sure, I was on the way-extreme end of the spectrum, but at the end of the day a choice was a choice, and everyone could make it, or some version of it, if they were willing to. I sometimes felt frustrated with my own feeling of being stuck in my hamster wheel of extremism, but I was just as frustrated to hear that people who were paid to make much easier versions of these hard choices couldn't figure out how to do it.

Somewhere amongst all this I ran Marathon #3 with Jack McDermott. He came over to Germany from Florida, his first time on the continent, to run Rotterdam with me. I was in what I thought was good marathon shape. I had just run a 1 hour 29-minute half mile on a hilly course and running probably about 45 miles a week.

Jack came to town wearing a beret which I rarely saw him without. We rode up to Rotterdam the day prior to the race, picked up packets, etc. accompanied by Jessica our spectating super-friend. I tried to eat some actual carbs the night before in the form of crackers and pretzels. As I would soon discover, they did not react well with my veggie-trained digestive system. Or maybe I picked up some kind of intestinal bug in the day of travel. I don't know, but I do know what it did to me.

The next morning started fine. I had an extra cup of coffee in attempt to make sure whatever was anywhere close to my bowels would make its exit beforehand (another bad choice), and off to the start. Jack gave me a Breathe-Right strip to put across my nose and supposedly aid my breathing and I looked goofy as hell. I tossed it soon after the start. The gun went off and Jack yelled "Viva La America." Another wretched omen. There was nothing not comical about that trip! Maybe it was Jack's yell that caused the extreme stomach disturbance that was to come, at the time, I just found it mildly embarrassing. Now, I think it's fair to blame Jack because everyone should know better than that.

The first kilometer went fine but by the 2k mark, I was in pain. My stomach tightened up in what felt like serious contractions. I managed to hold my first diarrheal explosion to the 5k mark and after that continued to stop about every 5k. I was in severe abdominal pain from kilometer 2 to 42, even making me keel forward from time to time. I clearly remember thinking, "My god this is horrible, but at least after this, childbirth will be a breeze." Add a healthy dose of naiveté onto the already ridiculous day. I had a lot to learn about how bad pain could get.

So, the big question answered: No, I did not PR but I finished and Jack stayed with me the entire time. Poor guy, but how sweet. Then we drove home. That ride deserves its own special mention. First, Jessica has a VERY sensitive nose. Second, on normal runs in Florida, Jack's running clothes had been known to get a bit odiferous. Third, a Toyota Tercel is a very small vehicle. We had gotten lucky enough that morning to find the one open parking spot in the entire city of Rotterdam and it happened to be not at all far from the start/finish. As is common at about every European race I have ever participated in, showers were provided, but by the time we finished and walked back to the car, there was not a single synapse firing in the direction of finding showers before commencing the journey home. Nope, not a single part of my body desired that freshly-scrubbed shower feeling over the feeling of sitting and not moving for the next several hours. Jack didn't argue and Jessica didn't have the foresight to force us. She probably would have, had she realized the olfactory sensations with which she was about to be greeted. We stunk. (I say "we" mainly to cushion the loneliness and the accusatory tone of saying "Jack stunk". And because you can't smell yourself, right, so I'm sure it was 90% him.) Jessica survived the six hours, but our return trip was driven very efficiently, and I think Jess was one step closer to madness than she had ever been before in her life. She had that certain glazed look of the insane when we finally disembarked, a stinky cloud wafting out behind us in silent escape. Jack returned to Viva La Florida, and I returned to my minimalistic ways.

Sometime shortly thereafter, I met the lunch-time guys. What a great bunch of runners. A collection of personable, mixed background speedsters, most of them were at least a decade older than me, but a couple were closer to my age. Mark was my favorite. He was a British officer with two small kids, a great sense of humor, and a charming smile. And there was Mick the Brit, Fred the Dutchman, Ritzi the Italian, and few more on rotation. I had also been promoted recently. My amazing cashiering skills could not stay undiscovered indefinitely and it was noted that I was good at my job. I became a "duty manager" and got a new schedule. The position involved much more responsibility and freed up most of my middays. The lunch-time guys met at about noon every day. They invited me to join one day, and I was hooked. Their training pace was faster than what I had been doing for most of my training runs on the treadmill, they typically ran four-to-five-minute kilometers for their training runs, with speed sessions that were sub-four-minute kilometers. So, it felt like a new challenge to me. We did speed work, tempo runs, hill workouts. It was like having a team again. It was great to socialize a little bit more and I could socialize while running so it was a perfect mix. I still kept mostly to myself, but I really enjoyed their personalities. Ritzi would run behind me if there was ever any ice on the trail so that he could try to catch me if I fell. One time, not an icy day, I did fall and came out of the forest with mud and dirt all over my backside. Everyone had a good laugh about four guys going out to the woods with a girl and the girl coming back with evidence that she'd been on her back. The training was just what I needed to recharge my running. I had been on a plateau just hanging for a while, still running about 19:30 for 5k's; not getting any faster or slower. Most of them were running eighteen-to-nineteen-minute 5ks and thirty-eight-minute 10ks. They were just enough faster that it pushed my training threshold without killing me.

My new routine of meeting and running with them also helped me through a new difficulty. I encouraged and oversaw a medical retirement for my mom. Her depression was not abating, her treatment not ideal, and not working like "they" said it would, and her job as a teacher was overwhelming. Though she had a small class of special needs students, there were days she couldn't even remember their names. Her bosses had worked with her the last several years, holding her job, letting her use FMLA as needed, and seeing changes that were trending negatively. My presence there had not helped as I had thought it might. The lesson that other people must solve their own issues was one I had not learned yet. It was conflicting place to be; my mom had been a rock, yes it was years ago, but sometimes I still hoped she'd get back there. Hope is such a hard thing to extinguish. My inclination is to trust, trust that people will do what they are supposed to, that the people who love me will be able to express their love, and to trust that things will get better. They weren't. I didn't want her to have to retire in her early fifties, it was something I never thought about as a kid, my mom, this bastion of strength, unable to work, live, and love. But she couldn't. I was angry that she couldn't. I was angry that she couldn't be my mom. I didn't want to be in my early twenties and motherless, but she wasn't able to mother anyone. It's hard to lose the emotional mothering when the physical body of your mom is still there. I wanted to be able to reach her, but I couldn't. I had to work through the grief of it. I was taking care of my mom and I didn't recognize her at the same time. And it was all so, so serious. I had gone from an abusive relationship to college cross country asceticism and was now taking care of my mom and my brother while working and grieving. Fun wasn't something I'd had a chance to experience except in small bursts, no wonder I tried to hang on to the bright spots so tightly.

Writing about my mom:

She feels my anger, but we will let it float

Her illness, seeming false

An imposter of a depression

And how we must rise to the sympathy
summons

Rise, rise

For her chair is too comfortable to allow her to
rise

She is stuck

She has crumbled,

Melted

Into the ease of the crazy façade

And smothered expectations

She licks her lips, her glasses droop, her eyelids
cannot resist the magnetic pull

Towards each other

That look. Drugged. By medical mandate.

I am mean, caustic, I don't mean to be, but I can't
watch her turn away from this life, from me

And worse, I record it, with this cold tractate

Angry,

No one has the power to dredge up these
emotions in me, why her?

She hears music, she says

Tunes from her childhood

They lull her into this semi-sleep, away, from this,
from me, from all that could be

Grief

There is supposed to be some sort of process-

Some grieving-

Yes, pain, maybe gut wrenching pain

Associated with the withdrawal or loss of

motherly love

No one would be surprised if screamed out

"but she was my best friend"

And sunk to my knees, wanting to be swallowed
up by the hardness of the floor

But no. Those emotions feel false to me.

I stand, wondering why I am numb

Touch my belly-my god-I can actually feel the veins
of my lower abdomen beginning to protrude

All feminine softness gone

I am hard, angular, serrated

With emotions to match

Wooden chairs: my enemy

I think of eating, of indulgence,

And decide, yes, I will do it, indulge

I'll have vanilla tea, unsweetened, alone

As her retirement was set into motion, I had a few rough days which were smoothed out considerably by just going with the guys for a few hard miles. Most days we got workouts completed in less than their one lunch hour, sometimes it went a little over, but we got in six to seven miles over varying terrain with various goals. They raced often, and I started doing more local races too. German races are fun. They tend be cheaper than comparable US events and more frequent, with most small towns hosting an annual 10k event. The courses are pretty accurate; the participants are well-trained. But there is one big difference in a German race:

Everyone is geared up and slender-ish so you cannot tell who the fast ones are. At an American race, I could always pick out the top contenders, not so at a German race. Another difference is they often offered warm fruit tea instead of Gatorade, especially refreshing at the end of a winter race. Of course, at that time, I still would not have indulged in a whole cup of the delicious brew no matter how parched my throat was at the end because it would have been a waste of calories. Ten kilometers was the standard local event distance. Fitting for me, as my coach in college had told me that he thought the 10k might be "my" event because I was so steady once I got going and I had great endurance while not quite the speed of a 5k runner. Although I could easily run a sub-twenty 5k, I still hadn't broken forty in a 10k. So that became my goal.

I ran a couple of races getting very, very close but just like my first sub-twenty attempts, always just off. Finally, I registered for a race in Zweibruecken, Germany called the Rosenlauf. It was a four loop, ten-kilometer course, some dirt, some paved, flat and fast. I got there feeling good despite my protruding bones that were held together by muscles which were equally visible. It was a little chilly, there was a slight breeze, but the conditions were almost ideal.

The start came and I was confident. I started ticking the kilometers off one after another, right on pace. Each one a little under four minutes and the first lap a little under ten minutes. My third loop I slowed (it's always the third, isn't it?) and I came through very close to thirty minutes with one lap left. I was still on pace, but there was no room for error on that final leg. I summoned all that I had left and focused on picking up the pace just slightly. A 2.5-kilometer loop is long enough that it's easy to misjudge. Too much push early would have sapped me at the end, too little and I'd once again miss the mark. My push had to be almost imperceptible, but enough. My legs were so tired then that I truly couldn't tell if I was going faster, if I had made the right adjustment, or if my speed had faltered even more and my exhaustion had increased enough to send me a false message about my speed. I neared the end of the lap. I knew it would be close. I crossed the line, done, my friends already finished and drinking tea came to support me. Only then did I realize I had done it. It was a big milestone for me. I had broken forty minutes, but I was broken down. I had become a girl defined by routine: running and restrictive eating. My bones and muscles showed with every move, my lonely heart did not. I was in my early twenties, living in Europe with none of the spontaneity or passion typical of my youth and position in life. I was watching life spin by me and away from me under the guise of being an athlete.

Chapter 8
Bodensee

"You must find your life."

-Captain Von Trapp, Sound of Music

My mom's early retirement happened a couple of months into the year. She moved back to Rochester, New York where we had some extended family, and the hope was that she'd be able to get some medical care that would finally help. I had sole guardianship of my brother while he finished out that school year. I was 23 and he was 15. I was living a very regimented and grown-up life, but I didn't feel like an adult. Still, I ran. It gave me my normal, but I was starting to feel just how abnormal my normal was. I didn't want to make up for missing the craziness of youth, of college, but I wanted something that I didn't have. Something ill-defined and out of reach. I'd walk in the evenings, sometimes, around the small German town where we lived and see the lights of family rooms illuminating glowing dining room tables with families huddled around. It looked like love and belonging. It looked like something I couldn't have. I didn't know if I wanted it, but that warmth looked so nice. I tried not to stare, but it was hard. Life was about to change drastically again, and I couldn't have predicted just how much I'd be broken out of my routine and thrust again into something new. A little warmth was, in fact, coming my way.

I felt like I was on the verge of something, but I also felt stuck. I think it's a feeling that happens before something new or an opportunity is about to be placed in front of us. Spring came with all its inherent promise. I felt that it would be hard to ever meet anyone whom I could let into my life. I dated occasionally – and smiled and laughed – but never connected. I had the dueling sensations of being content single and feeling an aching incompleteness. I was still feeling the effects of getting male attention day in and day out at work and I was getting tired of it. Similar to how I felt in high school, I was realizing that this was mostly about my appearance. Of all the things these military guys may have been interested in, deep conversation was not at the top of the list. My hair had grown long, and my brother's had gotten a little shaggy and he came up with the idea to shave our heads. While I couldn't quite manage to agree to a full shave, I did agree to chop it all within an inch of its origin. We made a pact and one night we cut. I wish I had thought to donate the eighteen inches of hair that fell from my head, but I didn't. I held up my hair to finger length from my scalp and chopped and chopped. It felt so good. I can say after that, that I completely understand how hair cutting can be associated with grieving and letting go. I felt free, free from some of the mom-grief, free from the femininity of long hair, free from some of whatever that feeling of restraint was.

I was still working at Pizza Gallerie in the Community Center on Ramstein Air Base. I was a duty manager with a reputation among the cashiers as a bit of a bitch. I was sarcastic and cynical towards most of them and did not tolerate much stupidity or laziness. I have since come to realize that there is a certain amount of laziness and stupidity one must allow for in any food service job, probably any job, but I just couldn't tolerate it without a little bit of an edge which could maybe come across as a little mean. We hired a new cashier, Jeb, not a momentous event, and initially, I took no particular notice. He was cute and young and had a charming smile, but I had grouped him in with the other younger-than-me cashiers who worked there. His dad was in the military, and he had hung around after graduating from high school while he figured out what to do next.

Try as I might to go about my normal routine, something was beginning to feel different. I was at the edge of the Grand Canyon on a foggy day. I could feel my proximity to the edge but I couldn't tell if I was about to plunge dangerously or if it was safe to behold? And how long had I been in this fog? I found myself beginning to anticipate excitedly the shifts during which Jeb and I worked together. I hadn't yet acknowledged to myself or anyone else that the heart flutter thing was happening. It had been so long since I had felt it, I don't think I even recognized it at the outset. In addition to that, I had halfway decided to work through the summer and then move to North Carolina where my father had a beach house. My brother would accompany me and finish high school in the states, and I planned to get my bearings and start graduate school. I still had a couple of things to figure out scholastically. I truly thought that finishing my one missing credit would be easy to remedy and although I might need a couple more post-baccalaureate credits to get into whatever grad program I wanted, it would be easy to do in a semester. So, with all of that on the horizon and heavily on my mind, the idea of a relationship didn't enter my consciousness, but flirtation certainly seemed embraceable.

So, there I was, working, running, taking care of my sweet, misguided brother, moving out of my mom's old house and into a small apartment, planning a move back to America for grad school, and feeling this amazing, comfortable, happy sensation whenever I was in close proximity to this dashing cashier. I remember one day his mom called into work to say that he was going to be late if he came in at all. He was at a junk yard with his dad and not back yet. My heart dropped to my shoes, and I realized just how much I was enjoying being around him. I looked at the clock confused about how I was going to pass the last few hours of my shift without him there. I turned my attention back to the conversation, letting her know that we had limited staff, it was important that he show up, etc. And yes, my motivations were somewhat selfish and somewhat related to actual work. He did make it in that day, and I think it was the first time I admitted to myself, that maybe, just maybe, I had a little bit of a crush.

There was also Dino Dash. We had some arcade games at the Pizza Gallerie, among them, Dino Dash. It consisted of two big, garishly lit buttons each corresponding to one dinosaur. Two players raced each other by pushing the buttons as quickly and efficiently as humanly possible to move their dinosaur from the start position to the finish of the race. Jeb and I Dino Dashed as frequently as we could allow ourselves without arousing any suspicions. We hoarded quarters and we dashed. Our shoulders would bump, we'd nudge, it was carefree and innocent, and I felt youthful and unburdened. This was easy. I guess it was what youth was supposed to feel like. We hadn't officially gone anywhere out together, but the cogs of change had begun to rotate.

About that time, I had a conversation with Jessica who was waitressing at one of the adjoining restaurants. We discussed the difference in sexuality and sensuality and how, for many men that we encountered, it was clear that they were looking for sexual connections and sensuality wasn't usually part of the equation. I, of course, thought immediately of Jeb, and told her that I thought he seemed to have the sensual side to complement the sexual side. I thought that he'd definitely be someone from whom I could get a nice kiss. It had been a couple of years since I'd had a nice kiss. Jessica lurched her car, looked at me severely and said, "From the kid?". What could I say? "Yeah…." Didn't seem to cover it, but that was all I came up with. I guess I felt like I was still a kid too, he was 19 and I was 23, it was a difference, but it didn't seem like anything to prevent us from kissing. That kiss sounded so nice, and I wanted to remember what the warmth of a nice kiss felt like.

That weekend, a group of employees were going out in downtown Kaiserslautern. It was *the* place to go and still makes me smile to think of downtown Kaiserslautern on a spring or summer evening. Crowds out and about on cobblestone commuter walkways, slow meals and long drinks, laughter and closeness. I agreed to go and since Jeb and I were closing up, it was agreed that he would ride with me. I stopped home to pick up my brother and down we went. It was the first time we had conversed in an environment that didn't reek of pepperoni or offer the solace of competing dinosaurs. There was a bit of first date discomfort even though my brother was with us, but mostly I just liked being with him. We hung out at a bar, trying to be together among a group of ten or so, and it didn't work all that well. He left to go to a dance club from there and I declined despite repeated entreaties. As I walked back to my car, sad that the night was ending, but happy at the prospect of where this was going, I happened upon Jessica in the midst of what appeared to be a very nice kiss. Of course, I interrupted her. The same cogs of change had begun to rotate for her too.

The next weekend approached, it was mid-May and the prospect of going out with the work crew loomed again. This time we were all headed to a sleepy place called the Holzwurm in the small village that I lived in. As it turns out, it was only a block away from my apartment. Travelling together with Jeb made sense so we went back to my place after work so I could get ready. I relished the giddy effervescence of initial attraction. I truly couldn't tell what was happening with him emotionally, but after such a dearth of romantic anything in my life, the feelings that I was experiencing were more than enough to sustain me. We walked around to the bar. Though it was May, a chill still permeated the air. We walked in and were greeted with the Friday night melee of coworkers who are drawn together only by commonality of employment. We were multi-national, multi-age, multi-ethnic, and multi-interested but for me there was a very singular thing going, and that was Jeb. We socialized separately but seemed always aware of where the other was and how and where the sparks between us were flying. As the night wore down, it was decided that most of the group would go back to another coworker's house within walking distance and sleep as no one (except me) was in condition to drive. Among the guests sleeping at the coworker's abode was Jeb's recently ex-girlfriend. Jeb casually mentioned that he did not want to go where she was going. What could I do, but offer some floor space at my apartment?

As I transcribe these words about the outset of my relationship with Jeb from journals and so many years have passed, I think about all that has changed. I hear my youth, my optimism, my ability to blindly see the very, very best in people and my inability to clearly see their faults. As the story progresses, I hope you understand that I have tried to stay true to the experience in the sense of describing what it felt like at the time, even as my mature self-recoils at my naiveté and wants to reach back and give a little more big-picture vision to the girl that was hurting and didn't know, that was lonely and reaching, and that wrapped her hands around a rose. I will progress, difficult though it may be, with how it all unfolded. When you wear rose colored glasses, all the red flags, just look like flags.

At this point, the probable outcome of the evening seems obvious. Further details about who this guy was, lend support to this seeming foregone conclusion. Jeb was the cool guy. He turned heads, he commanded attention, and he had a charm that was infective. He drove a Camaro, he skipped school, he smoked Marlboros in high school. He always had a girl, always had friends, always had that undefinable magnetic element which allowed him to travel the right direction doing all the wrong things. In short, he was my complete opposite.

But back to that night. We got back to my house late and he had no sleeping attire. My ever-so-giving brother offered him a pair of penguin boxer shorts which Jeb gladly took. With it, he got a nickname that stuck for years, "Penguin". Penguin-clad Jeb proceeded to attempt to sleep on the floor of my bedroom at the absolute furthest spot from where my futon lay. I told him he could come closer, which he eventually did until he shared the futon with me. It was small and a traditionally Japanese one, which was more of a very thick blanket on the floor. We passed the night cuddling close and that was the extent of our intimacy. To me, it was perfect. It was closeness and warmth; it was budding attraction; it was slow enough to not upset my fragile balance. From that night, until sometime far into the future, we only spent a couple of nights apart. That night, that silly night, in a tiny German bar around the corner from my house, something shifted.

I kept running the same mileage and I was still eating minimally and a bit freakishly, but it didn't affect Jeb at all. He knew that I was different than the other girls he had dated, but as long as I wanted to be with him during the time that I wasn't running, at the gym, or working, it worked for us. Most guys who I had dated seemed to react to my workout and eating regimen as if it guilted them into wanting to do the same thing or be more like me. They'd tell me that they might try being a vegetarian or ask me to go for a run, but it seemed somehow fake. With Jeb there wasn't an ounce of him changing anything about who he was, he seemed to accept me and I him, and that was that. That ability to be my quirky self was what hooked me. It was like taking a deep breath and thinking, okay, this is me, and this guy likes ME. Before then, I didn't really know if I was worthy of that.

The summer progressed, we were getting closer to our intended departures, him to family in Mississippi where he might go to college or join the military or just work, and me to North Carolina. Soon we'd have to buy plane tickets and make the actual plans to go along with these futures. I remember working that Fourth of July at the Freedom Fest on Ramstein, it was getting down to the wire. Weirdly, Jeb and I had been together for less than two months and we'd been living together that entire time. We had a very simple conversation. I said that I thought maybe I'd stay in Germany a little longer, he said that he would like that and maybe he'd stay a little longer too. That was it. We were deciding our future with maybes and loose language, and it felt right. Comfort was the single word I associated most. But that seems strange because there were other discomforts screaming at me that I just couldn't hear.

Jon was still living with me and was a constant source of worry. It seems strange that as he turned 16 and I turned 24, I was his guardian. To us though, it seemed normal, I'd always been like a mom to him and there was no question that I could care for him. I made him lunches, got him to school, picked him up when it didn't interfere with my schedule and did the best I could to make sure he felt loved. What must it have been like for him? I don't know. He was a teenager living without either parent. He too had said goodbye to my mom and felt, like many teenage boys, a sense of grievance with my dad. They'd divorced, she'd retreated into herself, and my dad had to re-figure out life too. This once-tight family unit had developed our own orbits and I wanted so badly to make sure Jon was okay, that he'd get through this. He was using though. And I was naïve. I knew he was drinking and that didn't seem horrible to me, we were in Germany, it was normal for teenagers to be drinking recreationally, but Jon's habits were more than that. I'd find clothes soaked with pee, I'd find bent spoons and I didn't really understand what they meant. I knew they meant use, but not the extent. It scared me to find the things, but I thought I could make enough homemade dinners to ease it away. I chalked it up to experimentation that would get out of his system as I cooked love into our meals. And then he threw up out his bedroom window and onto the kindergarten below us. The landlord was not happy. He filled squirt guns with yellow water and shot it out the front apartment windows onto the pedestrians below. It was a small town, the pedestrians too knew the landlord and thought they'd been peed on. Maybe it was pee, I don't know for sure. The landlord stopped by to talk to me and saw our ramshackle furniture, or lack of most furnishings, and decided we couldn't stay. I don't blame him; I wouldn't have wanted us there either. It made sense for Jon to try living with my dad again and we made plans for him to go, the intent was for me to follow sometime thereafter. It was very shortly after he left that I had the conversation with Jeb about staying in Germany a little bit longer. He'd slept over every single night since that first accidental night, except one night that we went to his parents' house.

Meanwhile, my mom was still unwell in Rochester and seemed to be getting worse. She was between inpatient care and day care facilities and was not yet at the point that she could even have an apartment on her own. My sister was back from FSU for another summer break. After the eviction notice and Jon's departure, I looked for another apartment. Jessica went with me to a couple and then I found this cute, little place. It was the ground floor of a two-story house and the landlord, Gudruen, lived on the floor above. She was a single, older lady who had lost both her son and her husband young. She smiled, but you could tell it was to cover some deeper ache that never went away. I liked her immediately. She asked if it would be just me and I had to think about my answer. I said no, it wouldn't, I had a…. was he a boyfriend? Did I have a boyfriend? I said that there was someone else who would stay sometimes too. Oh shit, I had a boyfriend, and he was going to live with me. How had this even happened? We had never, not one single time discussed our relationship and yet here we were. Informal and comfortable.

It was summer romance at its height, and nobody expected it to last through the fall. For me, it felt like respite. My mind had been buzzing for years, I was too young to have been acting so adult, and I wanted a break. Jeb was a break. We didn't need to talk around each other, to me that was huge. It seemed like a lot of people I knew needed to fill up space with words and I desperately wanted quietude, but I didn't quite know how to express that need.

Jeb offered quietude; I felt this slow recharging. His dad was going to retire from the military in about a year, so although we were living together in our apartment, we still visited their house frequently. I sat with his mom one summer evening and she asked me, bluntly, about our relationship. She asked me where it was going and said that she could tell by the way I looked at her son that I loved him. I quickly informed her that I had been in love before, and it didn't feel quite like this. The casualness betrayed the seriousness. Everything had softly progressed without either of us realizing what was happening or acknowledging it. To me, that made it seem magic. I never understood that something could just feel that easy. He just came over one May night and never left. It was that simple.

Eventually, some time that summer, we did go on an actual date and admit to "loving" each other but we were very hesitant to label it. Mostly we just let our relationship define itself. All of this happened in just a few months. It seemed so long then and life had been happening so quickly; my mom's retirement, moving out of her house and into the eviction apartment, Jon's living with me then leaving. I felt at times like I couldn't keep up. To have had three months with Jeb, that felt like peace, was huge, but how ostentatious to have been told that it was love and to have believed it myself. I was in no condition to love, but I wanted it badly. Being a little broken isn't usually the best spot to start anything, but I was being swept along and all I knew, right then, was that it felt better than anything I'd experienced before.

Shortly thereafter, I asked my boss if I could change the location of employment from the Community Center Restaurants to the Officers' Club. Both facilities were operated by the same management team, and I could keep my role as a duty officer. Jeb had been promoted at the Pizza Gallerie and was now a duty officer too. I thought it might be a conflict of interest to having us both work the same position, and I was also still somewhat sure that it wasn't going to work and was protecting myself from the discomfort of the aftermath of working with someone post-break up. I was given permission to make the switch and with it came a schedule change that almost completely cut me off from the lunch time guys. I was still running with the same speed and frequency but had somehow put on a couple of pounds. I had broken the 120lbs mark for the first time in years and I was more than a mite frustrated. In retrospect, 120lbs was still too low for my build, but I could not understand how with my extreme dietary restrictions, daily miles and weights, I had gained the four pounds. These were the kinds of things I obsessed over. They would get in my head and take hold and ultimately challenge my sense of self-worth. My frustration, my inability to understand that my body was begging for some sort of equilibrium, for enough calories to menstruate, my not-yet-repaired psyche led me to begin purging. Now, eons away, it seems so impossible and so unlike the person I am. I hurt for that girl. I would love to hug her and tell her she was so beautiful, but it was too soon for her to know.

With all that I had experienced, abuse, college running, the removal of normal motherly love, I kept it all together on the surface and I had held my sanity together pretty well. But I did have some lapses, and this was one of them. I didn't do it frequently and I kept it very well hidden, but even as I did it, I could feel that it wasn't who I wanted to be. And really, the little bit of purging that I did was just the tip of the iceberg of years of overly controlled eating and exercising. I still needed something to hold on to.

I was holding onto Jeb, and I was holding onto running. I hadn't been doing much speed work, mostly maintenance running. I was still doing a long run either weekly or bimonthly when Jeb slept in. One of my coworkers mentioned that she had a friend doing the Drei-Laender (Three Country) Marathon. It was in October, and I found out about it in August. They had same day registration which gave me a training goal without a 100% commitment. Perfect. The marathon was flat, fast and went through Germany, Austria, and Switzerland. It was about a five-hour trip from the house and seemed ideal. I followed a training plan that I got from the internet and altered it to fit my needs. I hit most of the long run goals but wasn't doing much speed or tempo work.

That summer had been rainier and colder than normal and early fall followed in its footsteps. The race approached and I felt ready. I really wanted a sub 3 hour 40-minute Boston qualifying time. We got to the Saturday before Sunday race day, and I had somehow gotten to that point without a reliable car or a secured rental. I think I expected Jeb to help with the logistics of the planning, but like most things, we hadn't really talked about the details. I began to feel the crushed hopes of twelve weeks of training and no trip to Bodensee for my PR. I tried to pretend that it wasn't a huge deal for me, and I had left a backdoor open for not participating by planning to register on the day of the event. I made a shrug-off attempt, but Jeb could see how much I wanted to get there. He went to base, got a rental car, and basically told me to hop in. We packed a few things and off we went for our first road trip, my first race during our relationship, and our first hotel room together. We made good time getting there, the Autobahn and Jeb got along famously, but we still had to find a hotel. We drove around, found a spot to park, and got out to look on foot. We walked among fountains and ancient cobblestones, the same ones where Sound of Music was filmed. I recognized them from the movie and felt the same romance and charm I do from watching what is still my favorite movie. Unfortunately, though, after hours of cramped car riding through the afternoon and evening of pre-race day, the absolute last thing I wanted to do was sight-see. I wanted a hotel room, I wanted it quickly, and I wanted to stretch, eat, and relax. We found a place to stay and pretty much collapsed.

The morning came early and made gray and rainy look pleasant. The sky was so dark with frowning, angry clouds and rain poured forth. Keep in mind, I was still unregistered. At this point of the story, any normal person would have taken a day to visit a museum or a cathedral, somewhere indoor and dry, make up for missed hotel sex the night before and simply enjoyed the trip. But we went to the start of the race. They asked me repeatedly at registration if I was sure I wanted to register for the full marathon. Even the volunteers at the marathon were questioning my sanity as they looked ominously towards the heavens. Every time I was asked, I wanted to back out, but the little runner inside me, the little engine that could have turned around, spurred me instead onward. I registered. I found Jeb and we made our way to the start.

I have a sharp picture in my head of a man in tight fitting clothes doing a German Bon Jovi-esque song and some sort of warm-up aerobics on a stage. His presence made me feel comfortable because I realized there was at least one person a little crazier than me out there that morning. Jeb was already soaked at this point, and we had checked out of our hotel room, so he had nowhere to go after the start. I was frozen as well, not sure how we'd meet up at the end and very unsure about the whole experience. But we were young and lovey so it all still felt alright.

The gun went off and I started steady and strong, wet and cold. The race progressed and the rain did not abate. I remember it was picturesque, the mountains dwarfing us and putting the runners in our place in the universe. We may have been competing in a marathon, but the mountains had withstood time's marathon in way that the best and most resilient of us never would. We ran around the Bodensee, golf ball sized raindrops plunking down onto us. The volume of water in that lake must have increased two-fold as I ran. I didn't really enjoy the scenery as I was already thinking mostly about persevering and pushing through. I was chilled through and through, water squished out of my soaked shoes with every step. Still, I felt good enough at halfway that it seemed reasonable to break 3:40. By mile eighteen, or kilometer thirty, I felt myself fade a little, but I drew on all the resources I could muster. I held myself together as well as I could, knowing the conditions had caught up with me. The rain had not let up even a little the entire time and I finished in 3:41. It was a PR but so close to meeting my Boston goal that it hurt to have missed it. Anything anywhere could have taken off a minute. Probably, had I been physically comfortable, I could have finished in under 3:35 but the bone-chilling, constant rain took a lot out of me. I found Jeb close to the finish, he had stood outside in the rain almost the entire time. I had never seen him look so frozen; at least I had the benefit of moving the entire time and chasing down a goal. He had endured and had no medal to show for it. I was emotional at the finish. I think I held back my tears, but I was feeling totally and completely in love with this guy who had waited in the rain for four hours. If our first overnight defined the next many years of our life, that first marathon together certainly made me acknowledge just how deep my feelings had gotten.

We travelled home and traffic was thick. The five-hour trip stretched into six, then seven, then eight. Our rental was not a compact car, but it certainly felt like it after spending five hours in it the previous day, four hours running that morning, and eight more as a passenger. I have a vague residual impression of that ride back as being physically uncomfortable, but mostly I just remember feeling like everything was perfect. Not much had gone my way that day, but with him, it just didn't matter. The trip could have been ten or twelve hours, as long as he stayed right there in the driver's seat. We had completed our first marathon together, different but together. And that phrase, different but together, seemed to sum up a lot about us. I knew that evening as I glanced at his profile in the setting sun, speeding along the Autobahn that we'd be travelling many more roads together on our individual terms, but solidly together.

Chapter 9
And a Baby Makes Three

"Who, being loved, is poor?"

– Oscar Wilde

Fall trudged along mutely into winter. Jeb and I had been living together for about six months. I was working full time at the Officers' Club as a Duty Officer and running and enjoying coupledom. When I thought about it, it was amazing to me that I had gone from feeling so irretrievably single to the other half of a very entwined couple in such a short period of time. For the first time ever, I wasn't worried about graduate school, or finances, or life beyond the day. I felt happy in a simple way that had eluded me in my late teens and early twenties. My eating behaviors were still unbalanced, but somehow it was easy not to consider that part of me in my assessment of the relative normalness of the time. I don't remember if I was still vomiting after eating, it was not a very long time that I did it, and I guess even after I had mostly stopped there was still a recidivistic time or two. It was never a daily thing for me, or even every other day. I do know for sure that I was still very restrictive and still vegan, but I had begun to incorporate more carbs from non-fruit and vegetable sources. As it turned out, a few extra calories and regular sex was all I needed to start menstruating again. This had happened during the first or second time Jeb and I had been intimate, thank you Universe. It certainly took me by surprise, I didn't think I was consuming that many extra calories. Now, I cannot imagine viewing menstruation as a symbol of excess caloric intake. I had resumed a level of intake to allow my body to complete its normal functions. In my early twenties. I had abstained from so much. And here was life, literally.

Jessica and W had also moved in together after that first weekend, though Jessica was hesitant to admit it then. Strangely enough, W and Jeb had the same last name and were unrelated. Jess and I found it weird but weren't prescient enough to suspect that the result would be that all of us (and our kids) would share the name. Around Thanksgiving we found a deal for a week trip to Turkey for 99 Euro (about $100) including air fare and hotel. The four of us booked our vacation for early January and anxiously awaited our getaway. Jess and I had been to Istanbul the previous winter, but this would be a trip to coastal Turkey and this time we would be bringing men!

I continued to run through the early winter and attempted to keep my fitness level at about the same point that it was when I ran Bodensee. Christmas season was particularly busy at the Officers' Club. Squadrons, groups, and clubs from all over wanted to book parties with us. Jeb would come over from the Community Center when his shift was over and wait for me while our functions ended. I'd help get cleaned up, get the rest of the staff out of there, secure the money, and lock the doors. We were alone together a lot of late nights in that huge, dark club and although there was a rumor that lots of couples would find deserted corners for intimacy, we never joined that group. I took my job, as all my jobs, even sandwich maker, very seriously and it just didn't seem like something a serious person would do. All those possible corners for exploration and all I ever did was my job. How was I that serious, that young? The folly of youth was never my folly.

Our Turkish vacation approached, and the position of maintenance manager had opened at the Officers' Club. I talked to the manager about Jeb taking the role. It would mean that we'd be working under the same roof again, but it also meant a significant pay raise.

I guess I had pretty much overcome the fear of things not working out or I wouldn't have made the suggestion. It was decided that right after our vacation, Jeb would start training for the position.

So off to Turkey we went. It was as amazing as we could have hoped. I would get up before everyone and run, scope things out, and then return to the Turkish style buffet breakfast and my freshly wakened co-vacationers. I bought a beautiful Turkish scarf that I could use as a veil and added a few words and phrases of Turkish to my vocabulary. I was mistaken for a local several times on the trip, which I loved. And it was kind of nice to wear a partial face covering and be a little incognito. There is something about not feeling at all judged by your appearance that makes you really think about the other ways you come across to people. I did turn a few heads being veiled and with a red-headed American; people seemed not to be able to figure us out. I loved the feeling of fitting in and taking in as much of the culture as I could, it just felt a little bit easier to sponge it when I looked a little more Turkish than American.

Upon our return from our first big trip, life felt right, or righter. Jeb and I were working together, living easily together, and still getting to know each other. It had been about seven months of cohabitation. Although I had formerly eschewed our working together, it was easier than working in separate facilities. We would often drive in together and then I would run home or go to the gym after my shift. After a couple months of this easy pattern, I was displeased with the fact that once again, I had gained a couple more pounds. I decided to go to two-a-days for my runs to boost my mileage and try to figure out what was going on. I'd add a twenty-minute run in the morning to whatever my normal workout for the day was. I figured that if I didn't change anything else, it should get those couple of extra pounds back off too. I stuck with the double running for about four more weeks and then it happened. I was putting on a pair of my favorite work pants, probably size 2 and they were too snug right in the lower abdomen. I immediately got upset, threw the pants away, and ranted about there being something wrong with my metabolism. The next day I was reading the newspaper on the way home and started sobbing uncontrollably. In my defense, it was a list of young soldiers from our area who had recently been killed in action, but seeing their pictures brought me to such an abnormal state of raw emotion that Jeb began to suspect something else was going on. He bought me a pregnancy test. I thought that was a drastic overreaction on his part, I'd had amenorrhea for years and had only recently resumed some still irregular menstruation, we used protection most of the time (there had literally been maybe two exceptions), and it just didn't make sense to me. And then I saw a little plus sign materialize before my eyes. I couldn't believe it; I didn't believe it. There were too many reasons for it to be impossible, but some part of me, once I saw the test, knew it to be correct. I was pregnant. I was going to be a mom. I was unmarried, uninsured, and living in a foreign country making twelve dollars an hour. And it was the happiest moment of my life.

We made an appointment at a German hospital for mid-May. At that point, Jeb and I had been together for about eleven months. Hardly any time at all. The day of the appointment came and with it, beautiful lilac blooms and wildflowers brightening the hills all around us in Germany. I sat in the office of Dr. Monika Mader and she had the most fragrant lilac bloom that I've ever smelled in a vase on her desk; I just wanted to keep inhaling. And then she did an ultra-sound, and I heard the most amazing little heartbeat in a tiny little lima bean and lilacs became my favorite smell. To this day, when lilacs start to bloom, I associate them with motherhood, fecundity, and life. I called my dad and he and my brother, who was still living with him, got on the phone together. I told my dad he was going to be a grandpa and my brother he'd be an uncle. I could hear the emotion in my dad's voice. For years I'd joke that no dad was ever happier to have a daughter call him and tell him she was pregnant out of wedlock because of all that had happened up until that call. That wasn't true, of course, my dad had loved me for who I was and it was me who had taken longer to realize it. He was happy to be a grandpa though, if a little worried about the circumstances under which this life would be brought into the world. I think he trusted me to parent, he just knew it wasn't going to be easy. As usual, he was right.

As Jeb and I adjusted to the idea of being parents, spring turned to summer, and we were walking every night. I was still running with no problems, no nausea, some tiredness, but I felt physically better and healthier than I had my entire life. On one evening walk, we were on a paved path outside our quaint German town, he stopped and asked me to marry him. Up until then, we hadn't really talked about what we were going to do, how we were going to parent, support a child, live our lives. Jeb was 20, I was 24. I told him that I thought he was too young, it was too much of a commitment, and that we could figure out how to take care of our baby together, but we didn't need to get married to do it. I also told him that he was free to not have to feel obligated to the baby, I knew, without any doubt that I wanted this, but if he wasn't sure, he was free to go. We could carry on with our pre-baby plans and I would still go back and live with my dad while I figured out my plan and they baby's. He said no. He wanted marriage, he wanted family. He had already been thinking about it and although he was young, he had lived all that he wanted to before my pregnancy and was ready for everything that marriage and a baby would bring. What could I say to that? Here was this guy who I felt had brought me equanimity, I was carrying his baby, I was happy, our baby was healthy, and he wanted to marry me. I said yes.

The pregnancy progressed and the baby was growing well. I went from being vegan to vegetarian because I felt like I needed dairy and eggs. In fact, I don't remember ever feeling sick during my early pregnancy except one time I got a little light-headed and nauseous at work and came home early. I made a sandwich with egg and cheese, and it was possibly the best food I had eaten in my life. I learned in a new way, pushed by my little lima bean, to develop a different relationship with food. When I was hungry, I ate. I ate to nourish, to grow a body and to take care of my own. In the moment of knowing that I was pregnant, all of my other bullshit stopped. I became a scholar of nourishment rather than denial. It's interesting to me that all it took was knowing that I was taking care of someone else to push me right back to normal eating, when it was just me, I had to take care of, it had never hit me. The other life lessons I'd garnered so far had taken work, they'd taken time, reflection, and synthesis. A slow row to hoe. Not pregnancy. It was instantaneous. It was me and the lima bean, growing and glowing.

I ran, I worked, I ate, I watched this perfect little life grow. These were again some of the happiest days of my life, it didn't seem that happiness could keep compounding, but somehow it did. Still, though happy, my life stayed at the serious tempo it had always had. I'd had a few months of respite, of living with someone, and now there was a baby on the way. What little glimpse of easy youth I'd gotten, quickly became caring for another little, tiny youth who would be my own. I have no question that I was truly and purely happy, yet I marvel at how adult I had to be. From sixteen when youth crashed around me until twenty-four with a baby on the way, I was a grown up. And now, it was almost time to be a mom, something I'd be practicing for, for a very long time. Jeb decided to join the military after the baby was born and began talking to a recruiter. I would quit work once the baby arrived and he would work a couple more months and then join the Air Force. It was all coming together. It seems weird to me now that I didn't feel any stress at least consciously about anything that was happening. I had an inherent ability to think that whether or not I made any big decisions, the path would always just emerge in front of me. I know that since then, the universe has forced me to several crossroads where I had to pick. One or the other.

Chapter 10
Vows

*"Having children just puts the whole world into perspective.
Everything else just disappears."*

– Kate Winslet

Pregnancy, blissful pregnancy. I loved so much about it. After the first trimester tiredness went away, I felt beautiful and glowing and like the epitome of health. I felt like this was what my body was made for, and I got my boobs back. The baby grew and so did I. We decided not to find out the gender and my due date was December 15th. I kept running the whole time and felt so good. I read the only book I could find on aerobic exercise during pregnancy because it had been studied so little at the time. It was called Exercising Through Your Pregnancy by James F. Clapp, M.D and between the book, my doctor's encouragement, and the way that I felt, I knew it was okay to keep going. That Thanksgiving, just a few weeks before the baby was due to meet us, Jeb and I registered for and decided to run the local Turkey Trot on base. It was a 5k course through some forest trails and paved roads on base. Since he was already signed up for the military, he was feeling like he should have been pretty fit and although we didn't ostensibly set out to race, I'm pretty sure he wanted to at least keep up with me, if not beat me by at least a few seconds. That didn't happen. I ran the race in about twenty-five or twenty-six minutes which was about six or seven minutes slower than my non-pregnant pace. At about thirty-seven weeks pregnant, that was my slow pace. And yes, I did beat Jeb, by a good five minutes, not that we were racing.

December arrived and I was as big as I was going to get and was still very mobile and comfortable. We had had all kinds of hang ups getting our marriage to happen. Jeb's parents had moved to Mississippi and had to send his original birth certificate just like my dad had to send mine. They had to be officially translated, and the list of steps went on and on. Finally, we had all the paperwork we needed for a small ceremony at a Germany courthouse. I didn't want to or really didn't even consider buying a dress. I borrowed one from Jessica's mom. It was black and stretchy and fit over my full term belly no problem. We needed two witnesses and the town with the closest courthouse was about fifteen minutes away from our tiny apartment. On December 9th, 2003, Jess and her mom sat in the benches as Jeb and I exchanged vows. We promised each other to always put the other person first, to never let anger grow, and to respect the bond and the permanence of the vow we were taking. It was the most beautiful thing I'd ever participated in. We walked down an ancient cobblestone sidewalk afterwards to a small café for some hot drinks. It was another one of those perfect moments that I felt like I could watch from outside myself. I was married, I would meet my new baby in just a few more days, and my best friend and family sat there with me. Everything, everything, was a dream come true. Jeb and I drove to a windmill atop a hill after our little ceremony and looked out at the world around us at our fingertips. We embraced, we felt forever.

I had one more appointment two days after that. I was so happy to be able to change my last name on my hospital paperwork. Now, it was official. Baby would have the family name. I ran/walked the evening of December 13th and began to feel the onset of some mild contractions. Late that evening, as Jeb was finishing a closing shift, I called him home from work thinking it was time. We went to the hospital in the early morning hours of the fourteenth and I was contracting regularly and painfully. They examined me, no dilation at all, and told me to go home. We did, but I couldn't sleep, the contractions were five to ten minutes apart but stayed regular. Finally, the evening of December 14th, I went back to the hospital, already feeling tired. I hadn't gotten any rest and hadn't been able to eat much. This time they said I could stay because I'd been having regular contractions for over twelve hours, but they said I had made no progress. They sent me outside for a walk. It was December, in Germany, in a hospital surrounded by forest on a hill and it had snowed for the first time that year. I went out and walked the cold, slippery paths and continued to contract every four to five minutes. I held on to Jeb with each contraction, hoping upon hope, that the walk with helping with something. Back in we went, still nothing, but they did give me a room.

A word about German hospitals and birthing: They emphasize and make available everything homeopathic and natural. Water births are available for everyone, midwives are used instead of doctors, unless there are complications, and there are birthing balls and wooden rungs on the wall to grasp onto and squat. Everything is designed to give the mom all the options for everything natural and that's usually what happens. Not quite my story, but so cool to have every natural option available.

I kept moving at their direction, spent some time in the water bath, tried squatting and sitting on the ball, I was not dilating, and my water hadn't broken but I was getting exhausted. At twenty-four hours in, not much at all was happening and I was starting to get anxious. I labored through the night, Jessica and W arrived sometime on the afternoon of the 15th and still no baby. Finally, the staff decided I was so tired I needed an epidural if I was going to be able to push. In addition to contracting, the pain had been so bad, I was throwing up and dry heaving and when the epidural decision was made, I was so ready for some relief. It took another hour for the epidural guy to get there and then finally, with people holding my arms, my back, and my head while I heaved and contracted over and over, I realized I no longer had control over my body to even hold myself up successfully. They use walking epidurals in Germany so the pain is dulled but you can still move. Movement is the key to giving birth. You wear what you came in, with nothing on the bottom and you move in whatever way you need to, to coax the little one out. It was awesome, even if that's not exactly what my thoughts were then. I continued to labor until about 9pm on the 15th, when they decided a doctor was needed. My water still hadn't broken, and they were beginning to worry about the baby. The doctor. Ugh. He was from Turkey and spoke decent German and broken English. My German, normally decent conversationally, wasn't good enough for his German as a second language, so we used English. He decided to stop the Pitocin drip to get me ready to push. For the next few hours, he tried all kinds of things among which was a huge leather belt across my stomach with people holding both ends to push the baby down. It felt horrible and a little barbaric. I was screaming in pain and crying and sometime, in very heavily accented English, he told me two things. One, I cannot work with you if you keep making noise like this. And two, and this is the one that stuck and that has stuck through every phase of my life since then… "Did anyone tell you this was going to be easy?"

I was so mad. How could he say that to me? I was almost two days into laboring with my first baby, I'd been throwing up, shitting, pissing all over the place, I was exhausted and no, no one had told me it was going to be fucking easy. But no one said it was going to be that hard. I had done everything right throughout that pregnancy. Stayed active, eaten well, no caffeine, no alcohol, no anything that might in any small way have impacted my baby's health. I planned a natural birth, and I was sure I could do it. No, no one said easy, but my body wasn't acting like I was expecting it to. This was my first time with the experience that despite the best intention for life to go a certain way, it may not. And it might be very hard, harder that you ever understood it could be.

At 11:58 pm on December 15th, my beautiful baby boy Zeffrey Leif was born. He had the largest head possible and had to be suctioned out, but out he came. So perfect. After everything I had read about how to get ready, nothing prepared me for that moment. I couldn't believe he was mine. They put him in my arms after doing the basic tests to make sure he was healthy, and they left the room. I really don't know why everyone left at once, but they did. I was there in a hospital bed with a baby in my arms and I realized I had to throw up again. There was no one there. I was able to call out or press a button or something and someone came back just in time for me to heave my final heave of the evening and take little Zeff as I passed him off. I realized in the moment, that life as I had known it was completely different. I had a new life to be concerned about all the time. I needed, for a moment at least, to hand him off and throw up, I was too exhausted to know that I could hold him safely and do both. I was momentarily dependent, but now, my biggest and most important job would be keeping this little life safe. He was mine, mine to take care of, mine to love, and mine to shepherd through life and it wasn't going to be easy. Beautiful Zeff, with his beautiful cone head, was perfectly healthy and he breastfed right away, no problem. He would continue to do so at every opportunity he could get for the next several months. That boy could always eat.

After a couple days in the hospital, we went home to our tiny one-bedroom apartment. I think it was probably six or seven hundred square feet. Our bedroom had room for a queen-sized bed against the wall with a crib right next to it and a changing table adjacent to that. And that was it. Not that Zeff ever slept in his crib. Although he ate very well, sleeping for any stretch longer than about an hour was not his gift. I was no longer working, so this lifestyle of short bursts of sleep, constant feeding, and having to sit around all the time to do both at someone else's whim, was a huge transition for which I was not prepared. Jeb kept working without interruption, going back to work immediately, so I went immediately into solo parenting. I was exhausted, my body felt weird, and I didn't know what to do with so much time at home. Zeff was eating about every ninety minutes and would fuss anytime I put him down to sleep. I started taking long walks with him in a front carrier zipped up in my coat against the German winter and we circled our town, the town next to us, the trails all around. I could feel his little warm body and his longer breathing as he slept against my chest, and it was better than anything I'd ever felt. On Christmas Eve I decided I was ready to run again. My stitches had pretty much healed, and I was walking comfortably. So, I put on some warm clothes and left Zeff with Jeb for my first thirty minutes away. When I returned from the run, my pants were soaked down to my knees, I had peed all over myself, and had not even felt it a tiny bit until I came back into my warm house. Obviously, my body wasn't ready, but I was not at the age to listen and so I kept at it. It was only that first day that I peed so fully without awareness, but I continued to have incontinence problems while running for the next couple months. I got a running stroller and as soon as I could, I'd bundle Zeff up and he'd sleep in there. Paradise.

Chapter 11
Maryland, Motels, and Mice

"I got dreams. What can I say?
Sometimes life gets in the way
Well, getting by and wanting more
Baby, there ain't no shame in being poor"

– Whiskey Myers, Trailer We Call Home

Jeb's enlistment date was in mid-May. We kept our schedule of me staying home, nursing, nursing, nursing, and running most days and Jeb working. Sometimes then, if I'd run in the evenings, Jeb would sit in a rocking chair with Zeff on his lap and play video games. That was my break. It would have been so nice to have some house help during that time, to get maybe a run *and* a shower or anything. Yet, I was thankful for the break and even if that was his major contribution to family life in those days, it felt like enough. The change of life pace had caused a little bit of the post-partum blahs but being able to run and still do the activity that made me feel like me, helped immensely. As soon as that became regular again, everything else started to feel like it was normal too.

Because Jeb was joining the Air Force from Germany and I wasn't working, we would lose our base sponsorship as soon as he quit his job on base. This meant we had to move out of our meager dwelling because Zeff and I couldn't stay in it without someone having a job on base. Still, weirdly, I wasn't stressed. How was I never stressed then? It all just seemed like part of the journey, and I never questioned where the path was going. I just knew to keep going. A moving company came and packed us out, which was funny because we had so few belongings and nothing really worth hanging onto. It was all to be put in "storage" until we had a duty assignment, so with nothing left except what we could carry, we went to stay with Jessica and W for a couple days.

Then Jeb left for Basic Training. I had a baby, no home, no car, and now no husband. Basic Training was six weeks, but it would have been a long time to be couch surfing with a five-month-old. I stayed with Jess and W a few days after he left and then flew back to my dad's house. I literally had a duffel bag, a stroller, a cheap car seat and a diaper bag. It was a life that fit on my back and in my arms. I stayed at my dad's a couple weeks, went to see my sister, and tried to figure out how to fill up my days. It was both lonely, fulfilling, and amazing to know that I was feeding and protecting this little life with so little structure. Having him felt like enough. I held him all the time, slept with him, nursed him every two to three hours, but I didn't care. Well sometimes I did. It was a lot, but a lot in the best way. While Jeb was at Basic, I got back into pre-pregnancy shape. I stuck with vegetarianism rather than veganism, it was a good fit and something I could easily manage with a transient lifestyle. My running-incontinence had abated, and I felt like I had my body and fitness level back where I wanted them. For me, breastfeeding and figuring out how to resume my choice physical activity made getting back into shape easy. The baby weight literally melted off. It took several months to get back to the shape I wanted to be but getting back to the same relative size didn't feel like a challenge.

Finally, the day approached for us to travel to Texas in early July for Jeb's graduation. We got to Texas in the July heat, I figured out a rental car, and made it to the motel. We saw him march in a parade the evening before his graduation and my heart was so full of pride and longing and the future that was to come. I wasn't sure if he saw us, but we saw him. He couldn't come see us or talk to us that evening, it was an exhibition only. But after six weeks, my goodness, I wanted to be able to touch him so badly. This little tease made him real again, but it also made the fact that I'd been so alone even more poignant. Graduation day was the first time I had felt pride that brought me to tears and caused a veritable swelling inside. I can't describe it. Jeb was one of the only ones graduating with parents not there, but he had us. We met up after watching him graduate in the hot Texas sun. His ginger complexion and was so tan and not the image of the man who had left. He was chiseled, exact. Wouldn't break any rules. Was this the guy that had stolen a tamarind from the Commissary in our first days together just to show me that he could with no compunction? He wouldn't even cross a street without permission. I couldn't understand how the Air Force had changed what had seemed his core nature prior to joining, but Basic Training definitely knows how to grow compliance. Different yes, but there was the same Jeb too. He held Zeff. He held me. After six weeks of going it alone, it was shelter from the storm. We were so broke. The trip had taken everything, I was travelling with what had become my norm: backpack, diaper bag, stroller, car seat, and baby. It was a refrain that was getting too familiar. We spent a few hours together over the next couple days and tried to figure out what came next. I didn't want to couch surf anymore, but we didn't know for sure where he was going. Just before I left, we were informed that he'd be in Aberdeen, Maryland, in welding school at an Army base. It would last until October. God, I couldn't imagine being homeless with my baby for the next three months. That felt weighty, but I didn't feel like there any other options.

Zeff and I flew back to North Carolina, Jeb flew to Maryland, and we planned a weekend trip. Like so much at that time, I just kept believing that everything would work out, sure I was without a home, but homes are transitory, this thing we were building was bigger. I'd drive eight hours with a baby in a borrowed car. We'd stay in motels or with people we knew, we knocked it out a day at a time. I don't remember thinking much about the future. I knew we'd be making a home together and I knew that it wouldn't be too long before we'd have the opportunity to do so, but my days mostly, were just spent waiting. I'd be up with Zeff at six, if he slept that long, in whoever's guest room we found ourselves in.

I'd nurse, I'd plop him in a stroller, I'd run, I'd make food and play and read and maybe do another stroller stint later in the evening. We just were. It was simple and weirdly both full and lonely at the same time.

On the second weekend visiting Jeb, I decided not to leave, I couldn't do any more time without him. There was no temporary housing in Aberdeen, but I was going to make it work. My sister had come with me that weekend and we found a motel with a weekly rate. She didn't really want to leave me there in the motel, but I assured her it was fine, it would all work out. Jeb could see us evenings during the week, and weekends, but he had sleep in the barracks. We'd need a car, though, for this whole thing to work since there weren't grocery stores close enough for us to walk to and we'd have to get to and from base to pick Jeb up so that we could see him. I'd need some way to transport Zeff and myself around even if it was a rig that wouldn't get us far. We had a few hundred dollars to our names, and we started searching for a car. After a couple days and a lot of dead ends, we found an old Chevy Nova for sale for $200. It ran. We test drove it, or Jeb test drove it while Zeff played in the grass of the owners' house, and I sat with him. The Nova had a rust hole in the driver's seat floor and a bad exhaust leak. Exhaust somehow blew into the car from the leak and the hole in the floor. But the damn thing ran. We bought it. I had talked to the wife of the owner a little during the transaction. She asked me if we were going to put the baby in the car. I didn't understand why she was asking. Of course, we were going to put the baby in the car, there was nowhere else for the baby to go.

A day or two later, there was a knock at the door of the motel room. There she was. She told me she was taking the baby in her car, and I was to follow her in the Nova to a repair shop. I hadn't been apart from Zeff at all in the last few months, or ever really, save for the runs that I went on before Jeb joined, and I hated packing him up in someone else's car, but I did as she asked, feeling uncomfortable the whole time. We got to the shop, and she knew the people, she asked them to fix the exhaust leak. I stood there ashamed and freaking out. There was no way I could pay for what she was asking them to do. I didn't know what to say to anyone. The humility of poverty is a weighty thing. I could compartmentalize it in my head most of the time. We didn't have money, but we weren't poor, I felt like they were different things. Then there were moments when it was so obvious it hurt. Yes, okay, we were poor, though never in spirit. I knew in that shop, though, without question, that even over the time span we were there in Aberdeen, there'd be no way to have enough extra money to pay this bill. She didn't know how destitute we were, or maybe she did.

She dropped us back off at the motel and said she'd come to get me when it was ready. And that's just what that angel did. She took me back to the repair shop and paid the bill, which was more than the price of the car. Now she let me put that baby in it. She was satisfied that he was safer this time. This woman sold us a car for two hundred dollars and paid something close to three hundred to get it fixed for us. She did it so certainly and sternly that there was no question. I started to tell her that I couldn't accept her help, but she wouldn't even let me get the sentence out of my mouth. She wouldn't let me speak my shame out loud. I never heard from her again, but I wish I could say thank you. I know that wouldn't be enough, but I hope she knows. And I also hope that someday, I can make that kind of difference in someone else's life. I had a motel room, a baby, and a few hundred bucks and I needed a vehicle. The Universe delivered and did a little extra to take care of me. Did that lady know how significant her gesture was? Do we ever? The only other thing we ever heard from them was a couple days after that, her husband stopped by the motel. With a crowbar. He told me to keep it under my bed and to be able to reach it all the time at night.

That moment is one that restored my faith in goodness and my belief that no matter how bad things get, there's always a tiny window of a way that things that can work. I drove that car until October, until tech school was over, until it was time to head to our first duty station. Jeb and I had called from a payphone to get insurance on the Nova, I drove it every day to base to see him and bring him back to the motel for dinner. We'd eat together whatever sparse meal I'd cooked in the eight square feet of kitchenette that I had, and we'd walk. We'd speak of things other than motels and money and I'd bring him back to base to say goodbye. There were so many goodbyes. And how did I fill the days of those months? Zeff spent at least an hour a day, usually more, in the running stroller, and he spent time nursing, still always wanting to eat. I found him a few books and toys at the cheapest thrift store I could get to, and I held that little boy every moment he wasn't on the go. There were hard days, days when the few dollars a week I had to get us through didn't seem like they'd stretch enough, but they always did, I made them. There was a day, towards the very end of motel life after I'd dropped Jeb back off at base that I saw a mouse run across the floor of our room. When the options before you are so narrowed that there's just a lone door at the end of long hall, it's both easy and hard to keep going. You have to, but you long for other doors. But with the scope narrowed, like with everything else, you adjust to what's available. By degrees, your norms adjust. The long hall becomes a long haul. But then a mouse running across the stained carpet of a one bedroom with kitchenette motel, brings you back to the reality that poverty sucks. Just getting by with a little baby doesn't seem like it could possibly provide all the things you want to give him. It's easy to feel like it's unfair.

Jeb got orders that let us know where we'd be going next. It was Ramstein, we'd be heading home at the end of October. As I made loop after loop in the town of Aberdeen with my running stroller, I had seen a sign on a church that said they accepted car donations. I wanted to pay the car favor forward and this seemed like a good option. I talked to the pastor, and we made arrangements for a drop off. I was hoping the car would go to someone who needed it, but I think they probably sold it or auctioned it. Either way, it was given as a gift and with the hope that it might help someone the way it had us. Jeb, Zeff, and I rode to the church on our last day in the country. We dropped it off, walked to the train station with all of our belongings on our backs, and rode the train to Baltimore where we caught a flight back home to Germany. Goodbye and good riddance to Maryland, motels, and mice.

Chapter 12
A Taste of Loss

*"Don't be scared...Women can handle the worst kind of pain.
You'll find out one day."*

— Gayle Forman, If I Stay

We got to Germany towards the end of October. It was beautiful, it was fall. The trails called and that running stroller and I answered the call. Jeb went right to work, we had ten days in temporary housing, and we got our first house. It was the most amazing thing I could ever have imagined. About twenty kilometers away from base in a small German town. It was two stories with a basement, three bedrooms, two bathrooms, a kitchen, a living/dining area. Space. Space for babies to grow, space to be human, and no space for vermin! We made quick friends with the landlady, Liesl, whose heart had broken, and would never be fixed. She had lost her husband early and then just a couple years before we moved there, lost her son to a car accident right outside of town. She smiled the saddest smile a woman could wear, and it never covered up her pain. The house we lived in would have gone to her son had he survived. Liesl's daughter, Stef, and her family (Fred, her husband, and Anna and Lukas, her children) lived down the street from her. Fred's parents, Walter and Inge lived right around the corner from us and this whole family unit became our second family. Walter had survived a Russian internment camp during WWII. He didn't talk much about it, but he did tell a story of having been so hungry at one point that the prisoners drank motor oil, it was shortly before they were released and, somehow, they survived. Suddenly, a mouse in a motel wasn't that bad after all, perspective is always a gift. Walter had the bluest, most honest eyes a man could have and was good through and through. And Inge was his perfect counterpart. She was a compact fireball of energy who swore by her post-dinner peppermint Schnapps to keep her healthy.

It was so good to have family again, I soaked in their love and relished its warm embrace. This was a life I could live. Our town was surrounded by an endless circuit of well-maintained German trails, and I could have gone up to forty kilometers without touching the same trail. I should have gotten off road tires for the number of miles that stroller took on the trails, but the standard ones sufficed. I'd bundle Zeff up and out we'd head, exploring, learning, never really getting lost, and loving every moment of it. He usually slept in the stroller and sometimes it was my only down time during the day, but it worked for me.

We had a bed, a crib, a couple of beach chairs, and a kitchen table set. Still not living a life of luxury, but those days were idyllic. We settled into a pattern. Jeb was up and out the door by 6:30 or 7:00am, I'd make him breakfast before he left, then feed Zeff, or the other way around depending on who was up first. Zeff and I would play and read for a couple hours, then I'd pack him into the stroller. We'd do an hour to an hour and half in the stroller most days. We'd walk to the Baeckerei, the grocery store, sometimes to get coffee with Inge and Walter in the afternoons. Jeb got home about 5pm and I'd usually be finishing up some nice dinner with fresh ingredients. Zeff would go down to bed about 8pm and Jeb and I would have a little time to ourselves before we did it all over again. A couple times a week, I'd drive to base and do Commissary shopping and use one of the gyms on base that had a parent and kid room where the kids could play in a center area of the room and all the workout equipment faced it. On really bad weather days, I'd use the gym option as my back up to get my run in. My mix of stroller training and the occasional treadmill training had gotten back into racing shape. I could easily have broken twenty-one minutes in a 5k anytime. Twenty minutes would have been stretch, but I could have gotten close. Fall turned to winter, and we spent our first Christmas in that house; it was a gift. It was warm, it was light, it was the type of house whose windows I'd walked by longingly just a few years back. We still didn't have much, but I finally knew that warmth. I felt it in my soul.

That summer when Zeff was eighteen months, we went to the annual fest in our town, with all of our neighbors/family/friends. Zeff was bubbly and mobile and well-loved. Strangers would tell me they could tell he never missed a meal. I looked around at the beauty of our lives and wanted another baby more than anything. That night I told Jeb my thoughts, we made a couple attempts, and within a month I was pregnant. This time, I knew the routine. I was so excited when I saw that positive test. We made an appointment at the hospital where Zeff had been born and had the first confirmation ultrasound at six weeks. The first ultrasound showed a cystic hygroma. Hopefully, not many have had to look that phrase up to know upon reading it that it's a usually the first sign of a genetic problem. It presents in most of the common abnormal genetic patterns such as Downs Syndrome and many other less common ones. It looks like a webbed neck. And that's what we saw, a little ball with a tiny heartbeat and a pocket of fluid around the neck. Mind you, at this time in my life, I still believed that everything would work out and that babies who were loved, survived. Genetic issues or not, this little bean was going to grow into the most beautiful, perfectly imperfect little one who had ever lived. I was worried, but thought I probably just needed to do some research and figure it out. We scheduled an amniocentesis to try to determine what the cause might be. The procedure worried me some even though the risk is relatively low. The results showed that she was a little girl with Turner's syndrome, or only one X chromosome. She would need hormones to develop during puberty, would be smaller than average, and might have a few learning issues, but Turner's babies lived and had full, happy lives. Our doctor, Dr. Buechler, told us that when found at this point in a pregnancy, a baby has about 30% chance of survival. I took those odds. She gave us a thumbs up on the ultrasound and my world was back in order. I researched what I could, I talked to a couple people from a mom and kids play group about special needs families and the military, and although I still had some residual worry, I was feeling like was something I could prepare for and handle like anything else.

However, the military insisted on adding one more challenge to our lives; Jeb got orders to deploy to Iraq and was going to have to leave on very short notice. Like less than a week. I was left with an atypical pregnancy, a baby who was not yet two, and a house to maintain. It didn't bother me all that much, though. I'd gotten a thumbs up on the ultrasound and had full faith in our second baby's ability to fight and to get through this pregnancy. The first time I felt her move, at about eighteen weeks, I sobbed tears of joy, alone in my bed at night, my hands around my belly. Unfortunately, my little girl had some other issues that went hand in hand with Turner's. The ultrasounds were revealing more problems and finally I went to a specialist who found a serious and fatal heart defect. She told me that the baby had no more than ten days to live in utero and she pointed out that the baby had stopped processing amniotic fluid. Her midsection circumference was growing, but she wasn't getting any longer. The waste elimination process wasn't working, and it could have serious side effects for me. They explained that the waste could cause toxicity for me and that a sudden influx of waste into my system could cause all sorts of different complications. If it happened during the day, chances were good that I'd be able to call emergency services and get help, but there was a possibility that if it happened at night, I may not wake up. They gave me a couple days to think about what I wanted to do. I talked to Dr. Mader, the one who had the lilac on her desk when I found out I was pregnant with Zeff, and she told me that most moms do better later in life if they let their babies who can't survive pass naturally and don't make the choice to end it. I called the American hospital too, hoping to get some advice and maybe a second opinion. My first call answerer was some Airman who, when I explained the situation and that my baby had Turner Syndrome and other congenital defects, thought I meant "genital" defects and sounded disgusted. I finally got to speak to a doctor who told me sharply, "We don't end pregnancies here." Not the discussion I was hoping to have.

I was single mothering with a toddler at home. I had a baby who couldn't survive much longer inside me, definitely couldn't survive after she was born, and I was twenty weeks pregnant. I talked to Jeb and made the choice to end the pregnancy. I also talked to my friend Paul who was an officer deployed with Jeb and he pulled a few strings and got Jeb sent back home on the next flight. Paul was another angel, there when I needed him. I was a mess. I loved and wanted this little girl so much. The last several days of the pregnancy when I was just starting to show, people were commenting on how excited they were for me and telling me congratulations and I'd break down in tears because I knew she couldn't survive. I remember one of these instances happening at the Commissary. Someone that I knew vaguely congratulated me, I started reflexively crying and said the baby wasn't healthy and couldn't survive. No one knows what to say in these situations. I don't know if I would, even having been through it. She told me that she was sorry to hear it and then gave me some version of saying I could try again, before walking away. And just like no one really knows what to say, no one who is losing a baby they love wants to hear that they can have another one. Life doesn't work like that. We love these babies; the ones we are losing or have lost. Of course, we can love other babies, but in the moments of loss, thinking of putting something in the place of loss doesn't help, and might even hurt worse. Having Zeff kept me going and Jeb got home less than 48 hours after I had called him with the news. A couple days later we went to the hospital where I had to give birth to the tiniest, most beautiful little luminous being that could be. Her lifelessness looked so incredibly still. They brought her to me wrapped in a tiny blanket, inside a small basket. My heart was broken. They gave us time to spend with her and said we could have as long as we wanted. Making the decision of when it had been "long enough" was impossible. I didn't want to say goodbye to this little life that had been growing inside me for the last twenty weeks. No mom should have to be in that position, but there I was, saying goodbye to little girl, who we named Phoenix. I loved her wholly and completely. In the years since, I have come to understand Dr. Mader's advice that mom's feel better in the long run if they let nature take its course. I had a choice, but it didn't feel like one. How could I, as a mom who was the only parent home, take a chance of not waking up for Zeff? How or why would I have continued to carry a baby with a diagnosis of lethal Turner Syndrome? I couldn't. So, I chose, and I said goodbye in a planned way that was no less heart breaking. They gave us the option to have no ceremony, have a ceremony for just her, or to have a joint ceremony with babies that had passed. We chose the joint ceremony not knowing when it would be. Although it sounds morbid, they wait until there are enough angels to have the ceremony.

Coming home from the hospital was horrible. I don't have any words for it. I felt so empty and so desperately, achingly, sad. I didn't want to lose my sadness because for me, it felt like the truest way to hang on to her; it was the thing I had left. I wanted to stay in bed and cry. I felt like it was such an injustice. I felt like I'd had to make a choice when there wasn't really a choice to make, and I felt so confused. Until that point in my life, I didn't really think things like this happened to people like me. And I maybe didn't even know what I meant by that. It wasn't fair. I had so much love, I wanted this little baby so badly. I wouldn't even drink a drop of caffeine during my pregnancies, why couldn't a loving, healthy mom who wanted her baby, have it? But, of course, that's not how it works. All the other big changes had felt like shifts that I could adjust to. Seeing my mom change and having our roles shift, it was incremental, I dealt with it. I still had moments that it was hard, but I had shifted with the change. My abusive relationship, even, had gotten there incrementally. My disordered eating, also in stages. I could adapt to anything when it happened slow. But the swift loss of my beautiful girl was different. It was when I finally, like a slap in the face, learned that bad things happen to good people, that good things happen to bad people and that maybe there really aren't even good or bad things or good or bad people, we all just get to experience the whole spectrum. And there will be times on that spectrum that your heart is ripped from you and lying in bed seems like the only way to get through the next five minutes, or half hour, or day. Thank goodness I had sweet Zeff and all of his needs to keep me moving. Movement was key. In a merciful moment, the Air Force decided that Jeb did not have to return to his deployment and would be able to stay home. It was right before Halloween, and he'd be home for the holidays. It was a small glimmer of something positive amongst some of the saddest moments of my life.

Losing a baby, one that you've felt move, one that you haven't, one that happens early and naturally, or one that happens late when you are ready to welcome them home, is a rite of passage for so many women that I know. How we make it through still isn't clear. But we do. For me, no surprise, running helped. I was able to get Zeff back in the stroller some days, or get out on my own others, there was something about that one foot in front of the other rhythm that was therapeutic. It had been an antidote for me for the past ten years, but this time it felt different. The trails, the cooling weather, the crisp leaves, seeing Zeff fall asleep in the stroller, that immaculate, loving face, one foot in front of the other. Keep moving. Keep moving. Let a little sadness go at a time, rush through the trails when you need to, but don't rush through the sad. Let the sad just be. I took comfort in Jeb's presence and that meant physical comfort too. We knew we didn't want to get pregnant again right away so that we could have time to deal with the loss. We were using condoms, but not regularly. Well, that doesn't work for preventing pregnancy. Less than a month later, I was pregnant again. And I was so worried. This time the Air Force said I needed to go the American hospital so I couldn't continue with Dr. Buechler and Dr. Mader, whom I had come to love. I had a new, handsome, male, American doctor who had a whole different approach to patient care and I got to know the American approach to pregnancy. Or should I say obstetrics and gynecology. They medicalize every piece of it they can. While for some cultures, it's seen a symbol of health, the American hospital seemed to treat pregnancy as it were a symptom or disease. Pregnancy with the Americans felt like something to treat, not to experience.

Chapter 13
The Thousand Mile Pregnancy

"Sometimes the strength of motherhood is greater than natural laws."

– Barbara Kingsolver

For this pregnancy, because my last one had had genetic problems, we knew we'd need some extra testing. From the first ultrasound though, everything looked healthy. Like my other two pregnancies, I felt fantastic, pregnancy brought out the healthiest in me and I loved every moment of it. I wished I could be pregnant and nursing for all of my fertile years. It was the thing that finally made me feel whole. It was around the end of 2005, Zeff was a healthy two-year-old, Jeb was home for the holidays, and it looked like this new baby was healthy too. Although I was still sad, I was beginning to feel like life was on track again.

In February of 2006, Jeb and I decided to go out for one of our first dates since Zeff had been born. We dropped him off with some friends and went to the movies where Jeb had a couple of beers. We watched a movie in the German Kino, I thought about how Zeff was doing the whole time. I still wasn't in any way used to being apart from him and then we went back to pick him up from the friends' house. They said Zeff had done fine (phew!). On the way back home, the roads were icy, and we came up to a construction spot.

Jeb was driving, I was in the passenger seat, and Zeff was in his car seat in the back. I was coming to the end of my first trimester. We hit an icy spot and slid. The car tipped up on its side suspending me in the air by my seatbelt. I immediately looked back at Zeff and saw him perfectly safe and still completely buckled in his seat. I breathed a sigh of relief when he giggled as if it had been fun. We were able to get out and my legs were extremely shaky. Because Jeb had had a couple beers, he asked me to say that I was driving when the police arrived. He didn't want to take any chances of getting a DUI. So that's what I did. When they arrived, I said that it had been me who flipped the car. An ambulance came and we said we didn't need it, everything felt fine. Finally, after waiting out in the cold for what seemed an eternity, a tow truck came and drove us and the totaled car home. I was exhausted, emotionally, and physically, and got Zeff put down to bed. I made myself a small meal and couldn't wait to put my head on my pillow. Why Jeb wasn't doing any of these things for his pregnant wife after a serious car wreck and hadn't insisted I go to the hospital when the ambulance arrived, we will never know. As I was getting ready for bed though, I felt a warm rush soak out of me, down to my knees. I looked down and I was covered, I mean covered, in blood. My pants, from crotch to knee and all across the lap were wet with bright, red blood. It was everywhere. I screamed. This was the only time in my life I have screamed a guttural, heart-rending scream, it came out of my soul. I couldn't go through this again. I couldn't. I just knew that I couldn't survive this loss. That scream coming out of me wasn't even a conscious decision, it was my emotion escaping in some visceral way. My wail switched to a silent, constant sob. I changed my pants, put on a big pad that I had left over from birthing Zeff, and we called Liesl's son-in-law, Fred, to take us to the hospital. After the accident, we didn't have a car to get there ourselves and we thought an ambulance might take too long. I rode in the backseat of the van and by the time we got to the hospital, I'd soaked through the jumbo pad, through my clean clothes and covered the seat in the van. The quantity of blood was incomprehensible.

Fred dropped us off and told us to call when we were ready for a ride. We got checked in and waited, they did let me go to a room to wait, but there was clearly no rush. It seemed everyone knew what had happened, it was a foregone conclusion, so they dealt with the other emergencies first. I think we waited a solid hour before a doctor came in to do an ultrasound. I was dreading it with all that was in me, but I also had to know for sure. I had been alternating between crying and quiet desperation with maybe, just maybe, still a little bit of hope. I was far enough along to do an abdominal ultrasound and as he put the instrument to my belly, we all looked to the corresponding screen and there it was. A heartbeat. It was so strong and steady. My tears immediately turned to tears of joy. How could this little miracle still be okay? I had seen the blood. I knew I'd been suspended in the air by a seatbelt across my belly. But the heartbeat was there, I saw it on the screen with the same eyes that had seen the blood. The doctor was doubtful still. So was I. He told me that there was a chance the baby could be okay, but there was also a good chance that a miscarriage was in progress and might happen sometime over the next several days. He advised me not to run and I was ready to listen to that piece of advice. I was willing to do anything just then. However, he also told me that if it was in progress, not much that I would do or not do, would change it. So, he said a few days of reduced activity should tell us either way and to come back if I started bleeding like that again. He certainly didn't tell us there were any other reasons that I could have bled that much, basically it was, you're likely miscarrying, pay attention, don't do too much, and call us back. I didn't need the doctor's hope though, I had seen the heartbeat. I wish he would have told me that the amniotic sack wasn't ruptured, that he saw no obvious signs of damage to my uterus or the baby, but he didn't. Probably he didn't want to give me false hope, but at the same time, those things were true, and it would have been awesome to know.

I had another appointment coming up soon and by that time, the baby was still healthy. I'd had no more bleeding and once again everything was on track. I asked my doctor if I could run again and although he wasn't that supportive of me running overall during my pregnancy (totally different from the German doctors), he said that I could. He actually told me that since I was a few years older than I was during my first pregnancy, running would "probably" be different this time. I shouldn't expect to be able to do it with the same ease that I had the first time. I was twenty-eight!?! My body had not miraculously aged to a point that physical exercise wasn't healthy, the opposite was true, but that didn't seem to be where his advice was coming from. So, I went back to it. This was the difference between the American treatment to pregnancy as a "condition" and the German treatment of pregnancy as a phase of life. Huge difference in the perception of pregnancy and in how both women and their babies have gestation and birth experiences.

In March, we booked a cheap flight to Rome for a weekend with a friend of Jeb's from work and his wife. I woke up before the rest of the group to go for my run before the day got started and went out exploring. Early morning Rome in the spring was amazing. I knew that our hotel was close to the Colosseum, but I didn't know how close. I'd gotten maybe a mile or mile and a half into the run and surprisingly came upon the monstrous structure of the Colosseum. It was breathtakingly gorgeous. My eyes went up to the top, boggled by the size, and I completely ignored my footing on the cobblestones around it. I fell completely forward, hitting my knees, belly, all the way up to my chin. It was a flat-on-my-face fall. I didn't hurt anything, my belly was fine, my knees were a little banged up and sore, but I took this as a message to just slow down a little. I decided not to run the rest of the weekend and just enjoy the time walking around Rome. Zeff had a disposable camera and was toddle-running all over the city taking pictures. We ate pizza, drank Italian hot chocolate, and had a good, cheap time. I was starting to get back to feeling like life was normal again, but my definition of normal was always in flux. The wife of that coworker developed a friendship with Jeb. One night on the way home from work, he'd stopped to check in on her while her husband was away. Jeb had come home late from work after not letting me know he had any other plans, and I'd been worried. One of the first things he told me, after saying that he'd been at their house, was how heavy she was. How heavy she was!?! You mean you lifted her up?? Well, she was drunk, and I had to get her to her bedroom. Yes. I trusted him wholly and completely and didn't think anything untoward had happened, but I couldn't believe this revelation. I wrote him a letter to explain how and why it had hurt me and he promised never to do it, or anything like it, again; he understood. It was also during that pregnancy that I got a call from a woman who'd bought a car from us. She told me

Jeb had put his hand on her leg during the test drive and played sexually explicit music. I asked him about what she'd told me, and he responded by telling me how crazy she was. He couldn't believe there were crazy people like that in the world. He said that maybe it was possible that his hand had brushed her leg while he was showing her something in the car. Duh. That could happen during any test drive. I was so angry at her for coming up with these lies and sharing them with me while I was pregnant. How dare this crazy woman insult me and my family? I didn't have any reasons not to trust my husband completely, one anomaly, and then two and he was right, there are crazy people in the world. Trust is a beautiful thing, but with it comes blinders.

Running was still feeling great and I had decided to take a measured approach to my running during this pregnancy. I had been running about forty miles a week prior to getting pregnant with Phoenix and that was kind of my happy mileage point. I wanted to aim for thirty miles a week for the first ten weeks of pregnancy, twenty a week for the middle twenty weeks and ten to fifteen a week for the final ten weeks. My goal was to hit 1000 miles total, but I gave myself the leeway to switch to cross training, if I needed to, or stop completely if there was a medical reason to do so. So far, these goals were totally reachable and were working out well.

At some point during the pregnancy, I went to a German fetal medicine specialist to make sure that everything was healthy. While there, they did an ultrasound and could see what looked, to me, like scar tissue on a part of my uterus. I told them about the car accident and the bleeding, and they told me that it had been a uterine hemorrhage and could clearly see where the injury had occurred. It had never even been close to the placenta or a risk to the baby. They seemed shocked that my doctor hadn't seen that and explained it. I was glad to have the explanation, but again a little confused about the American approach to medicine compared to the German care I'd gotten. The results were good though, heart, lungs, growth, everything progressing as it should.

In May, some of my running friends were doing a 10-mile race at an American base close to the Czech border. Several people were driving up the night before and camping or staying there and then racing the next morning. I wanted to do it too. Where did I start? With asking my doctor. I explained my planned approach to the race and the logic behind it. I was still regularly running at least one run per week of six to eight miles as my long run and it felt very comfortable, the racecourse was a flat out and back course, 5 miles to the turn and then back to the Start. There were water stops every mile or two. My plan was to go out slowly and stop and walk at every water stop and drink at least one cup of water and if I felt off at any point, I wouldn't continue. The doctor appeared to listen to my reasoning and then looked at Jeb and said, "If she was my wife, I wouldn't let her do it." Let me tell you, there was one pissed off pregnant lady in that exam room. I wanted to know if there was any physiological or medical reason that the choice wasn't healthy, he didn't have one, nor did he even have the courtesy to look me in the face and answer my question. Um yeah, I was running the race. We planned to go up the night before and rented a tent and some sleeping bags. At the last minute, Jeb got called to do an exercise at work which meant that he had to be on base basically Friday through Sunday and couldn't join me. Did that deter me? Nope.

One of my very good friends, Marty, was going to be there. He and I had met at the base gym years prior and still regularly did long runs and training runs together. I'd discussed my running plan with him and with Paul who was going to be there too. I was excited to be heading to a race, camping, and to have some friends there with me. Zeff and I made it to the campsite around 8pm and it was dark and buggy. I was 6-ish months' pregnant setting up an unfamiliar tent in a strange place and knowing that I was going to have to get a toddler to sleep here and figure out how to get ready to run in the morning. One more set of friends was going to be there, Donny and Blanca. Blanca was also pregnant, and we did some nice pregnant runs together. She had a toddler too and my hope was that Zeff would stay contentedly with her during the run. He was still not accustomed baby-sitters, but I figured for an hour and a half we could all make it work.

We woke up early, I got ready for the race in the tent, and headed over to the start area. I passed Zeff off, went to the start with

Marty, and shortly thereafter the gun went off. I started slow, as planned. I stopped and walked and drank a full cup at every stop and felt amazing. I saw Marty, Paul, and Donny after they had hit the turnaround point and they were flying. It felt good to be out there, see my friends, and be working through the course. I finished in right about 90 minutes as planned and relaxed. Turned out, I placed in my age group and got an award during the award ceremony.

I hit that 1000-mile goal later that pregnancy. I had told myself that if I needed to abandon that lofty mark, I could. I could switch to using the elliptical at any time. But like I had with Zeff, and despite what my doctor had said about my body being so much older this time around, I felt good. Running kept me centered, well, as centered as a pregnant woman can be. It felt like the most special time in the world I could have with my little unborn-ling. I also still ran with the stroller which gave me plenty of balance and also felt amazing. It was this perfect trio of everything I wanted on Earth out there logging miles, exploring, getting some sun together. I had some of the most perfect moments of my life running pregnant with toddler Zeff in the stroller. Lovely. Life was beautiful.

I had my thirty-six-week appointment and was not dilated at all. I had gained twenty pounds, baby and I were both healthy, and it looked like I would go full term. Several days later, Zeff was in the bath, and my water broke. Jeb was out in the garage, where he often was. Zeff apologized for my water breaking, and that brings us back to the opening scene. Him in the bath splashing, me soaked on the thighs, and his sweet little I'm sorry. I got Zeff out, called Jeb in and we got packed up and ready to go. We dropped Zeff off at Stef and Fred's house and headed to the hospital.

We got there about 8pm, I was not dilated at all, but the Americans make things happen. They do not let you wait for things to progress, they do not send you out for a walk, let you stay in your own comfortable clothes on top and get you naked from the waist down. They don't give you a bathtub and a birthing ball, they sanitize you, catheterize you, drug you, and then ask if you want an epidural on top of it. When they asked, I hesitated and the nurse told me that if I waited, I had the potential to be behind a couple other women who had just come in. I told them to hook me up and the epidural was on its way. Again, wow, was this different. It was not a walking epidural, and I couldn't feel anything. It didn't even feel like I was giving birth. So, catheterized, bed bound, unable to feel below my waist, and twelve hours later, Columbus Benjamin was born. He was perfect. Not quite seven pounds and a little spot on his ears that hadn't fully formed, but so, so perfect. Unlike Zeff, it took a little more cajoling to get him to breastfeed, but he started to get the hang of it. He would never be as avid of a breast feeder as his big brother had been, he did a lot of turning away that I had never experienced with Zeff, but he ate enough to grow and be healthy.

After he was born, they took him from me. I was so angry. I said that I wanted him to stay with me and stay on my chest, but they wanted to put him under a heat lamp and make sure that he was regulating temperature and some other excuse. Then they wanted to put me in a wheelchair to take me down to where he was. I told them, that I preferred to walk. They seemed shocked at this request and over and over at every opportunity, tried to make Columbus and I patients not people. We needed to follow rules, adhere to procedures, and sanitize and medicate when they said we should. I wanted my baby. So, I walked down to the nursery, waited until they were ready to give him back to me and never let him go again.

Jeb went to go get Zeff from Stef and Fred's house and Zeff got to meet his little brother for the first time, he was ecstatic. It was all so surreal. I got to go home that day, this time it seemed to make a lot more sense that the hospital was willing to give me this tiny, little being to leave with. It was August 20th, 2006. Zeff was two years and eight months old, Columbus was perfect, and miracles abounded. From the beginning, Col slept a lot more than Zeff, I'd have to check on him sometimes when he'd been sleeping for a couple hours. Zeff had never done that, but I got used to the rhythm of two little guys pretty quickly. Jeb went straight back to work, so it was me and the boys at home alone almost from the start. I got a little tinge of post-partum depression with Col as I had with Zeff, but this time I noticed it a little more. It was a lot to manage them both all of the time. Zeff had started German Kindergarten about three months before Col was born. I had gotten a double stroller, so from the time Col was about six weeks old, I'd pack them both in, walk Zeff to Kindergarten, drop him off and then run for about an hour with Col. I'd get back home, and he'd be sleeping in the stroller. I'd carefully pull the stroller up our front entrance stairs, put the lock on the wheels, make myself a decaf coffee, and just sit. I usually had about twenty minutes where Col would stay asleep that I could sit in the front doorway, enjoy the weather, drink my coffee, and watch the steady rise and fall of his chest. Sometimes I'd read, but mostly I'd just sit and watch him and breathe. He'd wake up, I'd do what I could around the house, and then at midday, we'd head over to pick up Zeff. Many days we'd stop at the Baeckerei on the way home and Zeff always wanted a big pretzel. We enjoyed so many moments of so many days. I had my struggles, but the routine gave me comfort. As Col became more mobile, he became a bit of a fighter. Didn't want to get dressed, didn't like his diaper changed, and wouldn't settle at night. It was tough. Zeff needed a lot of attention too and I never wanted to disrupt Jeb from being able to be 100% for work. So, I powered through on my own.

Chapter 14
Kindergraben

"Let me not pray to be sheltered from dangers,
but to be fearless in facing them.
Let me not beg for the stilling of my pain, but
for the heart to conquer it."

— Rubindranath Tagore, Collected Poems and Plays of
Rabindranath Tagore

In Col's first few months of life, we got an invitation in the mail. It was for Phoenix's service. The joint service for her and for the other babies who had not survived gestation. I had wondered what had taken so long and if we'd somehow been missed in the invite process. I'd been pregnant for almost fourteen months straight between Phoenix and Columbus and now had my healthy, little boy. We brought him to the service, he was still breastfeeding regularly, and I couldn't consider leaving him behind. Zeff stayed home with my dad who was visiting. Paul, the friend who'd helped get Jeb home quickly from deployment, met us there too. I felt like I was through most of my grief, though I didn't have a lot of time to think about it. It's ironic that grief requires the luxury of time to get through it, to heal from it, to think and feel your way through its edges, but it's also time that dulls it. If you are too busy to do the work of getting through, you might miss it and then, it comes in stark stabs at unexpected times. The service brought it back like a thunderclap. It was a beautiful ceremony. A celebration of life, but lives we'd never really known other than the feelings of these babies in our bellies, pushing on us, kicking around, the flutters of their motion. Moms and dads filled the small chapel. We proceeded to the front of it and got to write her name in a book and any words we wanted to share with her. Jeb and I wrote, *Phoenix*, and went back to our seats. It was hard to see her name in the book with the names of other babies who had passed, it was another goodbye. Some moms definitely noticed that I had a baby with me, I was the only one who had brought a baby. Was it insensitive? It may have been. Like always, I don't know what their stories were. Had they been trying for a decade when they lost these babies? Had they been unable to conceive since? Were their wounds fresher than mine? Probably at least one woman in that room could answer yes to each of those questions. I didn't consider at the time, and I am sorry. The service was in German and it was about rainbows. It was about storms and clouds and sun and how the mix of all of them makes the colors we know and see as rainbows. It was about pain and loss and growth and beauty and how everything has a place even if it's not the place we pictured. I held Columbus to my chest tightly, my rainbow, and I said goodbye again to my little girl. It was a cold day and we all walked out to the stone that marked their place in the ground. It was in the Kindergraben area of the graveyard. It was a small area with little toys and pinwheels with markers for ours and other babies' graves. There were so many joint stones like the one Phoenix was under. So many moms and dads who knew this, who had gone through this. Kindergraben and heartbreak. I went back only once after that first ceremony. Some of the toys had changed, but the stones screamed their permanence. Goodbye, sweet Phoenix, and thank you for the gift of Columbus. My intense little rainbow, who needed so much.

When Col was six months old, we found out that Jeb would be deploying to Iraq again, and he'd be leaving in April. Ugh. This was not good. Before Jeb left, I would be running one more marathon. It was the inaugural marathon in a German town not far from us. My boys were coming with me, and it would be the longest Jeb had cared for both boys together. I had pumped a bottle's worth of breastmilk for Columbus, hoping that he'd take a bottle. I'd only tried bottle feeding him a couple times and it was always only marginally successful. However, this wasn't going to be any more than 4 hours apart from him and I decided it would be okay. I started to flag a little during the seventeen to twenty-mile point and then I ran by a band playing, "Let it Be". I was a melody straight to my soul. Let it be, I could let it be, I could finish those miles, I could get back to my boys. I finished in under four hours, not a PR, but a solid effort for having an eight-month-old baby. I'd run my long runs with Marty during my training and even if they were only a couple times a month, my stroller miles had given me all the base I had needed. Jeb told me a story afterwards that Zeff had needed to use the porta-potty during my run. He'd found one that was not too disgusting to use, tried to get Zeff on the seat while holding Col and hanging onto the bottle. They had somehow made it through without a complete debacle and it was the first major kid juggling that Jeb had had to do. Welcome to parenthood. Jeb left shortly after that marathon, and he was scheduled to be gone until after Col's first birthday. Turns out, it was good thing I was far more accustomed to juggling than Jeb was. On top of the deployment, a few weeks before Jeb was scheduled to leave, we found out what our new duty assignment was going to be after Germany. I wanted to stay in Germany forever, but the adventure-loving side of me was excited about somewhere new. He called me from work one day and asked if I liked potatoes. I had no clue what he was talking about. He was trying to tell me that we were getting stationed in Mountain Home Air Force Base in Mountain Home, Idaho. I did some research online and the main thing that I found was that in addition to potatoes, Idaho was known for its white supremacists. What in the heck were we getting into? I knew nothing about Idaho, didn't know there was even a base in Idaho and could find not one good thing about it during my initial research except that were lots of sunny days.

Jeb left in April and there I was with a very active three-year-old and an eight-month-old baby. I remember taking him to the terminal and finding out that there was a delay. We had one extra night with him. What a freaking roller coaster. He came home another night and then we went to say goodbye again the next day. This time it was real. It was horrible seeing him walk away, I held my babies close and cried as their dad walked away to war. The struggles of women change and stay the same. I cried, but I knew

I didn't have a lot of time for tears. I had a lot to do. I decided to make this deployment a running streak, I'd run every single day that he was gone as a part of my countdown. Before he left, I had also gotten a few bags of rubber bands and counted out one for every day Jeb would be gone. I had one set of rubber bands for use and one set for Jeb to bring with him. For Jeb's pack of rubber bands, I wrote messages of love and longing on each individual band. We'd make our own rubber band balls and watch them get bigger as his return approached. My goodness that ball stayed small for a looooong time. It was excruciating. But as always, I kept moving. Movement, ever forward. One rubber band at a time; one run at a time. We kept our routine, Zeff to Kindergarten, Col for a run with me, Zeff back home, lunch, afternoon nap, time at a park, etc. I joined a weekly Mutter und Kind Turnen group for weekly parent/child gymnastics and it was awesome. I read when I could and rocked Col at night, sometimes crying right along with him when he wouldn't go to sleep.

Those days were brilliant and hard. I ran every single one. Sometimes with both boys in the stroller, lots of days with Col in the stroller solo and sometimes I'd bring them to the gym on base and let them play in the kid enclosure while I worked out around them. Some days I didn't feel like it at all, but I knew that each time I got out there was one day closer to their dad coming home. Also, one day closer to moving to Idaho which was happening in October. In addition to making a running streak goal, I also decided to figure out what I could do about getting my degree. I did some research online and I found out that to graduate from Florida State with a psychology degree, the Sensation and Perception Lab requirement depended on what campus you attended. If you graduate from the Panama City campus, the lab is not required to graduate, but if you graduate from the Tallahassee campus it is required. I reached out to the Dean of the Psychology Department and let her know that I'd been an athlete my last semester there and didn't complete the lab. I then asked her if there was any way I could still apply for graduation since it wasn't a requirement everywhere. It seemed like such logical, common sense to me. I had started at the Panama City Campus, I'd run for the school, I'd moved back to Germany a semester earlier than I planned to take care of my mom and I was missing a single credit that wasn't even required everywhere.

Someone who went to a campus an hour and half down the road could have their degree without this, why couldn't I? She told me no. Unequivocally, no. You didn't finish your credits there. No. I was shocked that there was nothing she was willing to do to work with me. Her response felt like she thought that I'd used my college athletics as a way to try to get around a requirement, which hadn't been my intent at all. I tried one more time. I figured, why not apply to graduate from the Panama City Campus's website following their graduation requirements. So, I applied. The application got back to the Dean. She gave me some version of, "What part of no did you not understand?" That one stung a little bit. I had over four years' worth of college work, I had met the requirements that any graduate from the campus I started at had to meet and still was told no. I wrote her an emotional email that wasn't the best version of myself and I decided I never wanted to have to interact with that lady again. I consoled myself with the fact that I didn't really need my degree to do what I was doing, which was being a stay-at-home mom, but it seemed like this great unfinished thing that I paid for with time, effort, and money. I should have had a degree. A single credit shouldn't have been that hard, there should have been an online option, but there wasn't. I put it out of sight and focused on the important things right in front of me.

Spring, turned to summer and Columbus' one-year birthday approached. All our German neighbors came; my mom even came to visit. My mom took care of the boys while I ran a fast half marathon, and it was almost time for Jeb to be home. I weaned Columbus, though he still wasn't a big eater and felt like I was getting my body back for myself. It was August of 2007. I'd known Jeb for just over five years and had been pregnant or nursing for about four of those. Wow. Early September was the return date, the last week both flew and dragged. I couldn't believe it was finally time. I got the boys matching sweatshirts and they were the cutest things on Earth. A picture of the reunion made the paper and is still one of my favorites. I look at that picture now and again to remember all the good and the love. We'd been through some hard stuff already, but it all felt okay. I felt like I had a partner to take on life with, I felt like my boys had a dad whom they could love and learn from, even if they'd have to get to know him a little again. The boys called Jeb "Papa", like the German kids did. September of 2007, their Papa was home.

Chapter 15
Readjustment, New Habits

"Things change. And friends leave. Life doesn't stop for anybody."

— *Stephen Chbosky, The Perks of Being a Wallflower*

Readjusting to life after deployment is its own battle. The parent at home is so used to doing everything, and being on edge, and managing ALL OF IT. The parent away has literally been to war. How do those things ever come together? We were made to go to a class on reintegration. Does anyone in the Air Force think a two-hour class really works for these things? The joy of seeing each other and the reunion was sweet, don't get me wrong, and having another set of hands was also sweet, but easy it was not.

Needs

He pulls,

Three years old and he likes the comfort of my
hair

Goes to sleep with it trailing between his fingers

He tugs,

My baby,

At my breast

Filling his little tummy with warmth and love

A smile trails across his sleeping face

He pulls and pushes,

My husband, until he too sleeps contentedly

I lie awake having given to all of them,

All of the parts which make me a woman

Eventually he'll sleep without my hair between his
fingers

And soon he'll be weaned

They'll move on, move away, grow

Needing less, wanting less

But you, husband, what will it be?

Less or more?

Four months away is a long time with lots of changes for babies
and toddlers; we all tried to adjust while we got ready to move. We
stayed in temporary housing for a week at the end of October 2007
before heading off to our new adventure. Jeb had befriended a
couple of fellow Airmen, before he'd deployed, the friends would
come over once a month, they'd get smashed and I wake up to find
all three of them with towers of beer cans in the living room. in
the morning. It bothered me, but I also knew that Jeb was young,

this was what young Airmen did, and I didn't begrudge him the occasional binge. While we were staying in temporary housing, he had the friends come by to say goodbye. I had the boys and was getting them down to bed, he told me he was walking the friends out and would be back in ten minutes. Two hours later, I couldn't sleep, he wasn't home, and I didn't know where he was. This was one of our last nights in country, and still relatively new time for us to be back together and ten minutes had turned into two hours. He came back eventually, reeking of alcohol and cried to me while he said he thought he might have a problem. We didn't think it would be anything like his parents' problem with alcohol, but it was just getting to the point, that when he started drinking, he had trouble stopping. We promised each other to not let it get worse and I promised to support him. But I had a bad feeling in the pit of my stomach. It felt like fear.

A couple days later, we left Germany. Atlanta was our destination for the first couple nights on the way back. Jeb's parents and my dad met us there. It was hard for Jeb's parents to plan trips because it disrupted his dad's needs to be home early enough to start his normal drinking pattern. Also, their finances were tight as Jeb's dad hadn't gotten another job since retiring from the Air Force. Limited -financial resources and a tight drinking schedule, make any kind of out-of-the-ordinary travel difficult. Nevertheless, they met us, and it meant a lot to us. Jeb, Zeff, and I had visited once after he was born and before Jeb joined the Air Force and then I had visited once with just Zeff. Though we didn't know it then, this would be the final time the boys got to see their grandpa and the only time Columbus ever met him. My dad had his camper at Stone Mountain and our family and Jeb's parents had a hotel room just outside of town. Stone Mountain was beautiful, and I had lots of people around to watch the boys while I got some solo runs. It felt amazing to power all the way up the trail to the top of Stone Mountain and back down, my fitness level was feeling great. I could have run that mountain two or three times, but maternal duty called me back after one up and down. There in Stone Mountain, Georgia, I was excited about the new start. Our family came to welcome us back to America. I had two healthy boys and we were on our way to a new duty station. Jeb's career was going well, we hoped it would be a while before the next deployment so we could get back to us. While there, I got a little bit of time to talk with my dad. I confessed to him what Jeb had told me about thinking that maybe he had a problem with alcohol. I downplayed it a little when I told my dad, but it felt good to get it out. I hadn't quite let go of that feeling of fear that had reared its head when I'd first been told. I was so confident in our love, though, I knew I could love him through this. We knew he had a family legacy; he was going to be the one to change it. I was going to be the one to protect, nurture and mother. Idaho here we come!

Idaho. What can I say? Flying into Boise at the beginning of November, we saw lightly snowcapped mountains, evergreen trees above the tree line, and all shades of brown fall below. It wasn't too populated. In short, it was gorgeous. And then we drove the forty-five minutes to Mountain Home. Bleak, desolate, nothingness. It was flat and brown and windswept. It looked like a moonscape compared to the green of Germany that I was used to.

We had ten days to stay in a hotel and find a place to live. Ten days in a hotel with a three-year-old and a one-year-old. And Jeb was starting work within a day or two. Our sponsor, Ray, picked us up at the airport with his wife and daughter. He was French and it was nice to have a small reminder of Europe, even though it was very small. Those first days greeted me like a slap in the face. Everything felt different. The air was dryer and felt different to breathe. The temperatures in early November were below freezing at night and would jump thirty degrees during the day. I took the boys out for a run in the running stroller and popped two tires on puncture vine, or goat-heads as they call them in Mountain Home. I tried to take the boys for a walk in the field by the hotel and it was spiky vine-covered, high desert terrain. There was nowhere to go. I felt stuck. I took both boys to the hotel pool and watching Zeff, Col took a mouthful of water and choked and sputtered. I went to the hotel gym and tried to turn the TV to Scooby Doo and let the boys sit and watch. They would not sit. Zeff peed the hotel bed. Nothing seemed smooth or easy.

The first night in Mountain Home, Jeb walked to the gas station by the hotel and bought a beer. He drank it before he came in. The second night we were there, he walked to the gas station again. This time when he came home smelling like beer, I asked him about it, and he told me he only bought one. Later I saw the receipt and he had bought two big ones and had them both before coming in. I couldn't understand why he lied or why he didn't bring them in and have a beer while he relaxed around us. Why was it something to hide? From there, there was hardly a night that Jeb didn't have a drink. In writing it, it doesn't sound that bad. Here's a guy back from a deployment, readjusting to family life, moving to a new country, having a couple beers at night before he came home. But it was more than that because it immediately came with lying about quantity and hiding it. It wasn't just relaxing after a hard day, it was getting a couple of forty's, downing them in less than a half hour, and then trying to cover it up. Something wasn't right.

The economy in Mountain Home wasn't great at the time or probably ever, really. It's an interesting mix of agriculture, blue collar, and Air Force retirees. There were three houses we could afford to rent. They had stained carpets, badly converted garages made into bedrooms, no yards, it was such a downgrade from the beautiful, spacious, well-constructed home we'd had. And the Air Force pays you less in the states than overseas so Jeb's meager paychecks would be decreasing. I couldn't wrap my head around what was going on. We found a townhome that was new and shoddily built but looked nice. It was more than our Living Quarters Allowance would pay for, but we didn't have much choice. Now in addition to having less total income, we had to pay more than we were allotted for rent, it was more of a cut to the income. However, I was happy to have a space to make our own. It had a fenced yard, three bedrooms, and a decent garage. Finally, something was starting to feel a little more normal. We needed so little to get by back then. We had a mattress on the floor, I cut mine and the boys' hair (well, Col was still bald), and shopped at thrift stores. Enlisted military income encourages spending on credit at its subsistence level, but when it's what you have, you make the choices that go along with it. It was going to be hard to pay the bills, I think our total annual family salary was around $40,000. We qualified for WIC and had in Germany too. I didn't feel quite comfortable using this federal benefit that provided milk, cheese, beans, cereal, and a few other staples. The more I thought about it though, if the military paid its member with kids and young families a low enough amount to qualify for federal benefits, then taking advantage of the offerings made sense. They had also provided me with a breast pump after Columbus was born which was another great benefit and something I wouldn't have been able to purchase on my own. Even with that though, I have no idea how I stretched the paychecks and still kept us comfortable, but I did, or at least I felt comfortable. Knowing with the military, that medical care is free, and groceries are 30% cheaper at the Commissary also provided a nice cushion and ameliorated some of the low-income stress. It's huge respite to know that if you or one of your children gets sick, it will be totally covered, no matter what. Thank you, military for that. On Mountain Home Air Force Base, there was also an Airman's Attic which was a thrift store that allowed lower enlisted ranks to get ten free items per month. I maxed out our free allowance almost every month. For the most part, that kept the boys and me in clothes. Those incidental costs, clothes and haircuts and the like weren't the things that were starting to add up and impact our budget though.

When we moved into the townhome, the drinking that had begun in the hotel continued, and began to escalate. It was that simple. Like a switch. In Germany, it had been an occasional thing and then literally from the day we moved to Mountain Home, it became every day. Looking back, I still don't get it. Part of it was the ease of access, with a gas station on every corner, all he had to do was go for a short walk or drive to grab some drinks. In Germany, by the time he got home, everything in town was closing up for the night. He had to plan to drink, in Idaho, it was a hobby of convenience. In addition to the consumption, he started spending more and more time in the garage. This became his place to drink. He'd stop for a six pack on the way home, pull into the garage, have a drink (or two) before coming in and then go back out to the garage after dinner to finish it off. I was taking care of the boys all day, making dinner by the time he got home, I'd clean up and start the evening routine; all of this without him around. It was feeling like deployment all over again. It felt difficult to decide when to tell him that enough was enough. I wanted him to be able to relax and to want to be with us, not be "forced" to, but I could also see quickly that this was getting out of control. How do you catch something getting out of control? If I had told him, no, come in when you get home, he wouldn't have done it. But by not saying anything was I telling him it was okay? I didn't stop to think about what my limits were or when I might try to intervene. I believed fully and completely in the sanctity of our love and marriage. I thought that even if this did get worse, it was something we'd conquer together. We could work through anything, we'd lost a baby, been through deployments, and an international move. We were a power couple! Not an affluent one, but I had no question that we were unbreakable.

That December, he'd been home from his deployment for just a few months and not much had changed in our roles for family care. One of the pitfalls of having a spouse get used to doing everything is that they are used to doing everything. He didn't change his away-ness and I didn't change my presence. It aggravated me, definitely I felt angry sometimes, but I was still so much in love that it seemed like some form of transition period was okay. The way I looked at it then was that he was working all day, he was the sole provider, it was my responsibility to make his time at home as comfortable as possible. I realize that just sounds like I was mired in traditional gender roles and that's how it was expressed, but that wasn't what it felt like. It felt like love. It felt like this was my ability to provide for him in a way that was equal to what he was providing for me. If one partner is at work and the other is at home, it makes sense for that person to prepare meals and domesticate. I didn't feel stuck, I felt like this was an opportunity. However, with that being said, I didn't understand how he felt okay going out to the garage while I managed the nighttime routine. It seemed like this was a good place for him to be a part of the family again, surely, it would be an easy way to reintegrate. Most nights after the boys were in bed, we'd sit together for an hour or so and watch part of a movie, or he'd watch something while I read. I lived for those hours of peace and togetherness. When the whole day had been purely kids, home, and forcing a run in somehow, having that final hour with him made it all seem perfect. I'd be exhausted most nights, but I didn't care.

My mom came to visit for Christmas, and we started to formulate a plan for her to move to Mountain Home so we could be closer and provide support to her. We thought that having the grandkids close to her would be a big benefit and we were hopeful that we could find some kind of psychiatric care that would work. She was doing better, but it all seemed so relative. I would still never have "my mom" back. She was forever changed and deeply medicated. I had adjusted, but still had moments of difficulty with it. If I stopped to think about "how she was before", it was like a knife, so I didn't. I had enough to think about aside from that, and I was excited about the prospect of having her closer.

As nice as it was to have had her visit, my body was starting to send me some messages. It had done the same thing in Panama City when I'd broken out in severe acne, and this time the message was just as disheartening. I started having a problem with blood in my stool. This is one of those embarrassing things that it's easy to let go longer than you should. It started as an every-once-in-a-while thing and then it became every day and then multiple times a day. I finally went to a doctor at the military hospital, and he checked for hemorrhoids and anything else that might have been perceived through visual or tactile inspection. There was nothing obvious. They had also advised me to bring a stool sample if I could to the appointment. I did not receive instructions on how this sample should be collected and brought in, so I used a plastic Ziploc container and brought it to the lab. The gentleman made a joke about how I was "giving him my shit" and I wanted to crawl under the floor. As there was no clear reason for this frequent and persistent bleeding, I was given a referral to a gastroenterologist for a colonoscopy. He scheduled me for Valentine's Day. The prep was unpleasant, but on Valentine's Day 2008, several months before I turned thirty, I had a colonoscopy. Nothing alarming was found, the doctor ended up saying that it may have been partially caused by running; that running could cause micro-tears to the intestinal track the same way it could cause them in muscles. Lab results from the stool sample also showed that I might have had a parasite commonly found in the Middle East. Who knows? I think it was just stress, it was my body telling me to pause, telling me something was going on. But I took my anti-parasitic, was relieved to not have colon cancer, and on I went. How loud do the alarm bells have to ring before they are heard? Apparently pretty loud when we have our anti-parasitic headphones on.

We also were realizing that the duplex was increasingly out of our price range and that buying a house would be cheaper. Yet another military "benefit" is the ability to buy a house with absolutely no money down. It was early 2008 (yes, just a couple months before the housing market crash) and there were about five houses in Mountain Home within our price range. We were approved for a loan of up to $140,000. How on Earth was a family of four with a household income of $40,000/year and not a single dollar to put down approved for a loan for $140,000? Oh yeah, the loan was backed by Uncle Sam, so anything went. We found a three bedroom, 1800 sq. ft. house for $125,000. It wasn't perfect, but it was affordable, and it was ours. I didn't have that first time home buyer sense of accomplishment. It felt forced and it was only an okay house, but I knew that we could make it a home. I applied my normal optimism and decided it would be great. It had a big, fenced yard with a swing set and a shed, was across the street from a trailer park, and it had asbestos in the ceiling (we didn't know that when we bought it). Ah, home, sweet home. Perfect or not, I resolved to make it ours.

We moved into the new place in April. It had been a long winter that year and stayed cold well into the spring. It was abnormally cold for Idaho, and I was having trouble adjusting. Even taking the boys to the park was still hard this far into spring because I'd be freezing long before they were done playing. Jeb's drinking had continued full force. He now went straight to the garage to down a few drinks before any of us ever saw him, but it was more than that. It seemed like he was starting to stay out there until I came out to tell him that dinner was ready. At first, it had been a drink or two and right in to see us and now I was having to call him in. And usually, he'd return to the garage as soon as dinner was over without even the pretense of participation. I'd do the usual clean up and evening routine and a little more resentment was building along with fear-tinged worry. He'd also started getting angry; this was new to us, but not new to me. He didn't do it in front of the boys, but we'd had several horrible bouts of him yelling, name calling, belittling. I'd end up sitting on the floor or in bed crying and feeling horrible. It all felt so familiar. The funny thing about abusive relationships is that once you've had one, it's so easy to go back to the same feelings and routines. Emotional habits are just as hard to break as the ones Jeb was developing. I didn't see it that way at all back then though. Certainly, the familiarity was there, but I didn't see that it was my habit to react that way too. I never yelled back, I never tried to leave, I'd take it. I'd try to remind him how much I loved him, how I'd always be there for him. I thought if he could see how much he was hurting me that he would stop. How could someone keep going when they saw pain on the person they loved? Some people can, though, and I was using my perspective on what would be too much to try to predict how he would react. As it turns out, we did not share the same frame of reference. He was the disher and I was the taker. I wanted to be able to take whatever he gave so that he knew how dedicated I was to us, to our love. I also started the reasoning game. When he'd tell me, for example, how I thought I was better than him and treated him poorly, I'd reason my way through. We'd go around and around and I was never right. I kept trying though. I would have saved myself a lot of energy and emotional trauma to have just stopped, but I didn't know. I was a woman, a girl really, in love and trying to save that love.

My mom moved to Mountain Home in July that year. We found her a nice, one-story duplex that was just a few miles away from our house and it met her needs perfectly. As much as I thought it would be a benefit to her to have us there to help her through her struggles, she was a great help to me. Just having the occasional option for help with the kids and seeing them start to develop a relationship with her was awesome. She wasn't the same mom I'd known growing up, in fact, her thinking patterns had changed so drastically you wouldn't think they could come out of the same brain, but my kids didn't know the difference. To them she was grandma. Just grandma.

As summer drew on, the verbal abuse from Jeb escalated. He'd started spending a lot of time with a girl from work, we'll call her Scarlett, and I didn't know enough to be concerned. I still believe in the sacredness of our relationship and trusted everything he said. In retrospect, there had already been enough glaring red flags, even from pre-Mountain Home that should have put me on high alert. In addition to the aforementioned instances in Germany, there had been another before we'd left. I'd found a note in his car telling a female coworker that he wanted to make crazy, monkey love to her. They were in an evening college course together. It was a total joke he told me, she smelled like cat pee, no one wanted to have sex with her, don't worry! I asked if he'd be okay if I wrote that same joke note to someone. Of course, the answer was no. He'd also invited Cat-Pee over to our house to do some detail paint work on her car. Apparently, she didn't smell so strongly of cat pee that helping her with her car was out of the question. I think I even brought them out some hot chocolate to drink while they worked in the garage together. Sweet, domestic, marital bliss. Jeb and Cat-Pee sitting in the garage drinking his wife's hot chocolate together.

At the new house, there was a neighbor who had just turned eighteen. During one of her first conversations with Jeb, she told him that she'd just been to the gynecologist and had a disease-free, clean bill of health. I told him, "No eighteen-year-old woman tells you about her vagina without ulterior motives." He laughed at the thought, told me I was being ridiculous. She was eighteen?!? And still I trusted him. I found them laughing together in the garage at midnight, Jeb drunk, his laughter loud. It was long after I'd put the boys in bed and expected him to come to bed. I'd tried to sleep without him until the peal of laughter had drawn me out. Another time, I found them together in the shed, laughing in the dark. This time, I'd known to go to the garage to look and when I'd gotten there, they hadn't been there. Somehow, I'd heard a noise in the backyard where our shed (with no light inside) was found. I opened our bathroom window with a direct line of sight to the shed and clearly heard male and female laughter, they came out together a few minutes later. I cried. It hurt. I knew, but I didn't know, which sounds so dumb. It was all changing so fast. Was it really just six months ago that we'd arrived in Idaho and marriage felt good and healthy and like it would stay that way forever? What happened and how did I not catch it as it was going? I'd been worried about not knowing when to intervene just a few months ago and now where were we?

Then there was Scarlett, the friend from work. She was beautiful. A fellow mechanic. I'd go to base some days and work out in the gym and try to meet Jeb for lunch with me and the boys. I remember him telling me he couldn't, he had plans with her. I can't describe how "into" the marriage I was. This was us, our institution, our kids' lives were because of our union, I didn't think that it was fallible. How silly to have never thought outside that very narrow box, or was it? Maybe it was beautiful naiveté. Every single time I came to base to see my husband, I was freshly excited. I was excited to have a forty-five-minute lunch with him, excited to see him interact with his boys, excited to be a family. I still didn't understand what was happening. I asked, he lied, and I'd ask some more. There is something about being a stay-at-home mom when your life and identity are wrapped up in the roles you play as wife and mother. I still hadn't completed my college degree. I didn't have a job. I had been out of work for years. It was Mountain Home, Idaho, for fuck's sake. Options were not abundant. I had started coaching that spring for the middle school track team, bringing the boys with me to the track. It gave me a little bit of an identity outside of the house, but it was a smidge compared to what I would have needed to feel like I had some level of personal power. The boys brought toys to play in the sandpit at the track, I'd push the double stroller if we went on runs away from the track and I got to work with Coach Root, a medical marvel, who'd been coaching for generations. He'd survived several bouts of cancer, failing organs, and other brushes with mortality and here he was coaching kids of kids he'd coached decades before. But oh, Jeb's friend from work, I felt like I had nothing on her. The feeling of the man you love and have given everything to, choosing someone else right in your face is something indescribable. I know there are volumes written by strong women who don't want men who don't want them, and who can eschew their former loves the moment they are mistreated or unloved. For some, simply feeling unwanted is enough for them to fall out of love. I was not one of those. My world was crashing. And Jeb was being mean on top of it. So mean. He'd pick me apart, break me down and I'd stick with my reasoning tactic and refrain from reacting in anger. Some nights, I'd escape into the boys' room to get away from him because I couldn't make him stop otherwise and I knew he wouldn't follow me in there. I'd curl up in bed with Zeff and feel his heavy sleep-breathing and cry myself to sleep, but I was safe. Then there were nights I could make Jeb realize what he was doing to me, and he'd apologize and pull me in. The cycle was back. Abuse and comfort from the same person. That is some mental fuckery, right there.

For Jeb's birthday that September, I got him concert tickets to a band he liked. I got him two, thinking he'd bring one of his male friends. He brought her. He brought Scarlett to the concert to which I had gotten him tickets for his birthday. Yes. He did. He said no one else could go, she was the only available, did I want him not to go? He reminded me that I knew nothing was going on between them, so if I trusted him, why would I care if he went with a male or female friend. They got back to our house hours later than they had planned. I found them that night around the side of the house, standing up, but wrapped in a sleeping bag together, smoking cigarettes, and laughing. It was closer than friends. It was obvious. And I was so torn apart, but he told me it was nothing. He said it had taken longer because they needed to wait to drive back until they were sober enough, the sleeping bag was wrapped around them because it was cold. He would NEVER, EVER cheat on me. NEVER. Who was it that said when you say always or never, you're usually lying? Yeah, I don't know, and even if I did, I wouldn't have listened. I believed him because I wanted to, but some part of me knew, of course. The desire to believe is a fairly unbreakable thing, though. My story, that my husband wouldn't hurt me like that, couldn't lie to my face, was more real to me than all the facts around me. The real story was obvious, but I was telling myself a different one.

Writing from the time:

Flight

the anger oozes out of you

like oil-dark and thick

it is stuck now

in my feathers

preventing my flight

leaving me earthbound and tainted

Darkness

and I wonder if the black of your lungs

has spread

and corrupted too

your soul

Trails

I have sweat and cried

bled, spit, snotted, and peed

out here on these trails

territory marking?

I have definitely sprinkled myself

I have owned them, they have been submissive to
me

and I to them

they call, I come

I have given hours

Shaped their surface with my pounding feet

They have sucked me in and built me up

Shaped me and nurtured me when I had nowhere
else to go

My outlet, coddling, caressing, convincing me

That the rest is possible

Chapter 16
Running Group, Deployment, and Work

"A friend is someone who knows all about you and still loves you."

— Elbert Hubbard

Sometime in this mix, I found a flyer at the base gym for a running group. Charlie and Brad's running group. I met them for the first time at a trail about twenty minutes outside of Mountain Home. It had been rough getting up that morning, trying to get Jeb up from his hungover slumber, trying to get him to watch the boys, feeling like they'd all be okay. I /kept telling myself that I deserved this little break, but I did not feel that way as I worked the logistics to get out of the house. The group was amazing. A perfect antidote to a life feeling like it was crumbling. There was Charlie, at least twenty years older than me, a hardened, wizened, leathered, bony runner of a man. His wife, Sherry, did not run, but came to every run to support. She'd bring fruit, bagels, water, and her serrated personality. She seemed so mean that first day, questioning why I was there when she hadn't seen me at races before, but the heart on that one was a thing of beauty. She'd been married to alcoholic in a band at fifteen and had two kids by seventeen. She fought her way out, left him, and was single parenting as a teenager herself, when she met Charlie. They raised her kids together and had ended up in Mountain Home, with Charlie working at the base. There was Brad, another older, hippie runner with a long gray ponytail. At the time, he and Charlie were best friends and had a depth of trail and race knowledge between them. The others came and went; Charlie and Brad were the staples.

I met Jamie a month or two later. My next angel. We were both stay-at-home-moms and she had recently had a baby girl, Elaina, and also had an older son, Gabe, who was between Zeff and Columbus in age. We did stroller runs together and, as we got to know each other, we did run exchanges. I'd watch all four kids while she ran, and she'd watch them while I ran. We went to parks together, we'd meet at the gym and workout with our kids in the play area. Then suddenly, it wasn't just running, I had a friend. A friend!?! Little did I realize how much I needed that friendship. And somewhere in the mix, Al joined the group. Jamie, Al, and I became training and pacing partners. To be able to run, talk, laugh, and get the miles in. What sweeter joy is there? (Maybe a couple, but that's pretty high up there!) We did our long runs on weekends and covered every mile in and around Mountain Home. Mornings that I ran with them were weird, I'd feel guilty leaving the boys, I'd usually make them muffins or some kind of breakfast and hope that Jeb would be able to get up, but it didn't quite feel right. As Jamie and I became better friends, I'd often drop them off at her house on the way to the run and her then-husband would watch all four. It was pretty awesome that he was willing to. This niche became my tribe; how grateful I am to have had them. All things in the right place at the right time, even when things were feeling wrong in so many ways.

Despite hoping that Jeb wouldn't have deploy again anytime soon, a little over a year after we moved to Mountain Home he was scheduled to go again, to Kyrgyzstan this time. He left two days after Christmas. I kept a journal the whole time he was away, he was gone for six months this time, I called it Around the World for 180 days. I wrote of how much I loved and missed him, how he completed the family. He was, of course, sober while he was deployed and so when we did talk it was all "never again" and "I'm so sorry" and "I've changed my ways". And did I believe every one of those pronouncements? You bet I did! Heart, line, and sinker. I couldn't wait until he was home, and we could get back to being a family. I willed it, I believed it, I knew my husband was who he said he was. Although, even there, even sober, there were times he'd get mad at me and tell me I was being a bitch or some other unkind epithet. We'd only get to speak once or twice a week and could email in between. Though some of those conversations left me rattled, mostly I just missed him and wanted him home, back to who he was before and who I knew he could be. No one reading this is probably surprised to hear, it didn't happen. He got drunk before he even made it back into the country. They stopped in Germany on the way back and got completely trashed, so trashed that he couldn't even follow through on the phone call he'd promised me. He told me, he'd been sober for months, he was ready to stay sober, it was just the guys having fun on the way back. He was still fully dedicated to everything he'd promised. It was such a roller coaster for me. He returned, he promised, he lied, he hurt, he went out, he went right back to everything he'd been doing before. The longer and longer it got between the interludes of him treating me with respect, saying sweet things, the more I held out for them. He definitely had me trained. And I let myself be trained. Here are a few excepts from that journal which pains me to read:

<u>Day 1</u>

We walked away from the airport gate. Crushed and leaving a trail of tears. We turned back to watch your plane take off, our hands pressed to the glass in one final, futile goodbye. It was a comfort to know you weren't quite gone, but unbearable to know just how fleeting the proximity was. Finally, Zeff said, "Let's just go, Mama." And we did.

<u>Day 5</u>

I found your hat in my car. You, you, you. I put it my face and breathed you, inhaled you. New Year's Eve…

I drove around while the boys drifted off – couldn't quite bear the house alone. I was glad when they slept badly and needed me tonight.

<u>Day 9 (after an apology conversation)</u>

Frigid Sunday Run. In the book I'm reading there's a family falling apart. I think of how close we were to that. Now I'm wishing you were here so we could work on us but maybe somehow this deployment will help us reassemble. Maybe without it you wouldn't have realized your bad judgment and self-imposed alienation from us. Maybe it came just before I reached my limit so that when you come home to us, I won't even have to contemplate limits.

<u>Day 34 (after an email admittance to some of the things I'd suspected)</u>

Finally, your response email to my inquiries. You spoke of your alcoholism and the other girl relations, the lies you had spewed like lava from a volcano. I was a little bird surprised by the lava wash and now I'm a bird shaped pumice – a little floating stone where once beat a raging heart.

Where do we go from here? There's only up.

<u>Day 96</u>

April…can it really be April already? Elongating days and windstorms to the blow the hands of time just a bit faster than normal…

I miss your nighttime presence again. I long for the privilege of being able to stretch out my foot and bump your calf, to drink in the beauty of the rise and fall of your back as you slumber deeply, long before sleep has found a way to pull me under.

<u>Day 99</u>

I feel like words could pour forth deluge fashion tonight. In one phone call tonight, I saw, knew momentarily that you weren't done with the man you were before you left. The man who bled my heart dry or the man to whom I handed my heart for a beating time and time again. I felt something drain out of me. I saw myself, how I look to other people, a picture of self-confidence, contentment, and inner surety and I knew that as little as I care what judgment other might dole in my direction with no effect whatsoever, a few easy words from you can send me into a tailspin.

Unease welled in my throat like bile. I expected my run to revive me, to renew my strength, to no avail. I saw a dad holding hands with his son of five or six on a walk. I tried to recall if you had ever taken such a walk with Zeff, but I knew the answer. I look at the pair with a pensive smile, wondering, questioning too many things. I feel tired and worn like no matter what, it's never quite enough.

<u>Day 125</u>

April, unbelievably, comes to a close. I thought today if I were telling the story of my life's hurdles and at a particularly intense moment, I were asked, "So what did you do?" I would be able to answer over and over again, "I ran".

"So, what did you do next?" "I ran, I ran..."

Not away, never away, okay occasionally away. I ran and returned to the start, breathing heavily, glistening sweat, a beastly gleam in my eye. I ran and I returned, stronger, better, ready.

Ready for it to get worse, ready to make it better.

"And then what happened?"

"I ran."

I had kept up with the coaching and it was my favorite thing ever. I worked with Coach Root still, and the boys came with me most days. Sometimes my mom would watch them, so I had a couple of hours of kid-free time. It felt strange to have moments without my babies. And the high school kids were so fun. Full of intelligence and spunk and talent and ambition. It seemed so recently that I'd been there, but a lifetime away too. Zeff was going to a preschool a few mornings a week and they also offered day care. I got the wild idea to start substitute teaching and that was pretty amazing too. I made eighty dollars a day when I subbed, and I was finally starting to feel like maybe there was a little more to me, maybe something inside I could work with. Don't get me wrong, I didn't feel incapable as a stay-at-home-mom, that was exactly what I'd wanted to be. In fact, I felt supremely capable and like I was fulfilling one of the most important roles a human could fulfill. I hadn't wanted anything more than that for so long. I wanted to have more kids and stay home and cook their food and read to them and support their education and tuck them in at night, every night. I wanted to be at home with my kids and have a house full. The circumstances of my new reality were changing what was available to me and thereby caused a change in who I needed to be. I remember the first day I subbed for a whole day. Dropping the boys off and heading to work felt so far outside my normal reality. I was being paid to do something outside of my home. I felt a sense of purpose as I got through that day and then picked them up at 2:30, right after nap time, knowing that Columbus wouldn't have slept for someone else. But he did. They were fine, I was fine, we'd done it. A day of day care and I'd worked. Whoa. The changes kept a-coming!

I continued to sub until early spring while Jeb was still deployed. I had an offer to go full time and work as a teacher aide, but it wouldn't have brought in as much as full-time day care would have cost for both boys. Then there was an opening at the day care itself. Full time, no benefits, minimum wage which was $7.25. But day care was discounted 50%. I could work full time, afford their care, and be with them all day, every day. It was a dream come true. And the women there, they set me on my way.

Dee and I had similar stories. Her son and Zeff were best friends. Shortly after she'd started working there, she and her son had left her husband because his drinking had gotten out of control. He had a beer in his hand as they drove away. But she went back and was trying to make it work. She was trying for both of them.

Suzanne was tough as nails. She was an Air Force veteran and a single mom of three kids who had always figured out a way to make it work. She was working there for less than eight dollars an hour, living in a small, extra house on someone else's land and providing for her kids. I had no idea how she kept it all together. But she showed up every day with a smile (or a smirk, or a grimace) and didn't put up with anyone's shit. The kids loved her and so did I.

Amanda was the owner. She had hired me even when I had no experience because she knew me from having had the kids there. She lived with her parents and loved her dogs. She'd been abused by a man and could never get past it to have a relationship, but she loved kids and animals. She was caring and loving and owned the business, even though she didn't always take home a paycheck and wasn't really hard on parents when they couldn't pay. You wanted to tell her to move past her past, but she was where she was, and it was enough for her.

So, I became a preschool/day care worker, and I had these wonderful women around me every day. I could run during nap time and used it to my advantage, getting a full hour or sometimes more almost every day. It kept me sane. And slowly, ever so slowly, I started drawing some strength. I listened to Suzanne's no bullshit approach, I watched with sadness as Amanda stayed stuck and could love only the kids, and I watched as Dee battled it out with herself on the best choice for her and her son. We laughed, they listened, I got my feet peed on, I made melted crayon wax drawings. The job was simple, the growth complex. I'd run on my hour lunch, come back exhilarated, I was balancing it: motherhood, full time employment, and running. The paycheck was tiny, but the income was so much more than that.

Jeb got back that June, when I'd been working full time for just a couple of months. As became my pattern, even when I knew somehow inside me that Jeb wasn't capable of going back to who I thought I had married, I held out hope. Still, things remained dismal at home, they'd gone back to pre-deployment status almost immediately, with a few reminiscent days thrown into the mix. I kept running with the group and between the job, the coaching, and the shared miles, something akin to strength was growing in me. I started to get the idea that maybe I didn't have to stay in the situation I was in. Maybe there was some control to be had.

Not to say that I wasn't conflicted. I believed so deeply in my marriage, I wanted, more than anything to be able to look back on this struggle as just another "hard time" that we got through. But it was getting hard to think that that would be possible. The verbal abuse was getting worse again, the emotional control and manipulation, making me feel puny. And the gaslighting. It was fucking working. I was feeling a little like maybe I was the crazy one. He was certainly telling me that. Telling me I was crazy to think he could be cheating again, that if I was paying attention, I'd be able to see how much he loved me. The list went on.

At home, every evening, he'd be in the garage, I'd hear the pop, crack of beer after beer opening. What had gone from a couple of forty ounces those first nights in Idaho, had become a six pack, then a twelve pack and then he was buying something like a twenty pack a night. When I write that, it seems impossible. It seems like no one could drink that much, stay up the garage until one or two in the morning, and then be at work by 7:30. In the military no less. But that was exactly the routine. No wonder he couldn't get up on the weekends. The week was so full of alcoholic ups and downs. He'd be mean a few days, be apologetic another day, and almost every single Friday, he'd tell me, "I just want to hang out with you and the boys tonight. I can't wait until I'm done with work. Make something good for dinner, we'll get a movie to watch with the boys." But then he'd come home, hit the garage, come in slightly bleary-eyed and get a call from a friend. The work crew would be out downtown in a couple hours. They'd see him there, right? Yes, they would definitely see him there. Sometimes he walked home, sometimes he drove home, sometimes he went somewhere else and then came home. Sometimes he'd wake me up, sometimes angry, sometimes horny, sometimes nothing at all. I'd never know. I wanted him to come home, but many nights I dreaded it. I remember the nights spent sitting on the floor, crying, feeling like this was not supposed to be my lot. I remember wrapping my arms around my knees because it was the closest thing to an embrace I could feel. I remember almost running into the boys' room so I could get there and close the door and lock it soon enough for him not to open it and come in. He never came in there. He'd stay on the other side of the door and tell me to get out of there. He'd tell me I was being a bitch for not being willing to finish a fucking conversation with him. I'd find a warm spot to curl up and smell the sweet little boy hair smell and cry and sometimes I would sleep.

As the thoughts of leaving him started to form, I was emboldened by this great friendship with Jamie. It wasn't a tough-love friendship; it was an understanding "you got this no matter how long it takes" type of love. She guided me through. At some point, I went to one of the low-income apartment complexes to see if they had availability. They rented apartments on a sliding scale and I wanted to see whether this would be a feasible move. The idea of a fresh start with the boys where evenings would be peaceful, was like a drug. It took a lot to make that trip. I was literally making 7.50 an hour, working forty hours a week, and paying for day care. I was still married, I just needed to know that I could get out if I needed to, and I could have a safe place to live.

I went there and talked to the rental office lady. She judged me from the moment I started talking. I told her that I had a husband in the military, but that I was leaving and needed an apartment. I told her how much I made. She looked at me. She told me there were only a handful of apartments that they slid to the very bottom of the income scale and they were all taken and had a waiting list of at least eighteen months. And then she said, "Maybe you should just work things out with your husband."

Ugh. I was demoralized. The one small action of strength that I could take was shot down. I was stuck. I couldn't afford another place, I couldn't wait that long, and I felt my barely-there power shrink back to its former nonexistence. That sentence haunted me and in some ways it still does. I wonder how many women she said some version of that to. How many women in abusive relationships of some type drew up courage to come ask this lady for a shrapnel of hope and ended up being cut by it instead? I would like to hope that I was the only one, but I venture to guess that would be overly optimistic. After this - what next, what options did I have? I evaluated my situation, and I knew that the only possibility I might have would be to get another job and it would have to be a job making much more money than $7.50 per hour. But what? I didn't have my degree; it was a small rural town.

I had been cowed down and a stay-at-home-mom for the past few years. Nothing seemed possible.

Another holiday season was coming. It was the winter of 2009. Columbus was three, and Zeff was turning six that December. We had a small party for him, Jeb had several drinks before his friends and coworkers arrived. Of course, the drinking continued. Later that evening, after everyone was gone, Jeb went out to get more beer. He called about twenty minutes after he left and said that he'd just been pulled over. He had a taillight out, or had an expired registration, or didn't signal. Something minor, but his car was known. He'd been drinking and driving regularly for months. As soon as the cop walked back to the police vehicle, Jeb called and said it was going to be a DUI. He'd call again when he knew more. A few hours later, I bailed him out, which we barely had enough money to do, and picked him up from jail. I was upset, but truthfully, I was so hopeful that this was the thing that would cause him to turn his life around. I had heard all those rock bottom stories, and I knew that this would be it. How could any dad who had to call his wife to come pick him up from jail after a DUI, knowing that there would be career consequences, and knowing that we could already barely afford the bail, not feel like this was a turning point? Well, there are lots of alcoholics who feel that way it turns out, and here was an example. The Air Force has a no-DUI-policy, however, this guy was so loved by his superiors that he convinced them to let it slide. He said it was his son's birthday, he didn't realize how much he'd had, and hadn't eaten enough throughout the afternoon, he'd made a bad choice and had never, and would never, do anything like it again. He recognized his stupidity, etc., etc., etc. They let him off easy. He actually started giving presentations to other flights of airmen on how easy it is to be just past your limit and how you have to be adult enough to never make choices that put people's lives in danger. Everyone believed him. They actually felt bad for him. And he came home and drank and drank and drank and he showed up at work with cologne to cover the smell of alcohol. I bit my tongue, and I didn't know what to do.

In February of 2010, I was getting somewhat desperate. One of the people that I ran with somewhat regularly was the manager of the local Idaho Department of Labor office. Jamie had worked for him as a temp employee a couple of times, and I figured I could at least ask him if there was anywhere hiring that he knew about. He knew all the jobs in town. I mustered up the courage and asked if he was aware of anything. This was a Saturday run. He said he was hiring two temps and told me to show up on Monday for an interview. An interview!?! Bring a resume and cover letter and show up for an interview. At the Department of Labor. I had no idea what the Department of Labor was or did, but you bet your ass I was going to be there. The boys and I were staying with my mom for a few days; it was getting so out of control at home. Jeb would come over and knock on her door, drinking, always drinking, and apologizing and then blaming me for why things were the way they were and how could he work on being more of a family man if I was taking away the one thing he really loved and needed, to be a family man. Half the time I believed that I was at fault. The power of those mind tricks is staggering. I put the boys to bed Sunday night at my mom's house. She didn't have beds for us so we slept on the floor in one bedroom together. But after I got them down, I researched and created a resume. I tried to figure out how to make my day care work and coaching sound appealing. And then I wrote a cover letter, trying not to let it express my desperation. They were horrible. Absolutely atrocious. And little did I know that I was applying to work at a place where part of the job was helping people create resumes. Had I known how bad mine was, I wouldn't have had the blind courage to show up. But I did. I interviewed and I got a job offer. The starting salary was $13.41 an hour. I was close to doubling my salary. However, it was a temp job, so I didn't know how long it would last. Conversely, I could stay at the preschool in a very safe job, forever. I made the leap, I had to. It was my first big leap of faith. And a huge lesson in taking chances and faking it until you make it.

Chapter 17
Workforce Consultant, Mom, and Runner Extraordinaire

"For me, becoming isn't about arriving somewhere or achieving a certain aim. I see it instead as forward motion, a means of evolving, a way to reach continuously toward a better self. The journey doesn't end."

— *Michelle Obama, Becoming*

I couldn't afford any business casual clothes. I had maybe a couple outfits that I could have cobbled together to even be close to work professional. Fortunately, Jamie came through and gave me a bag of her old work clothes. One problem solved. The other problem, maybe a little bigger, was that I didn't really know much about using a computer for work. That sounds strange now, but other than using the college library to write a couple of papers, and using my home computer for checking emails, I did not regularly use a computer. This was a job with a desk and a computer. What on earth was I supposed to do every day? When the manager showed me how to create folders, navigate through my email, switch between the multiple programs we used, I watched every tiny move and practiced replicating it. I didn't have to ask a lot of questions, but I felt like a total fraud. Nothing seemed too hard to get, but it was an overwhelming amount to remember and so drastically different from how I'd been spending my days. But just like I'd pretended I knew what I was doing when I created my resume and cover letter, so I could pretend here too, and that's what I resolved to do. I never lied or misrepresented my abilities, however, I definitely tried to make myself look like I wasn't a fish out of water when my new job was being demonstrated to me. I looked around, feeling like if the others here could do it, so could I. One mouse-click in front of the other.

One of the things the manager regularly did was check the local newspaper to see who in town was in jail. This let him know if anyone on unemployment or our training programs was incarcerated and not telling us they were unavailable. Well, on my first day at IDOL, Jeb was in jail for his DUI. He was in for ten days and got to pick when to serve them. The manager asked me if he was any relation. It was a small town. Yes. Yes, he was my husband. And we were having problems. I was embarrassed and worried about keeping the job on so many levels. So much was hanging in the balance. Could something like this tip the balance to being let go? And if it didn't work, could I even get my other job back? This was a big and uncomfortable leap. I just had to decide to be all in, but it felt scary as hell.

They had hired another temp about a week or two before me. She was outgoing, gregarious, she approached customers with a friendly demeanor. I was quiet, I was absorbing everything and learning quickly, but that wasn't visible. My coworkers found me unusually quiet and had told the manager there was no way I would fit in long term. I found out later, the consensus was that she would last, and they'd need to get rid of me soon. But then cracks appeared. The other staff started to notice she lied. Like, blatant, bold-faced lying. A customer would let her know they needed to file a complaint against an employer, and she told them with complete assuredness we didn't do that there when one of our primary functions was to help people with that type of issue. Another time, they had her call an employer about an unemployment claim, and she lied about what was said even though the conversation had been overheard. Move over crazy, the quiet one is here! Fortunately, I was starting to show my consistency and intelligence, even if I wasn't opening up as much. The manager devised a plan to get rid of her. This was state employment; we were temp employees. The manager could get rid of either or both of us at any time for any reason, no commitment to employment. However, he pulled me in on a Friday and told me that he didn't want to get rid of me and wasn't going to, but he wanted me to act like he'd just fired me. WHAT!?! He told me to storm out of his office, grab my stuff and leave for the afternoon, and he'd pay me for the whole day. Fake get fired, and get paid for the day, this didn't sound right. He said he was really going to let her go after me and wanted it to look like he was getting rid of both of us and that I was getting the ax first. Was this what professional employment was like? Of course, I listened. He was my new boss and my co-runner. I stormed out. I grabbed my stuff. He let her go. I showed back up on Monday. She didn't. However, given that, as mentioned, it was a SMALL TOWN, it was somewhat obvious that my car was still parked out there every day after the fake firing. So weird. But I made it through the first test.

Jeb got out of jail. There was no respite from drinking. I got my first paycheck. My confidence ticked up. I kept working one evening a week at the preschool and Amanda gave me half off day care costs. How can I describe that feeling? From being a woman beaten down, with no hope, no place to go, and two babies to take care of, to getting my first paycheck that wasn't minimum wage and working a professional job. Fuck Yeah. That's the feeling. The universe was giving me exactly what I needed when I needed it. I just had to start asking. There it was, a way to get out, a way to pay for my kids to stay in day care. A way to feed them. There it was. I asked. I asked one runner on a bleak, February day if he knew of any jobs that were available and a new world was handed to me. But I had to ask, and I had to accept the answer. I had to fake a resume, fake computer skills, and fake just a little bit of confidence to show up and fake it some more. Fuck yeah, the Shalane Flanagan winning the New York City Marathon feeling. Okay, maybe I didn't quite have that, but slowly, ever so slowly, it was gathering.

Enter into my life, two more life changers with whom I worked. The amazing, Dr. Ray Cotton. Not a medical doctor, a doctor of life. Some of his sayings include but are by no means limited to, "You have to feed and water your own," "She was so fine, made me wanna eat corn through a fence," and, the famous, "Sometimes you have to get your pee-pee stepped on." He took care of my heart and soul. And Athena MacMillan. I was scared of Athena at first and did not want to piss her off. She was beautiful. One of those women who looks classy no matter what they wear or do. She exuded confidence and class. I wanted to be more like her and to be less scared of her. And she was funny and profane; she took the right things seriously and everything else lightly. She would come to imbue me with strength, be a friend and a model of a strong woman. I began to have a family at work. I started to have a place where I felt safe. Little by little, one grain at a time, confidence was happening. I say confidence now, but really it wasn't anywhere close to that yet, it was just a little less weakness, a little less of an open wound.

It was hard getting used to those days working away from my boys full time. Morning routine was an exercise in intensity. I rushed to get everything done that was necessary to get the boys to day care and myself to work (clothes that fit, socks that almost matched, three pairs of shoes on all six of our feet). And then the evenings: getting them picked up, making dinner, cleaning up, bathing, books and bedtime. And then before falling into bed myself, I'd clean up what was leftover, do laundry and make lunches for all of us. All the while, I'd be hoping that Jeb wasn't too drunk or too angry to take it out on me, and then I'd get some fitful sleep to do it again. Oh, and lunch break running. I made it work. It was a lot of work to make it work, but I moved forward. I put one foot down and then the other.

That May of 2010, Zeff graduated from kindergarten. I was off that Friday afternoon, one of the first bits of time off I had taken. I hated to miss work. Jeb was off of work for some reason that day. And, of course, had gone out the night before. He hadn't come home. He knew it was Zeff's graduation, or at least I had told him that it was. I never knew how much he retained/realized/cared about what I told him. But he hadn't come home. That much I knew. I tried to call him and text him that morning, nothing. Finally, he responded. He'd been at Scarlett's house. That's where "everyone" crashed, they were too drunk to get home. I was angry and humiliated. Here was a man who had two kids, one of whom was graduating from kindergarten, and he couldn't figure out how to get home on a Friday afternoon after going out Thursday? What was I doing? I went to the graduation. Jamie came with me. There was only one other child who didn't have two parent representation. Not all the families were whole, but everyone showed up. Everyone showed up for their kid. Except Jeb.

Then a couple of days later, I found myself walking into a lawyer's office. I told him I wanted to get a divorce. I told him what was happening in my life. I said that I wanted my kids. He told me good luck. He said that since Jeb mostly drank in the garage and didn't come home on the nights that he was super trashed, it was clear he was making an effort to not do it around the kids and family, so he had just as much right to the kids as I did. My stomach burns just to write that down. I was confident though, that Jeb wouldn't fight for the kids, he was still spending a lot of time with his female coworker, and he was getting angrier and more withdrawn at home. He was going through big twenty packs of beer every single night and sometimes I'd find bottles of hard alcohol stashed around the garage too. I could always tell when it had been one of those nights. Those were the nights to exist quietly. Also, he was about to deploy again, this time to Afghanistan. The second time I went to talk to the lawyer, he had an idea. He suggested that I could serve Jeb the divorce papers before he deployed and give him enough time to respond legally, but not enough time to really take action, that way I'd be almost assured I'd get what I put in the papers. I could do it a few days before he left Mountain Home, but when he still had a week or ten days before he actually left the country. And then it would finalize while he was gone. It was sneaky, but I was scared. I was scared of losing the most important things in my life, scared of Jeb, and scared of this version of myself I had become. I took the lawyer's advice. It felt bad, but amazingly empowering at the same time.

Jeb got served one evening a couple days before he left. I had told him I was going to file, but he didn't believe me. He was shocked; he had no idea I would or could actually do something like that. And he was angry. I knew I only had a couple nights to deal with it, I figured I could get through a couple nights of anything especially knowing what I'd already been through. I don't remember those nights, I remember only knowing that I couldn't believe what I had done, that it was happening. I think some part of me thought that *this* might be his rock bottom. He might realize he was losing everything, and it just might be enough. I should have known though, that even if it was, it would be arbitrary. He'd be sober because he wouldn't have access to alcohol and without the choice to procure it, his resolve, if he did feel ready to change, wouldn't be tested. Mostly I think I knew I couldn't go through the whole sober-deployment-promises/drunk-return, broken promise cycle. I was so simultaneously full of both love and hurt and I wanted to act out in a way that showed him how serious I was, showed him I couldn't put up with anymore, and removed me from the nightly barrage of mistreatment that had become our norm.

Jeb left. We brought him to the airport. There's something about watching your spouse deploy in uniform to defend the country that makes faults fall away. There in the airport, I loved him still. I was heartbroken about where we were, but I loved this beautiful, broken man who was treating me horribly. I thought somewhere underneath all that alcoholism, he loved me too. They went to Virginia for a few days before they left for good.

He called me every night, angry, apologetic, accusing, all the things. He called Scarlett too. I got the phone bill and saw her number over and over again. An hour here, forty minutes there. I reminded myself why I was doing what I had done. I went to work that Monday and one of Jeb's friends in the military came in to talk to Ray, the Veteran Rep. He had gotten kicked off of the deployment at the last minute and was frustrated with the military. I spoke with him for a few minutes. I reflected on how weird it was that they had only kicked him off. He said no, it wasn't only me. They kicked Scarlett off too. For the months leading up to the deployment, Jeb had known he'd deploy with the girl he was fucking. And as we went through all that we went through, discussing her, talking about why he was spending time with her, etc., it had never come up. He was planning to spend all those months deployed with Scarlett and thought I wouldn't know. He knew our marriage was on the rocks and here I was at work finding out that he had thought the entire time he'd be deploying with the other woman. At that moment, I began to get a glimpse of the level of dishonesty I'd been dealing with. I began to realize the narcissistic tendencies, the gaslighting, the convincing me that I was crazy for the past couple of years. Maybe he wasn't just a nice guy making poor choices, maybe it wasn't something I could just love him through. Maybe I could be okay, maybe I was okay. I didn't believe that all the time, but in the hours and hours of pain, sometimes I'd have a second when it seemed possible.

Writing from the time:

Airport—End of June 2010

I didn't feel like I thought I would

I waited so long to say good-bye and with goodbye

My bitterness, my anger, my hurt, my disillusions---
gone too

And it was just us,

Against the world and me watching the man that I
love walk away

And wanting to run and hold him and... live again

I loved you again, purely and wholly

It was July. He was supposed to be back in November or December. I was still in our house, but I knew I'd have to be out before then. I was making less than $14 an hour and I was going to have to support myself and the boys. I'd get some child support (according to the divorce paperwork), but it would be tough. I started to adjust to life without the constant emotional and mental turmoil and abuse, but I missed him. When he called, he'd be sober. I questioned everything. I'd go to the garage just to smell the smell of his car. To me, it was him. I'd spend a few minutes, breathe it in, cry a few tears, and question myself. He was their dad, he was an alcoholic, but I loved the man he was. He'd hurt me, he'd called me names, he'd cheated on me, he'd lied to me, he'd threatened me physically, he'd left me to single parent the boys more often than he'd been present. But I couldn't imagine life without him. I was so dependent.

I found a cute little free-standing house that I thought I could afford. It had one bedroom, a small kitchen, a bathroom, and a dining/living area on one floor and a loft bedroom on the second floor. It was less than a thousand square feet, but it felt homey. It was less than a mile away from our other house. Jeb kept calling me, I kept questioning myself. He'd call angry and hurt, accusing me of having slimy motives. I was still scared to make him angry. It gets inside you in a weird way, the need to please these men with narcissistic tendencies, the rhythms of your own emotions don't flow without ties to theirs. Because of his hardship, he was allowed to come home early from the deployment. He got there in October and again we spent a couple nights in the house together before my new house was available to me. I got him a return present, some new, fluffy bath towels and some other accoutrements of comfort. I wanted to do something to take care of him even if I wasn't going to be there to take care of him myself.

Moving out was one of the worst days of my life. I watched little, tiny six-year-old Zeff carrying boxes out to my car and packing us up. He carried boxes as big as himself without any question. He got the job done. He was six. I was a mess. He wasn't. We didn't have anything. Again. Did he know he'd been through this with me before? When I had to carry all that we had. Of course not, but he acted like he knew the drill. A couple of mattresses, some kitchen and house stuff. We didn't even need a U-Haul. I took the boys to Suzanne's house for dinner that night. I couldn't eat. My eyes were swollen from crying and I was sick to my stomach, but I knew I needed to be around people. And my people were there. As always, the Universe delivered.

I started going to Al-Anon around that time. I listened to others who had been through it all. My first time I just cried the entire time. I couldn't stop. It was admitting something to myself that I hadn't quite done before. I was a piece of an alcoholic puzzle. I told them one time, how at first, the quiet was so peaceful. When I knew every night that I'd be okay, that I could put my babies to bed and read a book and stretch. And then the quiet got loud. I missed Jeb's smile, I missed his presence, I missed his strength. I missed having what I thought of as a counterpart. I was broken. I didn't know which way was up. This would have been a good point in my life to start seeing a counselor and begin to work through some of the stuff. It was so much. It was too much. I was lonely and hurting and the way out of an abusive relationship was hazy. So hazy, in fact, that the way back in was the only thing that made sense to my addled brain. And I had those boys, they were everything. They gave me structure, they filled my time, gave me purpose, and reminded why the one step at a time was important. But they also kept me busy enough that I didn't have to focus on my own healing or didn't have time to think about it, except in moments when it came rushing out in a deluge that I couldn't control.

The first weekend after I'd moved out, I was supposed to drop the boys off at Jeb's house Saturday morning and then go for a long run. They were so excited to see their dad; it would be their first chunk of time with just him. I packed up some toys and snacks, not knowing what he had in the house, and we drove the less than a mile there. When we got there, there was a red jeep in the driveway. I thought maybe a friend had stayed over, it wasn't quite an alarm to me. He'd been so sure about wanting the boys there early that morning. We knocked on the door and no one answered, so we tried the front door, and it was open. The boys went barreling in and we heard some loud music playing, thinking still that their dad was ready for a morning with them. They continued running through the house looking for papa and got to his bedroom. That door too was open. Papa was on a mattress or blanket on the floor, with a naked woman and they were covered by a blanket I'd gotten for us when I'd redecorated our room during a deployment. I walked in behind Zeff and saw it too. If I thought that I could take anything, that I was ready to let him go, I was wrong. If I thought my world had crashed upon me before, that too was wrong. This destroyed me. Jeb woke and tried to talk to us above the music, I rounded the boys up and got them out of there. I made it to Jamie's house where her then-husband agreed to watch the boys. I was shaking and sobbing and Jamie held me. For a few minutes. I didn't want to run, I thought we'd be too late, I didn't think I could see other humans. Jamie knew. She held me and she got my ass out that door. I ran and cried. I think Al was there too that day. They took care of me. Got me moving, moving, ever forward. Zeff asked all day, who was that with all that hair? Who had that much hair? She had long beautiful hair, flowing out from below the blanket. It made me want long, beautiful hair too.

And how did Jamie manage my desperation and depression during this time? She was there for everything that I needed, every little thing, every big thing, everything. Jeb had called after he and long hair had awoken fully and been so angry with me. Why did you go into my house? You know it's mine. How could violate my space, don't you understand that this isn't yours anymore? The boys went in; the door was open. But YOU should have known better, he told me. AND this was still his weekend, so I needed to get the boys back there as soon as I could. I had NO right to take them out of his house. But don't bring them by just yet, wait a few more hours, he had some things to do first. I could not be without the boys. I didn't know how, but I brought them back later that afternoon. I dropped them off, I let my hearts walk away from me and into the only house our family had ever owned.

I drove straight to Jamie's. She had bunco that night and invited me. I staunched the tears as we got ready and went. I didn't know any of the bunco ladies. They alternated what house they played at and this time they were in a quaint, magazine quality, cabin-esque home. Family pictures adorned the walls and every shelf and surface. It was the picture of a perfect, family home. This was a hallmark movie incarnate. I tried to talk to all these happily married women having a night without kids and husbands. It was as if they had the luxury of choosing to have a kid and man free night. This was a jagged knife. I sat in the living room, looking at the pictures of happiness, listening to some soft country music and seeing and hearing the beautiful lives these women seemed to have. I couldn't do it. I went out to Jamie's car. Ran out probably. It was another moment, uncontrollable, like the Al-Anon experience. My god, I was a mess. Jamie left bunco and drove me around. I hadn't eaten all day so she took me to get some food. She probably was ready to be done with the day, we'd run two hours that morning, she'd dealt with my roller coaster, but I wasn't ready to be alone. We parked at my house and walked another hour while she listened to me, talked to me, and tried to distract me from my broken heart. Jamie, my angel. When I thought I was worn out enough to go back into my house alone, she said goodbye and told me I could call her or come over to her house still if I needed that night. This was a friend. This was love. Fortunately, it was only that night and one other that the boys stayed at Jeb's house, so I didn't have to get too accustomed to nights when I couldn't check on the steady rises and falls of their chests.

Ten days after I moved into the new house and out of the house I'd shared with Jeb, Lexi of the long hair moved in. More of a girl than a woman really, she had just turned twenty-one. They'd met in a bar one of his first nights back in country and she was in the military too. Lexi came with quite a reputation but told him her days of promiscuity were behind her. And really, she was so young, it was a good time to be promiscuous, but probably not a good time to be moving in with an alcoholic in his thirties whose life was falling apart. She may have been better off sticking to the one-nighters. Lexi also thought of herself as very religious, without, as far as I know, seeing any contradiction in that.

Our custody agreement was that Jeb got every Wednesday evening with the boys and every other weekend. That was the least amount of time with him I could put in the decree without having the divorce be for cause, or at least that's what the lawyer had suggested. Well, that it wasn't quite the way it went down. He'd start off Wednesdays texting me that he couldn't wait to see the boys and then something would always happen. Random, weird things. He had another guy move into the house who was a friend from a bar and that guy had a gun that was unsecured, so he didn't want the boys around it. Something happened to someone else that he knew, and he had to go help them out. It was always something. One Wednesday he did ask me to bring them over for dinner and asked me to pick up McDonald's on the way for them, oh, and he gave me his meal order to go along with it. Jeb hadn't paid a dime of child support and I was back to dollar counting, but I picked up the McDonald's including his Big Mac. I wouldn't have thought not to. The boys were ecstatic. They never got happy meals.

I had planned that if he did have them any full weekends, I would double up long runs and get sixteen or more miles each day they were gone. I was trying to think of ways to exhaust myself and fill up the potential time without them. I had never had two days away from either of them. The longest time I'd been away from either of them was when Zeff had his overnight with Stef and Fred when Columbus was born. Even thinking of that great yawning gap of time without them made me sick to my stomach. But I also thought there might be some value in a break, I just couldn't quite imagine how I might realize that value. When the weekends with Jeb didn't come to fruition, I kept my normal running pattern of the long run on Saturday with the group and a Sunday stroller/ bike run. Much preferred! And yet another thank you to Jamie's then-husband for all those Saturday morning hours with four kids under ten. I also tried to date a little bit. It wasn't very successful. Ultimately, I wasn't ready for anything like that, but I was yearning for something. I just didn't know it was something inside myself. The new house was perfect for us. I got a little bit of furniture using a loan. I was stretching my fourteen dollars an hour as far as it would go. I couldn't afford going out to dinner, buying expensive groceries like nuts and other healthy foods that were the mainstays of my diet. I did not get a single child support check that entire time. What I could have done, what a healthier version of myself would have done, would have been to either contact Jeb's first sergeant about it or Health and Welfare, but there was no way that I would have gone over his head at the time. I scrimped. I went without. I made it work.

I remember very distinctly, one incident that always reminds me just how broke I was. I needed to take an online coaching class to coach the boys' soccer teams and it cost $20 which was reimbursable by Parks and Rec after showing successful completion. I had $37 in my bank account before paying the $20 for the coaching certification and eight days until my next paycheck. I took the course, paid for it, and brought in proof to get my reimbursement the following day. They said thank you for bringing in the proof and the reimbursement would come in the mail the following month. I didn't cry, despite the blow. What could I say? It wasn't their fault I had $17 to my name. I sucked it up, I made it work. I stretched out that seventeen dollars and I got to the next payday. And I was a great coach.

Meanwhile, Jeb and Lexi were going out every weekend, taking day trips, having the fun of a new couple as we went into the holiday season. Everything was happening so quickly. I remember Jeb telling me he'd pick up Zeff one Saturday. I remember Zeff, who never sat still, sitting at the window watching for an hour. He knew, he had no question, that his dad would show up. He didn't show. I was so angry if I can even call it that. I don't think I ever really got angry then, maybe some muted blame-free version of anger, but not the real stuff. I was heartbroken for my little boy though, that feeling I recognized and knew well. The anticipation and dashed hopes and then hearing him justify it. He's probably busy, he's probably…I don't even know what. He couldn't blame his dad any more than I could. I had unintentionally passed that legacy down.

About this time, Jeb started reaching back out to me romantically. He'd gotten a pit bull and he'd walk it over to my house under the auspices of walking the dog so that his girlfriend didn't know where he was going. He'd tell me how much he missed me. He'd call me in the middle of the night after Lexi was asleep, to tell me how much he needed me and then he'd get angry and call me names. I'd call back to try to soothe him. I wasn't sleeping well anyway, and those calls made it impossible some nights. It was such a strange time. I felt like I still loved him and needed him. I guess I saw him as this tragic guy whom I could still love back to health. I'd seen what I thought may have been some changes.

He'd let me know that he and Lexi had made an early trip to go do something, because he'd never gotten up early for me. He'd tell me that she had taught him to cook, and he was getting really good at it. He told me that he had cut back on his drinking with the implication that it was now just a social thing, not an addiction and of course Lexi drank with him, so it was something they did together. He subtly, but clearly let me know that he was doing all the things with her that I hoped for from him and that he was able to do it while still drinking. Right. I'd listen, my heart would ache. I'd wonder how she could have convinced him that it was worth it to get up early to spend a day together, to cook together. Why hadn't I been enough to do that? I was the mother of his kids, how could this be happening with her? It was a jealous type of hurt, but also an aching feeling of not being enough. That was what it boiled down to, I felt like I had felt when we were married, like I wasn't good enough. It never occurred to me question how I should have been loved, what should have been enough for me.

So, I started seeing him again. Or at least that's how I thought of it. He'd stop over when it was convenient for him. He and Lexi had started having some spats, sometimes she'd go back to her dorm room on base and sometimes she'd be at the house. I was still running my long runs with Jamie and Al and doing what limited bit I could to process some of the pain and confusion. We never ran by the house; I couldn't take the chance of seeing her jeep out there. They looked so happy if I ever accidently saw them together, playful, smiling. It was too much, so we knew the way to avoid it whenever we went anywhere. The pain of that image was too sharp.

Between Jamie, Al, Athena, and Ray, I'd gotten to the point that they all thought I'd gotten stronger. I'd proceeded with the divorce, I'd moved the kids and myself into a house, I was supporting myself. Jamie knew I was still a mess and she'd talk me through and remind me how poorly I was being treated all the time. She'd remind me of the horrible things, the things I'd left behind. And it helped. I just didn't believe I was who she saw in me yet. Athena knew a little bit, but she was such a beacon of strength that I don't think she knew how easily I could sway back. When I told her I was "dating" Jeb again, she didn't talk to me for at least two weeks. She was so mad that I would accept that for myself. She recited the Maya Angelou quote she'd heard from Oprah: "When people show you who they are, believe them the first time" or some close variation of that. She was an example of resolve. I knew that this was never something she'd put up with and she wanted that strength of spirit for me. I just wasn't there.

And the truth of it was, I'd kind of become the other woman now. He was still seeing Lexi, hell, she was still living there most of the time. He'd come over, he'd pull me in for a hug and it would feel like home. It didn't take much. We planned what we were getting for the boys for Christmas, while he planned Christmas with her. She asked him to go away on a snow board trip for New Years and he agreed. He told me he felt like he had to even though he wanted to be with me. He'd agreed to it when things were new between them and there was a group going that was depending on him. Oh, and I could come over and let his dog out one of the days, he didn't have coverage? Of course I could. She was supposedly moved out at this point. I went over on the designated day, saw her shoes neatly lined up by the door, saw the sweet Christmas card filled with loving words that she'd gotten him on his table. Yeah, I was the other woman alright. She proposed to him on that trip, too. I was confused about she could have still thought they were together enough to be thinking of marriage and honestly, it stung. I don't even remember what he told me he said, something untrue, I can imagine. They came back, he continued to profess his undying love for me, and I did the same.

Then one night he came over upset. He said he needed to talk to me immediately, something had happened. She had an STD, that he had "found" and made her go get checked out. I had been sleeping with him too, so he came over to tell me. I was disgusted and hurt and crying. And what did this gentleman do??? He went back home to her to comfort her. Yes. That is what he did. He left me there crying and scared with his kids because she had called and wanted him back home. I guess he'd said and done some pretty horrible things on his way out of their house to mine, yet she called him back. And I wanted him to stay with me. Away he drove; my tears and feeling of being dirty continued. How was it that we both wanted him with us so badly under those circumstances? What was wrong with me? Fortunately for me, I did not get said STD. What luck.

Sometime shortly after that, they officially broke up. Lexi would try to reach out and come back over to get things she left there. I don't know, he probably let her, he told me he didn't, he'd put things outside if she really left anything. She reached out to me on Facebook and messaged me. She told me she'd never been so scared of any man in her life and that I had great kids. What on earth did she tell me that for? Did she think I didn't know that he had that side? Was she trying to remind me? Had he told her he always treated me well and that I was the one to mistreat him? Probably. I just couldn't believe she'd had the balls to reach out to me. I should have heeded her warning, but obviously, I'd had a lot worse warnings than that and they hadn't done a thing to deter me!

Writing about this time feels the same as writing about my brief interlude with purging. It feels just as shameful. It's not a shame to admit to the actions so much as being ashamed to have been that woman. I feel like I have to get it down because it's the truth, but I wish that I had been angry when I'd seen him with long hair and let my brain tell my heart to tell Jeb to fuck off. I wish that I'd been angry enough to see Zeff sitting by that window that I'd told Jeb to never fucking do that to his son again. I wish that I'd been a woman who would have kicked him out of my house when he told me about the STD and not felt hurt that he left me there crying, again. Just like I wish I had known I was beautiful enough in whatever body I was in that I didn't have to force any calories out of it. Strength and anger, they were elusive things. In the same way that I wish jail time had been rock bottom for Jeb, I wish that any one of these things had been mine. Jamie wanted me to see it, Athena told me I'd hit it. I just kept banging against it and bouncing up and back down to its painful surface. One more bruise, just one more. Maybe the next will be enough. Crash, crash, crash. but those running shoes stayed on my feet. A therapy mile here, a therapy mile there. Maybe I wasn't ready to acknowledge that bottom yet, to recognize it, but I had the shoes to run myself out. One foot in front of the other.

But at this point, our reunification was on! We kept seeing each other, it really did seem like he was drinking less. I mean, less than the twenty or more drinks a night he'd been drinking pre-deployment. But not always. One time he came over and passed out on my bathroom floor and his phone was open to a message he was sending not to the Lexi, but to the girl he'd been sleeping with before the divorce, Scarlett. I was livid and I told him I was. He convinced me that it was nothing and that it was my fault because he didn't know what was happening with us and Scarlett had always been there for him. I'd divorced him didn't I remember that, how did I expect him to behave?

Another time I found more messages from Scarlett on his phone. She was engaged to be married. Married. And she wanted one of the guys from the shop to do a boudoir photo shoot beforehand. Always the gentleman, Jeb volunteered. He asked her to wear that light blue undergarment set that he liked so much. He even knew her underwear sets!?! More messages asked if he could just come over and hold her, he missed the closeness but understood if they couldn't have sex now that she was engaged.

Those ones hurt the worst. Out of everything. He had convinced me that it was never about love for either her or Lexi. That Scarlett was just a drunken hook up and Lexi filled a void that I left. But to read that he wanted the closeness and the intimacy and didn't need the sex, painted it in a whole different light. Then I knew that I hadn't been enough. One of the things I'd always felt like we had that other couples didn't share was that we kept our intimacy alive despite whatever else was happening. I wanted to keep him happy and pleased in every way that I could. But he missed the closeness with her. I made him leave my house that night and listened while he told me he loved me and that I was being unfair. His love for me should have been clear to me and if I couldn't see it, then I was the one with the problem. I let him come back. I let him "love" me. And I must have hated myself.

This went on for months. We kept our separate houses. He'd go home to drink and sleep most nights but would sometimes have an overnight. He invited the boys and I over to the old house one night and it was so hard to go back. The furniture he'd picked with Lexi, all the painful memories. It was an icky feeling to walk back through that door. I recognize that feeling now as my instinct telling me that I was very wrong. My inner voice was screaming, "Get the fuck out!", but all I heard was it telling me that my stomach felt a little uneasy. I thought it was normal to feel uncomfortable to come back, I never really questioned if I should think of it as wrong. Like everything else, I thought it was me who had to adjust. I had to change, to accommodate their furniture, to accommodate being in the house he had hurt me in, the house I'd hid in. I had to change.

Chapter 18
A Scary Halloween

"Hey honey, you think that I'm a fool to be
So deep in it now that I can't see
I just wait for you to call my name
Ain't it always been the same"

– Nathaniel Rateliff & The Night Sweats, Still Out There Running

2011. In August of 2011, I'd made the decision to officially move back in. It didn't make sense to keep paying a mortgage and a rent between the two of us when we were having frequent overnights. He said that me keeping another place was just a reminder of what I'd done to him. Jeb had "cut back" on his drinking. He wasn't going out "as much". We were having fun together. I'd have a glass of wine with him sometimes, I'd stay up later than I had before, to try to show him that I was valuing our relationship and not just putting so much energy into motherhood. He never once, not one single time got up at six with the boys and I, but he appreciated that I was staying up later with him. We felt like we'd gotten back to some semblance of who we were before, but mostly I had just made more concessions. None of my friends thought it was a good idea, but they were trying to support me. Jamie loved me like always, but she was worried for me. She knew how alcoholics worked. She softly told me, others told me less softly, but I wasn't willing to listen. Or maybe I couldn't hear it. One of my arguments was: Alcoholism is a disease. It makes him mean and angry and make bad choices. If he had a brain tumor that made him angry and mean, I wouldn't leave him for that, so how could look at myself in the mirror for leaving him for alcoholism? How could I have thought that taking my vows that lightly, fit with who I was? I loved an alcoholic and I loved him fiercely. And I thought that he loved me too. And I thought that was a reasonable way for love to feel. I really, truly, to my core, thought that we had a special, unique bond that other couples usually couldn't achieve, and it was my job to recognize and protect that.

My dad was NOT happy about my choice to move myself and the boys back in with Jeb when he was still drinking. He knew that alcoholism was not a disease that one could remedy by drinking less. He'd been sober for almost fifteen years by then so he knew firsthand. But he also knew that I would live my own life and make my own decisions. I could see the lack of approval in the set of his jaw, but he knew that telling me don't do it wouldn't stop me from doing it. After all, he'd tried that with my high school relationship, and we all know how that turned out! He still came to visit, he'd stay in his motor home in front of the house and spend time with the boys, but he didn't want to be around Jeb if he didn't have to. I'm sure he spent a lot of mental energy figuring out how to parent me through that mess, how to have restraint and love me, how to hope for my strength, but give me the space to find it on my own. My mom had a different approach which I choose to look at this as her capacity to love and forgive, though that's not what it felt like. She fully embraced Jeb and my return to him. I'd stayed at her house with the boys to get space from him and the abuse in the past, she'd seen how he treated both me and the boys, but she let it all go. He was her son again. Why didn't she fight for me? Probably the same reason I didn't fight for myself. She didn't know how. But, God, how I wish she had learned. I tell myself too, that maybe she just didn't have the ability to, she was a different version of herself. Most of the time, I never thought about having a mom to mother me, but when I look back, there were times a mama would have been nice.

I have so many vibrant memories from this time, though much of it was a blur. When I think back on them, it feels like someone is sitting on my chest. Like my heart was beating in some strangled, suppressed sort of way. I remember so deeply wanting to be enough for him. I could go out more, I could get baby-sitters, I could party. I could be the irresponsible one some of the time too. One time he wanted me to go to one of the bars that he and Lexi had frequented. Of course, he had a drink or two before we went, and we walked into this small, dark, gritty bar. 100% dive bar, which might have been fun under different circumstances, with different company. I was uncomfortable from the moment I walked in, trying to so hard to look like a dive bar girl who wasn't thinking about her kids at home. He knew every single, old, broke-ass alcoholic in there and all of their sob stories about how life had done them wrong. He introduced me as his wife to all these people who had known him and Lexi as a couple. There was an older couple there who he seemed to know well, and they wanted to play pool. I hate pool. Plain and simple. I can see how angles are supposed to work and I'm impressed with the geometry of it, but I can't make it happen. I can't hold the stick right, and can't for the life of me, make the stick hit the ball right. It's just not my thing. The other couple and Jeb were all very good. I told Jeb I didn't want to play, I'd be happy to watch, but I really, really didn't want to play with these three. Not only did he tell them I would, but he paired me up with the lady. I tried to tell myself I could do this out of my comfort zone thing. But it felt like a betrayal. I was there, I was meeting his friends, I had a drink with him, and I didn't want to play pool. Why didn't he protect me? Of course, I wasn't comfortable enough with myself to say no and stick to it or to make a joke out of how bad I was. I just kept trying, kept missing, kept losing. It felt horrible and forced. After a single game and several dirty looks from the other lady who "didn't care that we lost", the game was over. I'd survived. After that, he *let* me watch him. I assured him, assured myself, that I'd had such a good time that night. I'd gotten a baby-sitter; I'd gone out to a bar. I'd let loose. Haha. Letting Loose. That was the one thing I didn't get. When we'd first gotten divorced, several people had said to me that maybe single I could loosen up a little. It sounded strange to me to hear it because I thought I was pretty laid back. I seriously didn't know what was being suggested. I didn't understand that they could see I was holding myself back, and in, and away, all the time. I was tentative. But they didn't mean that I needed to go out more and drink a little and have a good time, they meant that life should have been a good time for me and they could see that it wasn't. Making sure my kids were happy and healthy and oh so loved wasn't all that I should be getting out of my early thirties. One can't loosen up in a narcissistic noose, they can only move forward and watch where they step.

The drinking had been creeping back up around Halloween, and his desire to go out was getting stronger and stronger. He'd tell me he didn't want to go out, he just really, really, really liked playing pool and bars were the only place he could play. He and Lexi had been in a pool league together and he'd really found his passion playing pool. I bet he had. We were going to meet several other families at Jamie's house and go trick-or-treating from there. Jeb was getting off work a little early, Jamie was ordering pizza, it was going to be a fun, family night. Jeb got home and got angry. He didn't like that I'd obligated him to go somewhere right after work. He needed time, he didn't want to be around my friends, he only wanted to be around the family, and I should have known that. I tried to reason/compromise. I told him I'd go and he could take some time at home and meet us there before we alit. He accepted but was not happy and it was clearly my fault. He showed up at Jamie's just before we left to go hit the streets to collect the goods, and he'd been drinking. We all had cheese pizza and he'd stayed home to drink. He did his "life of the party" thing for a bit and ended up going back home. I trick-or-treated like all was well, but my seeds of doubt were blooming. When my sugar-rush boys and I got home, he was drunk. High-functioning drunk, but drunk. He wanted to go play pool and hang out with a friend. It was just after 8pm on Halloween night and there were kids ALL over the place. I pleaded with him not to go. I told him to get a ride, I tried to hide the keys, but he left. He had the keys, I couldn't take them, I didn't have the power or the ability or probably the will. I didn't know how to fight it. He sped off to the bar. Again, universe messaging me like crazy, I felt sick to my stomach. That was one of my worst feelings with him driving drunk. He usually drove intoxicated, but not usually like that night. I couldn't handle the guilt, I couldn't handle knowing that he was okay making that choice, I couldn't handle that he made that night my fault. How could I expect him to stay home when I'd gotten all that time with my best friend? I didn't even know how to argue that. It was ridiculous, but with a narcissist, the compulsion to explain yourself and readjust the glow of the gaslighting is strong! I knew that night that I had to leave again, and it felt like shit. How would the boys understand? Why had I put them through this?

He came home and hit something in the driveway early the next morning. I still feel sick writing it. Then, November 1st, 2011, he came home from work that day and started drinking. I was feeling confused and disgusted. He went out to get more beer with a taillight out. And he got pulled over. He called me while the cop was running his license and registration and told me he'd call me from jail when I could pick him up. And that was that. We knew he'd get kicked out of the military; his career as he knew it was over. He didn't have a degree, he didn't have his mechanic or welder certifications, and we lived in rural Idaho. I was making a little over thirty thousand a year. I called my mom, and she came over to stay with the boys and I went and got out enough money to post bail and I sat at the jailhouse until they were ready to release him.

He drank November 2nd, November 3rd, and November 4th. I had set aside all my dishes and towels and everything I'd need to leave in a hurry, I'd actually left them all set aside when I moved back in. They were stashed on a shelf in the laundry room where he rarely entered. I was making a plan; I just didn't know when to go. I thought I could stay until he figured out when he'd be kicked out and got over the initial difficulty that he must be experiencing. I seriously thought, I can't kick him when he's down. Kick him when he's down. Oh, the irony. The day after his DUI, another airman on base got a DUI. It was a big deal if there were two, two days in a row. Jeb hadn't answered his phone when his supervisor had tried to call so he sent another coworker to come to the house to tell him to get to base early in the morning. I gave him some excuse; I don't remember what. But the truth was, Jeb had been drinking again late that night and into the morning and I didn't want to send him to base with the coworker drunk or with a hangover. I wanted to protect him still. I felt so powerless. When he'd gone to base the morning after his second DUI his first sergeant couldn't understand how I'd let him out of the house. He'd asked Jeb why I had LET him leave the house. As if I'd had any control over this. How could his first sergeant have gone straight to how I had contributed? Blame was quick to go around, but no one blamed Jeb.

But then November 5th came. Jeb didn't have a drink that day. The evening wore on, still no drink. He went to bed that night without a single beer. I'd been talking to one of his superiors who I knew from the gym. I'd said that I thought Jeb needed inpatient dry out because of the twenty plus drinks per night he'd been used to. We'd been trying to figure out how to get him there, but Jeb stopped while we were plotting. He was sweaty and thrashy that first night and I slept lightly, if at all, making sure I didn't need to call an ambulance. I brought him cool washcloths, I blotted his forehead, made sure he had cool water available to drink. I laid beside him, I held him when I could. Through my nerves, I watched, I waited, I tended, and I hoped.

November 6th dawned. Jeb didn't drink. That night too, he sweat, my goodness did he sweat. He rolled around like a man outside of himself. I continued to take care of him. Everything he needed. More cool washcloths, some homemade soup, kept the boys quiet. He made it to November 7th and then November 8th. This was the longest, other than deployments, he'd been sober since we moved to Idaho. I held him, I loved him, it was too good to be true. Was I getting my husband back?

As each day passed, my optimism grew. I saw flashes of the man, who was really a boy, whom I used to love. My heart was singing but I knew it would be a long road. I began to feel a sense of pride for sticking with him, for knowing that there was more to our story. I felt like maybe my patience and perseverance were making sense. Maybe this was the reason there had been all those times I'd questioned the Universe, why things felt so hard. Maybe my kids would get their dad back. Maybe. Hopeful maybes permeated the very air I breathed.

November kept on trucking. Jeb was sober. He was getting kicked out of the military and had very limited career prospects, but he was sober. The kindness returned to his eyes. He began to open up. He told me all the stupid stuff he had done, all the lies. He cried as he told me, and we got back to us. That holiday season, the joy bursting out of me was palpable. I could literally feel it exuding from my pores. Sadly, though, things began to get a little strained between Jamie and me. She told me that she'd felt wrong to have given me the advice she had. She was worried that I couldn't ever see her as supportive now that I was back with Jeb after all that we'd just been through. I tried to assure her that her advice had a place and that she was right when she gave it, but that now he had changed and was a different person and I could still love our friendship and Jeb. She still felt like she should have kept her mouth shut and the tenor of our friendship changed.

The boys were both doing Little-man Wrestling that winter and Jeb and I were again talking about the rest of our lives. I still didn't fully believe in his sobriety but as the days added up, it began to feel more and more real. What else could I do but take the image that I saw as my reality? He made it through the holidays. He was home for the holidays. It was still slightly frustrating to me that he wouldn't get up with us on Christmas morning when the boys got up, didn't help me shop for, or wrap the presents, didn't help cook for the holiday meals, but these little frustrations were so easy to swallow. The story I told myself was that he gave up so much for us, he changed his whole life to be with us, the least I could do was all of the house, kid, and family stuff. Of course he could sleep in, of course I would cook him breakfast whenever he wanted to get out of bed, even though I'd made breakfast three hours earlier, of course I would do all the laundry, cleaning, and cooking when I got home from my full time job of helping unemployed people. Of course. I would work until I was exhausted. Of course I would run on my lunch breaks so it didn't impact my availability in the evenings. Of course. At the end of the day, hadn't he done even more than that by getting sober?

He got kicked out of the military in January. They worked with him to let it stretch into the new year and gave him a little time to figure out what would come next. And he was able to not get a dishonorable discharge, so it was still going to be a possibility to find decent employment after. I helped him with a resume, I knew all the employers who were hiring. He applied for two of the highest paying jobs in Mountain Home. The Cheese Factory, literally a factory which produced cheese, and a tow truck shop/ part company. They both offered him jobs with decent pay. He took a welding job at the tow truck place. Sigh of relief. I was making more than he was now, but we would have enough to pay our bills. He ended up on unemployment for two weeks total before his first day of work. I admired that about him. It was a promising new start. Jeb charms people and my coworkers, except Athena, were charmed too. They'd seen him in there on the computer looking for work, seen the way he looked at me, heard me talk about his new dedication to the family, and everyone, myself included, wanted it to work.

The new job was hard, the boss was a difficult guy to work for, but he was a successful, mostly self-made man in Mountain Home, Idaho. You didn't see that too often. Jeb learned a lot about Lean Process Improvement which was ironic because I was learning about the same thing at work. We both appreciated the simplicity of process mapping and how you could use it as a tool to boil down any task to its essential elements and then smooth them out. My career was going really well, it still didn't feel like a career, but I was getting confident. People were recognizing my intelligence, my diligence, and my contributions. I can't explain how much this impacted my self-concept. For the first time as an adult, I had people outside my family believing that I could do something, that I could make a difference, and that the effort I put into whatever I was doing could have an impact. My manager had wanted to hire me because he felt the people who came in could relate to me. I had tattoos, I had piercings, I had ever-changing hair styles. He hired me because the unemployed, down on their luck, low skill, fallen on tough times people of a poor, rural community could relate to me. Did he think they'd see themselves in me? He did. Did he know how poor I'd been? He did not. Did he know how well I could stretch a paycheck and still make my house into a home? No. Regardless, having been where many of our customers were, did give me an ability to relate to them, he was right about that. As I learned about process mapping and improvement, I never lost sight of how it would feel to someone just mustering the courage to walk in our door. It took a lot to take the ask-for-help step. I knew that intimately.

I was selected to be a part of the newly forming Adjudication Bureau and then selected to be on a team who was responsible for adjudication process improvement, and then I was selected to be the project manager for the team. The consultant who was working with the Department of Labor was one of the most amazing women I have ever met, enter angel number however many we're at now. Penny, my beautiful mentor Penny. She'd been married to an alcoholic, had single parented, had worked her way through her doctorate, kept working, teaching, and finally consulting and running her own businesses. She'd make process improvement suggestions wherever she went because it was who she was, and it got her where she was. I was in awe of her, I wanted to earn her respect and learn so much from her and I just liked her.

It was early 2012. Jeb was sober, we both had "good" jobs in Mountain Home, the boys were healthy and happy. One night at wrestling practice watching the boys tumble and wrestle and seeing all their little boy-ness, I was overwhelmed with love. Jeb had met us there and was sitting by me on the mat. He knew, we'd talked about how much I wanted, and couldn't wait for our family to grow. Ever since Columbus had been a toddler, I'd been wanting so badly to have another baby. When things were rough with Jeb and I wasn't working; when we were headed toward divorce it didn't make sense to want more children, but now that we were back, now that we were here, the desire was oozing out of me. I couldn't help it. I told him that night, I asked about when he thought we might start working on that. I didn't need for it to be soon, but I so desperately wanted to hear him tell me how much he wanted it too and that in a few months we could/should be ready to begin. He didn't say that. He was incredulous that I would ask. It was too soon. Of course it was. But for some reason that really hurt me. Not because of the soon-ness, but because he'd talked about it before too, told me how important it was and now, it wasn't. I didn't understand how he wasn't feeling the same grateful love that I was, and I didn't understand how an important thing, like a new baby, could be something he'd seem to waver on. The next time I brought it up and was told it was still too soon, I made him a deal. I asked if when we got to the point that I was making 40K a year on my own, we could start trying. He agreed. That was my benchmark.

But back to 2012. I started to notice little things. Jeb got stressed so easily. He was tense so much of the time, he'd have periods of happiness and joy along with a feeling that he'd gotten his life back. He'd be so thankful that I'd stuck by his side and holding my face, my hands, me, with so much love and then he'd be so angry at something one of the boys did. He chewed too loud, he swallowed wrong, it was all just too much for Jeb to handle. And then his weekend thing started. He felt like he'd missed all the years he was drunk and that he needed to make up for lost time, so every single weekend he'd have a list of projects to get done. New flooring, new blinds, new paint for both interior and exterior, new trim, new everything. Roof work, car work, yard work, landscaping. Everything. Now mind you, we both worked at least forty hours a week, the boys both played sports, I was running forty miles a week and I was doing 100% of all the housework and cooking every single day. I longed for a few hours of down time on the weekend, but this was not okay with Jeb. On top of wanting to "make up for lost time", nothing I ever did, the entire time, to help, was ever good enough. We had a brick façade on the front of our house that was maybe three feet high. When we were repainting the house, the brick was getting painted too. It was porous, but porous in different levels, in different spots. It absorbed paint strangely. He'd get so angry with me for the paint looking rough, looking like it ran on some bricks and looking thick in some places. I literally could not even paint bricks. I tried to paint interior trim, he thought this was something even I probably couldn't mess up. Well, in this area too, I was a complete failure. He came in to examine my work and yelled at me, "Do you want our house to look like all those places you go into where you see the globby, fucked up paint on the trim?" I had never seen globby trim at a single place in my entire life, but I guess there are some other places out there where people fuck up trim as badly as I seemed to have the capacity to do. He'd stress until explosion and then feel bad and I'd soothe and comfort.

I'd try to make things fun. I tried to get my running done as early as possible and with as little intrusion as possible into his schedules for the weekend. Basically, he'd sleep in until he wanted to, I'd be up doing breakfast, laundry, boy things until the moment Jeb was ready to put us to work. Of course, I'd make him whatever breakfast he requested first. Sometimes, he'd say "fuck it" let's go to Boise today and we'd load up the boys and take a day off, but it was always on his time and only when he deemed it okay. Then the aftermath would be that the next week would be hell because he'd have to make up for the "time off" that we'd all taken. It was crazy. But what mom who gets her alcoholic husband back doesn't understand that the road of sobriety has some bumps in it? I got it. I lived for those moments when he felt joy. We all loved those moments. He was so fun, so loving, so goofy. He'd be playful with all of us, and we all wanted to be in his presence. Audience: This is THE MOST DANGEROUS ROLLERCOASTER in the world to be on. In many years of reflection since I've learned exactly what this cycle does to a psyche. It is completely Pavlovian. I was the still rat on the intermittent sugar schedule. The ones who get the most addicted. The less the little rat can predict when she gets her sugar, the more she waits and waits and presses that button until she perishes or loses her mind. Okay I don't know if it goes on that long, but I know how it could. I will never, ever begrudge anyone for staying stuck until they get unstuck. I know how fucking good that sugar is.

Some of you will be reading thinking: "That could never be me. I know myself. I know who I am, and what I demand out of a relationship. I know how I deserve to be treated and I know how to walk away when it doesn't happen like that." And if that is you, I respect your power to do so. But there are just as many of you who were believers, like me, until they could believe no more, until the broken pieces outweighed the whole ones, until the putting back together seemed a task, almost, but not quite impossible.

In 2012, I was a believer. I was proselytizing at the altar of redemption. I believed in my family, my man, my career, and my house, which was getting more and more beautiful by the weekend. I believed that my life was on track, that I would bring more life into the unique miracle that was my world and my journey with this man. Zeff was eight, turning nine that December, and Columbus was five, turning six that August. When my birthday came around in June, I turned thirty-four. Jeb planned a weekend out of town. We got a break.

That Sunday, I woke up before the kids and Jeb and went for my run. It was still my favorite thing to do on vacation. I'd get a quiet forty-five minutes or an hour, usually with the sun just coming up, and then go back to join the family and get the boys ready for hotel breakfast. That Sunday, I ran down into Snake River Canyon in Twin Falls and back up, a nice, difficult loop, and went back to the family. I had showed them this cool waterfall off the side of the road there on a previous trip and before we left, Jeb wanted to take the boys back there. They got out and Jeb had something white and tubular in his hand as we walked toward this secluded waterfall. Can you guess what came next? He had Zeff help him hold open a sign asking if I'd marry him, and he had a ring. My first ring had been the cheapest, smallest diamond we could find when I was pregnant with Zeff. I still had it, I hadn't been able to get rid of it. This ring though, was me. It was a silver band a little on the thicker side with a tree landscape and a little runner silhouette. It wasn't expensive at all, but it was perfect for me. He knew me so well. I said yes. I put on that ring, and I put the other one back on too.

We set a date of September 22, 2012. I thought to myself that by nine months of sobriety, I'd have enough evidence that this was who he was, that I was what he wanted, that all the behaviors of the past were just that. They were alcohol behaviors; they were not Jeb behaviors. Jeb was a good man, who'd had struggles, who'd overcome, and who sometimes got stressed and could be mean. I could love a man like that. No one is perfect.

Sometime in this span of time, the manager position at the Mountain Home office became available. I applied for the job and got it. Within three years, I had replaced the man who hired me to relate to the town's most downtrodden. My process improvement skills had grown to the point that I was now analyzing processes independently and recognizing where and how to manage projects that made a big impact on the way IDOL did business. I was good at it. But most people hated that I was doing this. They didn't like that I was young and new and a bringing change. At that time, there was an office hierarchy with small offices like mine at the bottom of the totem pole and then there were two tiers higher for larger offices. Beyond that were area managers and a deputy director. The large office managers, who I was in some way subordinate to, wanted nothing to do with standardization and streamlining. I was completing projects that their bosses asked me to complete, and it rubbed them wrong. They'd listen, they'd attend my trainings, but then they'd keep doing their work the way they always had. I loved what I was doing even if it didn't have impact I was hoping for. I thought if I stuck to it for long enough, eventually they'd build trust in me and what I was trying to do. In the Mountain Home office, I was managing my small team of awesome employees and friends who had been there much longer than me, however, they supported me fully and I liked showing up at work every day.

Athena volunteered to plan my wedding for me, and we spent a day buying decorations and a dress. Everyone that we spoke to couldn't believe that I was buying a dress for a wedding a few weeks away and I wasn't stressed at all. Like my younger, more innocent self, I knew it would all work out. Jamie had a friend who was making me a cake. My dad was volunteering at a state park where we decided to have the ceremony and he was going to be able to get free parking for the guests. We found a barbecue restaurant to cater for a reasonable price and I bought a very modest array of flowers from a local shop also for a reasonable price. All in, I think the wedding cost something like $1200. Both Athena and Jamie still had their doubts, Athena's more obvious than Jamie's, but they supported me because they loved me. This was one of the first times in my life I had people volunteer to help and take care of me like this. These people showed up for me, they were my tribe.

Chapter 19
The Jon Interlude

"We bereaved are not alone. We belong to the largest company in all the world — the company of those who have known suffering."

— Helen Keller

While my life seemed to be on the upswing, my baby brother Jon's was not following such an uplifting path. Sweet Jon. He was twenty-six. He was homeless and he was a heroin addict. He'd dropped out of high school around the time Zeff was born and gotten his GED. He spent a couple of months living in a crowded apartment in North Carolina trying to go to a local community college. He wanted to reject the rules of society; commercialism, possession-based society, modern economics, the legal system, none of it made sense to him. He wanted freedom from all of it. He'd steal because he didn't think it was wrong, those rules didn't govern him. Sometimes this would include things like walking out of Wal-Mart with an entire grocery cart full of goods. He rolled his own cigarettes to avoid supporting big tobacco. And he read. He read everything and had thoughts and feelings about all of it. I visited his apartment sometime after Zeff was born. It was all dirty, on the ground furniture and remnants of recent parties, but he seemed happy.

Sometime shortly thereafter, he decided to be a hobo. He wanted to do it right and travel the country riding freight trains. So, that's exactly what he did. Evidently, there's a whole network of travelers who do this sort of thing and have various forms of shelter available all over the country. He literally hobo-ed across the country, north, south, east, and west, jumping on and off trains, dumpster diving, and carrying his life on his back. Of course, he was drinking and using what was available while he did it. He'd check in with my dad when he needed money or something bad happened, sometimes to be bailed out of a jail somewhere. The family worried, how could you not, but mostly when we talked to him, though infrequent, he sounded lucent and happier than he had for a long time. Then heroin became an issue. He was strung out, he got in bum fights, he stopped hopping trains as much and lived on the streets more. It was so strange to me that this boy I had loved so much was so out of my reach. I had told him, when I left home, that there was never going to be anything he could do, no matter what, no matter how bad that would change my love for him. That adage became the truth. I loved him so deeply and intensely that it hurt to think about. But the strangeness was that I now had my own kids. I had to take care of them, I couldn't go try to find him, to help him, to do anything other than be there if he called. He mostly called the rest of the family when he did because I couldn't help out financially. And maybe it was painful for both of us, so it was easier to avoid.

This little being of light, who I used to whisk out of his crib right after he was born just to be able to hold him. The child whose hand I held, who slept in my room, who I got up to go pee at night when he was potty-training, even though it meant setting my alarm for midnight and two in the morning when I was a preteen. This little smiley, rascally boy, was not a boy. He slept on the street or wherever he could find and did whatever he needed to, to get his next fix. He used to have his own version of peekaboo. He'd sit with his eyes closed and act like he didn't know you were there, then with extreme suddenness, open his eyes and nod his head up. I'd do it back, over and over, and get the sweetest, deepest, little boy laugh. That laugh was gone. To Jon, I owed my desire to mother, to have progeny, to build my life around being able to love and care for others. He made that what I wanted out of life because I loved him so intensely. It wasn't that my kids had replaced that love, but they'd certainly reset my love priorities. I wanted Jon updates, but I felt helpless, and through my helplessness I had to detach.

He'd flirt with getting clean. He'd try methadone and it would work for a little bit, but like most homeless addicts, he didn't ever have any of the anything that he'd need to get a job, to get a place to stay, get appointments, etc. Getting addiction under control is like step one of four hundred when you've been homeless. When he was little I felt like his guardian and I'd have these vivid dreams of losing him. I'd have dreams of him drowning and not being able to save him. When he was a toddler, I would never let him go to the beach without me so I could always keep watch. My childhood nightmares were coming true. This boy who taught me familial love was drowning, and I couldn't save him.

He met Anita somewhere in the crazy. She was my age and they fell in love. She was French and beautiful and weirdly classy in a homeless way. She was a transient too. When they were traveling together, Jon was better. Because she was a French citizen on a visa, they had to get out of the country every few months, so they'd hitchhike to Canada and Mexico as they needed to. Although Jon didn't fully believe in the institution of marriage, he knew she was what he wanted in life, and since she needed the citizenship, they got married. Sometimes they'd pass through Mountain Home and would usually stay in our shed in their sleeping bags which was at least as cozy as most of their accommodations. The boys loved them in all their unconventional ways. They'd come home with shiny golden shorts from the thrift store and Jon would wear them around with suspenders and tights. He was always on the edge. He had a big "Fuck the Law" tattoo on the back of his neck which was sometimes covered by his hair. He also had the pizza donkey tattoo on his chest. Because why would not have a pizza donkey tattoo?

They'd live places for periods of time after that, usually with groups of people in small houses or apartments where they could cobble together enough to afford it. Jon mostly panhandled, but he and Anita would work picking fruit or other odd jobs. Then he started using more seriously again. Anita was working at a restaurant and Jon would steal her money. Although she loved him, she couldn't put up with the addiction. She made the choice to leave. Jon was destroyed. He'd lost so many important women in his life, but Anita's leaving broke him. Of course, she didn't really have a choice. My mom was so mad her for leaving, but how could you fault her? I couldn't. I admired her, but I did hate that my brother was hurting.

He came to Mountain Home for a while after she left. He called my mom and said that he couldn't live that way anymore, he needed to get clean. He couldn't take another day. He showed up with his dog, Heavyset, the big Rottweiler, and they stayed with my mom. He'd gotten some methadone before travelling and then found a methadone clinic in Boise. We had to drive and hour and a half every single day except Sunday to get his methadone, my mom took the weekdays, and I took Saturdays. Jon always wanted to buy me a coffee when we went, it was a tiny thing, but it was the biggest contribution he could make. His way to say thank you, to tell me that he appreciated it. Me and him and some gas station coffee on an early Saturday morning. My Jon. Unfortunately, he'd also brought some heroin with him when he'd come to Mountain Home. His behavior started to get erratic, and we could all tell something was going on. One day when my dad was visiting, Jon tried to take the car keys, took a phone, was yelling and being aggressive with my parents so they called the cops. He got arrested and because of past charges in the system, he went to jail. The same jail Jeb had been in twice for his DUIs. Jon's first ten days there were absolute hell. He was detoxing bad, and they didn't get him any medical assistance. He got so dehydrated, his pee was thick brown, and he could hardly move. He was swollen and groggy, it was bad. When he was through the worst of it, I'd visit once a week for an hour. I was with Jeb then and he didn't really like me going there and I didn't like leaving the boys with him. He would get so angry when it was the three of them that I wasn't comfortable leaving them. Yes. You read that right. I wasn't comfortable leaving my kids with their dad for an hour. And it wasn't a huge alarm for me.

Visiting Jon was disheartening. I'd try to get him to look forward to anything. There wasn't much to talk about it. Jail was jail. I remember one visit clearly, he told me all he could think about was getting out to use again. He said it was the only time he ever felt happy. That was all he wanted, and he didn't want anyone to judge where his source of happiness came from. I didn't know how to feel about that. Was it my place to decide for him that his version of happiness wasn't right? His misery was palpable. Finally, the day came that'd he'd appear before the judge. We were hoping he could get out and stay in a recovery house. The first one ever in Mountain Home. When it was his turn, he spoke with the judge, and they talked about the likelihood of his recidivism. The judge told him he could go to any street corner in Mountain Home and get heroin, so he had to be committed to sobriety. Jon assured him that no, you could not go to any street corner in Mountain Home for heroin, he had tried them all. Darkly funny, but I'm sure he'd put forth the effort to get it. The judge didn't laugh. But they did let him out of jail and into the recovery house. My dad had gone back to North Carolina.

The recovery house was a hell hole. It had electric issues, heating/cooling issues, and lots of shitty stuff going on. One day, my dad got a goodbye message from my brother. He'd OD'd in an attempted suicide. My dad called the ambulance and they got there in time. I visited him in the hospital in Boise. He was mostly sedated and intubated. He'd have a moment of clarity and reach for the tube at his throat and then recede back into a fog, leaving the tube intact. When he had those moments and realized that he wasn't breathing through his mouth and nose, he'd have a look of abject fear in his eyes, it was horrible to see. I didn't know how to act. The nurse told me I could rub his hand and talk to him and that some of it might register. They told me to act normal. How can one act normal when they're holding their little brother's hand and watching him breathe through a tube? Normal, it was not. He got discharged into a mental health facility. One that my mom had also stayed in. That was short lived. As soon as he could get out, he was out of there. Caught a ride back to where he could use, and that was that. And actually, that last escape into the siren-y arms of heroin-led intoxication happened after Jeb's and my nuptials.

Chapter 20
Reunified

"Yeah maybe, we could find a place to stretch our wings
Rest upon cliffs overlooking scenes
Scenes we don't write and we don't fall between
Ah, we're just falling again"

-- Nathaniel Rateliff & The Night Sweats, Still Out There Running

September 21st, 2012. My sister Alycia, her husband, and her daughter arrived to the wedding venue. Jon was coming too. My mom and dad were there and all of my work family. I was spending the night before at Athena's house so that Jeb and I didn't spend our pre-wedding night together. Of course, I did not really want to leave the boys with Jeb, this was maybe the third or fourth night of their lives they'd been with just him. He was going to be getting them to bed, getting them ready in the morning, and getting them to the wedding. My mom was going to help with getting them into their tuxes and some of those things, but I still felt uncomfortable. It was so far outside of what we normally did, and Jeb's temper mixed with his need for perfection was something we'd all become accustomed to. Columbus couldn't moderate his behavior enough though to avoid consequences. I'd noticed from early on how different he was from Zeff. His defiance seemed more intrinsic and like maybe it was a part of something bigger that was going on. And he'd do this self-punishment thing. He'd get caught up in the way he was acting, impulsive as hell, then realize he'd gone too far, and ask us to take away his toys, especially his stuffed animals. That's how we knew how remorseful he was. When it was time for the stuffed animals to go, it was bad. He also had sensory issues. Socks were never comfortable, seams of pants or shirts could drive him crazy. Not the easiest kid to get into a tux and have behave before a big event like a wedding, even for an engaged parent. Nevertheless, I packed what I needed for the overnight and drove to Athena's house. It felt like a mini vacation with a very unsettled feeling, if there is such a thing, and I did not sleep well.

The morning of the 22nd, I got up, went for a run, and got ready for the day. Athena's daughter, Madi, was my flower girl and she went with me to a salon to get all done up before the big event. I looked beautiful; I was beautiful. Athena was already at the venue setting things up when Madi and I made our way there. Everything was perfect. There was no other way to describe it. Deep purple tulle decorating the columns of the pavilion, table decorations that matched gorgeously, and beta fish in fishbowls as centerpieces for the guests to take home. I couldn't have envisioned anything more lovely that what Athena did for me that day. For maybe the first time in my life, I felt like a princess. Jamie brought the cake, I was surrounded by love and marrying the sober father of my children. I. Was. So. Happy. We didn't plan it, but there was a ukulele band practicing together in the same park area. We asked them to come over to our pavilion and play the bridal march. They did. As usual, everything worked out like there was a master plan and we were a part of it. I think the Universe was like, "Fine, if you're going to do this, you're at least going to have the day of your dreams." Jon, Alycia, and I got a picture together. I think this wedding was the first time the whole family had been together in decades. My heart was full. Jeb and I had one night in a hotel, Saturday to Sunday, and were back at work on Monday. Married. Happily, ever after.

On November 5th, we took the day off from work to celebrate his year of sobriety. He started the day off irritated and telling me that he couldn't afford the whole day off, that we couldn't. But I persisted. We took the day off and went to a hot spring where we rented a private hot spring cabin. It was open to the sky, on a cold November day. It was lovely to have the day and the time with him. We went home refreshed and my mom was there with the boys. We were going into our second sober holiday season. Here's what I wrote about that year:

2012: A Summary

2012 was a great year for me. One of the best of my whole life so far. I met my goal to run at least as many miles as the year, logging a total of 2037.75. Which sounds pretty good, right?

But here's a look at years past:

2011 = 2152.25

2010 = 2731.25

2009 = 2670.25

And how about my Air Force Appreciation Day 5 Mile Race times? It's my favorite local race, kind of a yearly benchmark of my fitness:

2012 = 35:58

2011 = 34:10

2010 = 33:08

2009 = 33:56

How has it happened? How have I gotten to this point of decreased miles and speed and what does it mean? Have I succumbed to the grips of mediocrity? Have I unwittingly abandoned my throne of speed? It can't be age, yet..., can it?

I've been running now, regularly, for over 20 years. Twenty years. That is a long time. Twenty years of counting miles, clocking times, sweating, striving, working, speeding, and pushing, ever pushing, to be better, do more, take another second off. Repeats, track laps, phartleks, tempo runs, long runs. Runs when it's dark and cold and the world is still sleeping; runs in the heat of summer down long, empty highways where the only breaks in scenery are the mile markers and an occasional cow. I've run in Asia, Europe, Africa, and all over America. I've run in deserts, forests, through foreign cities passing women in Burkas and jeering men. I fell on my face (and belly, while pregnant with my youngest son, Col) when I came unexpectedly upon the Colosseum during an early morning run in Rome and I was stricken with its immensity and beauty. I've run through marriage and divorce, through friendship and loneliness, through births and through loss.....every distance from the 400m to an ultra-marathon. I've run away from things and to things. I've run to shut things out and invite them in. I've run through the empty, ache of deployments with bundled toddlers in a double stroller uphill in pelting rain (literally).

What, after all of this, has made this year different? And the answer is: Happiness. Contentedness. For the first time in my adult life, there is nothing that running is solving for me. I am not running anymore because of some great internal hunger for equanimity. Yes, I still have days that running provides me with a balance I would not otherwise have achieved. And yes, there are still days when every fiber of my body NEEDS to get out there for a long run and run until it's exhausted and dehydrated. Over the years, I have gotten so much out of running, taken it, stolen it, stolen every ounce of goodness that it could provide. And now, I'm just running. Sometimes on treadmills, sometimes outside, sometimes less rather than more. I don't race as much, but I have yet to miss a wrestling match, soccer game, or basketball game. I am slower, I am older, but I don't think that's why my miles and my times have dipped. I think that for the first time ever, most days when I leave my home for a run, I come back just as happy as when I left.

I'm pretty sure at some point in the next twenty years of running, I'll be struck with some wild desire to regain my former speed or beat former mileage. And maybe I'll be ready to do the work that goes along with it. And I'm pretty sure that other calamities will come my way from which running will give me that much needed refuge and respite. I'm pretty sure I'll have more runs during which I run everything in me out, in sweat and tears, and get to some point in the middle of the desert or forest an hour later a little bit unsure how I got there. But for now, I'm going to enjoy running for no other reason than I'm a runner and it's what I do.

Oh geez, was I right, those times of running everything in my out were not too far out on the horizon. And here's another thing I wrote. As you may guess, this one was retrospective.

It was eggshell happiness, those days between.

Rich on the surface, at its core unclean.

I was the victor, with my family back. Not feeling
the sharpness of those shells even as my feet
began to crack.

Chapter 21
The Ups and Downs

Life is like riding a bicycle. To keep your balance, you must keep moving.

- Albert Einstein

It was interesting how we made it work, or more accurately, how I made it work. This was the "lean in" phase of my life. I would get up early, get the boys ready for school, get lunches made if I hadn't the night before, get the boys to school, work all day managing a Dept. of Labor office, usually running or working out on my lunch break, pick the boys up, make dinner, clean up after dinner, do laundry, and get them in bed. Every night. Every single night. And weekends were not much reprieve. I was up early with the boys, making breakfast, doing housework, figuring out how I'd fit my run into the day. Zeff loved to come with me on his bike and Columbus sometimes would come as well. Jeb would almost always have some plans for the weekend, usually renovations or chores and sometimes that would dictate the course of the weekend. If he got up before ten to get started, it was an early day. He was working more than forty hours a week most weeks and his work was physical; I always wanted him to be able to rest, to have warm, healthy meals, to have it easy. I took all the hardship of two school age kids and a house to keep it easy for him. He'd notice sometimes which always made me feel validated. But mostly it was just our roles. If there was car stuff or house stuff to fix, he'd do that or plan to do it for a few weekends until it was absolutely imperative. The rest was mine. I didn't question it too much. And I'd love the weekend mornings he'd be lounging around lazily in bed, and I'd go in to get laundry or something and he'd pull me back down into bed with him. He was so warm and smelled of morning sleep.

In August of 2013, I reached one of the milestones I'd been aiming for. I was making $40,000 a year. Jeb was getting tired of his job and the non-living wage he was making working there, but we were doing fine as a family and my 40K solo contribution was my baby-making mark. I stopped taking my birth control. That September for his birthday and the one-year anniversary of our wedding, we went on a weekend trip together. It had been a month since I'd been off birth control. While on the trip, I got my period. Jeb could tell that something was wrong with me. I thought it would be as easy as the first few times and I'd get pregnant as soon as the thought entered my head. This was my first inkling that maybe it wouldn't be so easy. I told him that my period had started, and he had no idea what I meant. I thought he knew that I was off of birth control, the 40K mark had been something we'd agreed upon. I wanted a baby so deeply and intensely. I maybe had never wanted anything more. He was dismissive and incredulous. He told me the timing was still not right and that he/we were not ready. There would be no baby. He was angry and I tried to make him feel better. *I* tried to make *him* feel better. Yes, I did. I was heart-broken and on my period, and I comforted him. I guess that's the way it was. I did stand my ground a little bit though, I told him that if he wasn't ready that he was going to be the one responsible for birth control. I'd had an IUD after Columbus that migrated out of my uterus to between my uterus and large intestine and had to be surgically removed and most recently had been on the pill, which I didn't like. No more birth control for me. He could figure it out.

Columbus was starting to have more problems at school. He just could not conform. In kindergarten, he'd done things like leave his hand down when they were sitting in reading circle. and everyone got a marble for raising a hand when asked who wanted to be a better reader. He was the only one not to raise his hand. He thought he was a good reader already and the hand raising was for people who wanted to get better. He got bored easily and couldn't stay on task and he also had behaviors that just weren't like the other kids. First grade got a little worse, but he was still mostly successful. By second grade the teacher was isolating him from the rest of the kids, she really liked him, he just couldn't be around other kids without all of them getting off task and rambunctious. At home he was a very picky eater, he didn't want food to touch on his plate, he still had sensory issues with clothes, and he was impulsive and sometimes he'd throw all out, full body fits that made us worry he was going to hurt himself. It was obvious that he was different than most kids, but we weren't sure exactly how. His behaviors at home were often what sent Jeb over the edge in the evenings. I'd intervene between them and try to get Columbus to act in a way that wouldn't make Jeb leave the dinner table or be stressed and take it out in little ways on all of us. It's hard to know what it feels like to have little, subtle and some not-so-subtle retributions. When Jeb got stressed, we all knew the signs and how to react, for anyone who has been in a situation of avoiding someone with both narcissistic tendencies and a temper, you know exactly what I mean. He might get quiet for a couple of days and not talk to any of us. He might yell, he might tell me I wasn't doing enough, it could be anything. It was always some form of withdrawing love, affection, or presence, and I wanted him there and loving so much.

For the most part, life went on. Jamie and I never got back to our previous closeness. Jeb said he wanted me to have time with friends or girl time, but really, he wanted my free time to be spent with him. One time I'd gone to hang out with Athena and a couple of other female work friends. I had part of a drink when I was there. After a couple of hours, I came home. When I got there, I told Jeb how fun it had been and that my partial mojito had been delicious. He immediately got upset, how could I do that to him? I knew what his problems with drinking had been and I never should have considered driving hours after I'd had part of a drink. I was irresponsible, I'd risked everything he'd fought for. He'd say that I should plan things, but guilt me for being away if I ever really was. I thought that "we" wanted to spend our time together, but it was another subtle finger of control. Individually, things like this sound so mild and innocuous. And they were, it was the collective picture that was still doing a number on me mentally.

In May of 2014, one of my work friends had worked with a couple of other organizations to plan a huge Veteran job fair in Mountain Home. There were all kinds of huge employers looking to hire recently separated or retired vets. Department of Labor had a table there too to talk about what services we provided to veterans and to help make the connections with the vets we were already working with and all the prospective employers. All morning, I was by a table for an employer who worked as a contractor for a semiconductor manufacturer. They built and maintained the equipment that produced the microchips and they needed engineers. They were looking for vets who had troubleshooting, fabricating, and mechanical experience. They didn't need to be degreed engineers. I hear their spiel all morning. And Robert, the organizer, made me walk around and introduce myself and give my card to all the employers there. Even though I like being the manager, with my introverted tendencies, things like that were still hard. Robert was an extrovert through and through, and he walked me around like a pro. I texted Jeb and told him to come over on his lunch break, he was miserable at work, and I figured he could at least talk to a few employers. He was still making about fifteen dollars an hour and his employer went through staff like crazy. After a little cajoling, Jeb decided he could make it over there, but he'd only have about twenty minutes to talk to anyone. I felt like his twenty minutes would be worth it. He got over there in his work shirt and pants and we started with the table of engineers right next to me. How did the placement of that prophetic table happen? How had I heard them all morning going over exactly what they were looking for? Ask the Universe.

He talked to them for the duration of his time, and they were really hitting it off. When it was time to go back to work, Jeb went. At home that night, I asked him if he'd apply for one of their jobs. He said it was fucking crazy, he was not an engineer and that was the end of the conversation. A few days later, I got a call from one of the guys at the table. He introduced himself and said that he hadn't seen Jeb's resume come through and he'd been looking for it. He asked if I knew him. Yes, I did. I knew him.

The resume was on his desk the next morning. Jeb started the interview process which was multi-day and grueling and even involved dining with the prospective team. This employer was awesome, they travelled, they were an international company, they were smart, and they were successful. Jeb finally felt a glimmer of hope. When he had to do the online portion of the application, there was a section that asked about criminal history. Jeb answered truthfully but didn't have to put exactly what the crimes or charges had been. Finally, he got an offer letter with a start date of August 25th. The starting salary was over forty dollars an hour. More than twice what he was making. This would put our annual household salary over the 100K mark for the first time in forever. We hadn't dreamed of getting to that point ever really. Finances were something we suffered through, not something we were able to use to plan a future. It was always a question of how will it work, not how will the extra propel us in the direction we want to go. This was a game changer. Of course, he accepted. He gave notice at the tow truck place, and we felt like dreams were real and hard work really did pay off. We'd been working so damn hard.

Then he got a call. He hadn't passed the background check. The employer had a strict policy that you couldn't have more than one DUI in a certain amount of time and Jeb's were within that. They had to withdraw the offer, there was nothing they could do. Talk about getting your hopes and having them dashed. We didn't know how to feel. The letdown was palpable and heartbreaking. Jeb went back to the helpless, stuck feeling with a little bit of "I told you it couldn't work out for a guy like me" mixed in. He called the tow truck place, and they were willing to take him back. Ugh. Stuck. It's so hard to feel like there were options out of reach, we knew he'd turned this corner, but it seemed like the world didn't care.

A couple weeks later, he got a call from the same guy that had called to rescind the offer. He'd taken Jeb's case all the way to the highest corporate level to fight for an exception. This guy we didn't even know went to bat for Jeb, said he was willing to take the risk. Said that there hadn't been anything after the second DUI in years. Take a chance. He convinced them. He told Jeb that he'd understand if he didn't want to job anymore, that it must have been a rollercoaster already.

The second offer letter came in the mail with a new start date. We couldn't say no, but was it safe to say yes? What if someone changed their mind? He couldn't quit and get the tow truck job back again. It was do or die this time. He did. I think this choice was the one that changed Jeb's self-concept in a striking way. From that point forward, he believed that he could do things when he decided. Anything he decided. For the most part, this was a positive trait and the story of it was amazing. An Air Force mechanic and welder who got kicked out for not one but two DUIs, got a job as an engineer, making good money. And he was good at it. He decided to believe that he could do it. And that made all the difference. It had taken me a little longer to get there, but it was similar to me showing up for my first day as a Workforce Consultant. We faked it until we became it, and we were both good at it.

Around this time, a lady from Boise State University came to my office. She knew about a federal grant program run by IDOL which put people through school and paid for books, tuition, gas, and everything. She wanted to share information about the multi-disciplinary studies program at BSU. It was designed for working adults who had started college and not finished, who had life experience, and were ready to finish. The classes were online, and the program seemed reasonable. As she sat there talking to us about putting the people that we were working with through the MDS program, I knew she was talking directly to me. Right there, at that meeting with her, I committed to finish my bachelor's degree. I said it out loud in front of my colleagues and Vicki from BSU. I was going to do it. With our new family income, we could actually pay for it. Yet another voice that I needed to hear at exactly the moment I was ready to receive the message.

Even with my 130+ credits from FSU, I needed at least 30 to be able to graduate from BSU. 30 was doable. I made a plan, I applied, wrote my essays, and I was in the program. I started in the summer of 2015 and would graduate in December of 2016. That gave me the semesters from summer 2015 through fall 2016. Most semesters I took six or less credits, but that meant that spring of 2016 left me with nine credits. I think initially I was planning to graduate in the spring of 2017, but I just wanted to go once I got started and figured out a way to make it happen a semester earlier. And I committed to one more thing. I was going to study straight through until I got my master's degree. I only told a few people what the ultimate goal was, but I knew I had to get there. I'd spent so much of my adult life feeling "less than" because I hadn't finished my degree. I was always jealous of people who had finished their degrees, and in the military environment where degrees typically separated officers from enlisted, it felt like hard line in the sand. Even when I'd started at Department of Labor, the manager had asked about my degree. No, I'd had to explain, I'd gone to college for four years, I just didn't have a degree to show for it. He responded with an, "Oh. I thought you had your degree." Ugh. I still got the job. But there was always a but. I'd talk about college and refer to my last year. Most people assumed that I finished, and I always let that assumption be there. I couldn't quite own that part of my identity. Committing to finish also meant that I had to acknowledge what I hadn't before. It felt like coming clean and once I did, I just needed room to move.

Online classes seemed ridiculous. We had discussion forums where we had to introduce ourselves and people would seriously write things like "I like the color pink and pizza." Oh yeah, undergrads. I realized very quickly that first semester there would be a lot of game playing to get through, but this was a game I was good at. I played it and did the minimum that I needed to get A's. So that got added to the nighttime routine. I could do a lot of my schoolwork at work. I'd picked classes that were related to management, budgeting, team building and project management, all related to work stuff. Phew. Not too much to do at home, but there was enough. Fortunately, when it came to life stuff, I could juggle and adding one more thing in, always seemed possible. Guess what else? Jeb was finally ready to start trying for baby number three. This period of my life felt again like the things I'd been working toward for my whole adult life were within my reach. I could ignore all the little hard relationship things, Jeb had a good job, I had a good job, school was on track, the boys were playing sports and growing up into young men I was proud of. Ah, life.

Chapter 22
My Best Friend

"Everyone wants to ride with you in the limo, but what you want is someone who will take the bus with you when the limo breaks down."

— Oprah Winfrey

Something else miraculous happened in 2015. Jessica, my forever best friend and I got back in touch. When we lived in Germany, she and W lived in Wyoming, when we moved to Idaho, they moved to Germany. Our friendship was always such that we could take long pauses and pick up where we left off. No social pressure, no feeling of obligation, we could pick up and put down where and when we needed to. They had been double condom careful about getting pregnant before the time was right and when they were ready, nature had other ideas. They tried round after round of IVF while in Germany and it didn't work. Jessica could not get pregnant. After a few years of living there, they moved to Texas and decided to try one more time. It was a weird time for our friendship because I had healthy kids and my marriage had fallen apart and it seemed she had a perfect marriage and couldn't have the babies she'd dreamed about. We each had something the other coveted. W told Jess that one last try would be worth it. It was. Jessica got pregnant with twins. When it was far enough along to be past the risk of losing them, one of them posted an announcement. I wanted to be there for Jessica's baby shower. W and I worked it out as a surprise, I would fly to Texas the night before, and be there when she woke up. The surprise went off without a hitch and when Jessica woke up on the morning of her baby shower, her best friend whom she hadn't seen in years was standing in her kitchen. It took her a moment to realize it and fortunately the shock didn't send her into labor. Now that she had babies on the way and I was remarried, we didn't have these painful things between us that were hard to talk about. She wished she'd been more available to me during my divorce, and I wished I been there through her fertility issues. Even though picking up where we left off was as easy as always, we knew that we had to be there for each other and the hard stuff. Never again would there be anything so painful as to marginalize the love we had for each other. And that's what it had done, it had pushed the real stuff into a spot that we hadn't wanted to go to. We could talk easy stuff, but the hard moments had felt too hard when it came to babies and husbands. We rededicated ourselves to our friendship. Maybe, considering what we' already both been through, we had some inclination that we'd have a lot more challenges to get through. And that weekend, Jessica was resplendent, her belly was huge, the babies were healthy and life was good. It was interesting to us that we'd had some of these similarities. We'd both been model students in high school, the good girls, we'd worked hard, and hard work was ingrained in us. Neither of us could imagine life without hard work as a component. However, at the same time, our hard work always resulted in success. If we applied ourselves, we could do almost anything. Either of us could have gotten superlatives of "Most Likely to Succeed" or "Most Likely to Have Life Figured Out" or "Least Likely to Struggle Hard to Have Our Biggest Dreams Realized". Something along those lines. And yet, we had struggled. Mightily. The struggles had involved the things we'd held most dear. In your thirties though, it feels like what hardship has come, will pass and be done, or at least it did to us. I don't think I quite understood that ease is not on the horizon. It's not something you work towards as an end goal. No one said this was going to be easy and it wasn't. But then, at that baby shower, we both believed we could work hard enough to get there. Now, I think we both know we can work hard enough to know how to adjust to hardship when it does come. There is no avoiding it.

Chapter 23
The Worst Lottery
in the World

"Some of us think holding on makes us strong; but sometimes it is letting go."

-Hermann Hesse

Jeb and I had never had to worry about fertility timing before, but the first few months of "trying" hadn't resulted in anything other than me feeling sad every month when I got my period. There is so much wrapped up in periods for women. For me, it had been an embarrassment when I got it. It was something to hide. At home, we didn't talk about "feminine hygiene products" unless we needed more. Alycia and I both hated asking for them anyway though, everything bodies was not a discussion. Amenorrhea had stricken from the time I was twenty-one until I met and started having sex with Jeb and then I had been pregnant and nursing more often than I wasn't for our first five years together. Periods. Ugh. Every month right on schedule, like I hadn't been putting all this effort in, I would bleed and out of my body would go my hopes for a little embryo to be growing. I'd feel nauseous some months and my boobs would get sore; I'd be sure it was happening. And then, no.

During the month of September in 2015, Jeb was home literally one night the entire month. He was travelling for work and stopped home for one night before going to Japan. I was so tired. Both boys were playing sports six days/nights a week, school was in session, and Jeb was gone. One night when the boys were at football, I decided to sit in the car, instead of at the field and I immediately fell into a deep sleep. A few days later, or maybe a week, my period was late. After trying for months to time it and having Jeb only home for one night the month prior, I didn't really think much of it. The night hadn't been an "on schedule" night. A couple days later, my period still hadn't arrived. The hopes began to flutter. It couldn't be, it couldn't be. I didn't want to get too excited. I waited a respectable amount of time and bought a test. It was positive. Jeb and I had a video call that morning and I showed him the result. We were overjoyed. No, joy doesn't even come close. You want to think that there are words in languages to describe every human emotion, if you combine them right, if you have a big enough vocabulary, you can describe anything. There is no word for how I felt. You know when your heart is so full, it's like a presence in your chest, and it takes up all the space and you can feel it in your brain, buzzing, electric. It's all okay, everything is good and right and there. There, in that little plus. There. In my uterus. It was all there.

I wanted to savor every single moment of this pregnancy. I wanted to get big, I wanted to write all of it. I wanted to eat what I wanted and run when I wanted. I wanted every ounce of feeling that I could get out of this. I made my first appointment and they wanted to wait until eight weeks along. I didn't want to wait at all. I wanted to see that little heart beating and know that, that little bean was growing. Jeb was back home, and the day of the appointment came. We took a "before" picture and met the midwife. And then we went in for the ultrasound. Cystic hygroma. This little bean had the same fluid around the base of the head and neck that Phoenix had had. Except much more pronounced. The hallmark of genetic malformations. We knew what it was when we saw it. They measured it and it was big. They scheduled an appointment with a specialist early the next week. Between the Thursday or Friday of the appointment and the appointment with the specialist, it got even bigger. They told us the baby had less than a 5% chance to live.

I took the odds. We could do 5%. I started calling the baby Cinco. Cinco could do this. He was five-percenter. They made another appointment a few weeks out. The medical assumption was that the baby would miscarry by then. I didn't think so. The next appointment came, I got on the ultrasound table to wait. Another interminable wait to hear a baby's heartbeat, to see motion. To see life. A tiny miracle. The cystic hygroma had receded just slightly. A positive trend. Oh, how any little ray of hope was enough to keep me hanging on. We scheduled a blood draw to test for the major birth defects, it would detect all of the most severe and common defects.

And we waited. Waited for results, waited to hear what the fate of this little nugget be. How special? How would we accommodate whatever the needs were? We waited. I got the call from the doctor. He said: All major birth defects were ruled out by the test. He said I was having a little boy.

I called Jeb right away. I told him he was going to have another little boy. Cinco was already proving the doctors wrong!

In all of this mix, we had also decided to move to a bigger house. We found the perfect place. It was huge, it was on ten acres of land. It had space for animals, a workshop, a wall of windows facing the beautiful, barren, high desert landscape. It was a dream. The other house we decided to keep as a rental. Because I could not do anything properly, but Jeb didn't want me doing nothing, I would sit by him and hand him things as he did the work to finish renovations on the house. That I could do right. I could hand him peel and stick tiles while he tiled the bathroom floor, I could hand him spacers. I remember sitting there on the cold floor, troubled pregnancy in progress, exhausted, wondering why he wanted/ needed me there. Why couldn't I, this one time, just sit on the couch? But the move went on and I could hand him the tools and implements of betterment like no one's business. We moved into the new house in December and it was heated with wood and a pellet stove. One of the things we had to do every evening was get the fire going. One night Jeb was working later than I was and there was a rain, ice, windstorm coming. I knew I needed to get the fire going before getting the boys to practice. I worked on that fire and got a roaring one going. I knew he'd be so happy when he got home that it the house was warm, and he didn't have to worry about it right away. I left to take the boys to wrestling.

It was another story when we got home. Jeb was livid. I hadn't seen him this angry in a long time. The wind had blown the tarp off the wood pile outside. He couldn't believe I'd been so stupid to get a fire going instead of tarping the wood. He said that I'd risked a whole winter's worth of wood to save him a few minutes of starting a fire. He really and truly wanted his pregnant wife outside in an ice storm tarping wood. And that he assumed that I had any idea the tarp might blow off, that I had control, that this was my fault, was beyond me. Some part of me knew that this was crazy. I didn't know who this man was, I beyond hurt. I slept on the couch for a night. Thought I really taught him a lesson. He did not apologize. I did. I was sorry I hadn't known how to prioritize correctly. And this was the type of outburst I had gotten used to. Every once in a while, one, like this, would rise to the top and I'd recognize that maybe it was a little overboard. But I saw him yell at the boys for these kinds of things all the time. I saw rage and I saw it taken out and I apologized over and over again for being the way I was. I apologized for the boys being kids, for not behaving up to his standards, for all of us not being or doing enough.

Columbus started medication for anxiety and had his own outbursts, Zeff took it out on sports. I tried. Tried to love them through it and take care of all the hurts of everyone. I didn't have time to think of my own, which in some ways was good, because it got me through, but sad because of what I missed. I felt like this facsimile of what I wanted was close enough to the real thing and that I could keep working to get it. If I just did a little bit more, and more, and then some more. I wanted, more than anything, to keep my family together and to fight for it. When that feels like the ultimate goal, acceptance feels easy, or at least it did for me. My acceptance of wrongdoing felt like my version of fighting for my family. Fighting for what was right, should have been the fight for my family. I loved the image in my brain so much.

But the miracle Cinco was on the way, knowing this also made everything feel more okay. We could picture him in cowboy boots and a diaper running around all of that land. How great it was going to be to have a baby grow up with all that space, with family land, chickens, and maybe goats. Cinco was going to love it! His brothers would show him the ropes. Columbus's diagnoses of Anxiety and ADHD had finally given us some answers about his differences. It helped with the parenting; he was intense and took so much energy but understanding some of the why made every moment worth it. He had an insatiable appetite for knowledge and attention, and I wanted him to have all of it. Oh, and we'd also found out that because of the way his mouth was formed, it caused him to chew a little more noisily than most kids. Here, this thing Jeb had had a problem with for all of Columbus's eating life, was yet another thing he couldn't control. This kid. A good challenge and he was going to be a great big brother. Zeff was beyond excited too. He wanted to be the oldest brother, he wanted to meet his baby brother. He's a caretaker and wanted that role.

We kept seeing the specialist and there were more abnormal things in the ultrasounds. A tailbone that protruded, a kidney that wasn't forming right, the cystic hygroma was not going away, the list went on. The doctor wanted me to get an amniocentesis. I said no. We'd ruled out the major birth defects, the genetic counselor had explained that if it was something else, it would unlikely be something major. I wanted to accept whatever this little guy was bringing into the world with him. The doctor told me one thing that changed my mind. He said if the baby has a heart defect and having a specialist there when you give birth makes the difference between your baby living and dying, why would you not want to be prepared for that? He said that no other doctor would ever understand why he hadn't prepared the parents to have a single specialist that could change the outcome of this baby's life. That did it. Amnio it was.

I had passed out when I got the last amnio, so I was prepared to sit a few extra minutes, have some juice before getting up. It went without incident and once again we waited. I had an appointment with a pediatric heart specialist in a couple of weeks. Just before that appointment, I got a call from the genetic counselor. She had the results of the amnio and wanted to go over them, she could get us in right after the heart appointment. We had the heart appointment. While waiting for the doctor, I overheard a mom calling in that her baby's feeding tube had gotten detached, and she was calling for advice on what she could do or if she needed to come in. Hearing through the nurse's response, the struggle in the mom's voice made me reflect on the relative ease of mothering babies who didn't need such interventions. While that mom was probably accustomed to her daily routine too, there must have been moments, like when she was on the phone just then, that she was reminded of how not easy it was. I wonder if she had a Turkish doctor to impart that vital lesson.

They did an in-utero analysis of my son's heart. It appeared perfect. His little heart had all the chambers, they were functioning like they should at that point in gestation and it looked like any other baby heart at over halfway through a pregnancy. I was walking on air when I got up from that exam. There were those few other things on the ultrasounds that still looked off, but now we had both ruled out major genetic conditions and heart defects which are also often signaled by the cystic hygroma. I was so excited to go talk to the genetic counselor with the news. We floated from the heart doctor to her.

She asked us to sit in her office and pulled out the results. I told her what the heart doctor had said, I must have been smiling from ear to ear. Did that make her news harder to impart or was this part of her job that she was used to? She told us our little boy had a 6Q deletion. Basically, he was missing a huge chunk of genetic material on his 6th chromosome. It was very uncommon. Like one in a million. Completely unrelated to Phoenix's Turner Syndrome. She told us, and this is a quote I will never forget, "We hit the worst lottery in the world twice." A 6Q deletion with this level of deletion meant some serious things. It meant severe intellectual disability. I asked how severe, what were we talking? She said nonverbal, non-communicative, and that the very best-case scenario for the level of genetic material he was missing would be a couple of sounds that we might recognize as having meaning. He would never say or understand the word love or any version of that. He wouldn't know what I meant when I said it to him. And that was just the beginning. He would likely be dystonic, little muscle tone so he'd have an inability to walk or control his muscles well, he'd be wheelchair bound. Add to that, seizure disorders were likely, so he'd be strapped in. On top of that, both feeding issues and breathing issues were very common and likely with the level of deletion. He'd be nonverbal and strapped into a chair with devices to help him breathe and eat. She told us everything at once. We sat and listened. I cried. My heart stopped. It wasn't just broken. Brakes had been applied. Everything stopped. She told us there were options if we wanted to think about them. We told her no, we wanted this baby no matter what. We loved him and we had the capacity to love and care for special. She told us to call if we needed anything and we left. How many moms like me have walked out of her office like that? Were the receptionists used to seeing moms like me and having to avert their eyes and keep up the rhythm of their day? I don't know.

We made it to the car. We had to get away from that place. We drove to a parking lot probably a half mile away and just sat. What do you do from there? We had both started thinking about the reality of it, about the reasons for bringing a baby like this into the world. For us, the quality-of-life question had always been paramount. How could we bring a baby into the world who likely couldn't sustain life on his own, who wouldn't experience the joys of life? It felt so unfair to him to expect him to live like that. We started talking about what it would mean for Zeff and Columbus, how all of our lives would change. Would I have to quit working? We probably couldn't stay in our current house. There would be no little boy running around in cowboy boots on that land. Less than hour out of the appointment and we had started to change our minds about bringing this beautiful little boy into the world. I know there are so many deep seeded emotions on this question and I understand them. I understand making decisions that resonate with hearts and minds and religious beliefs, but I would ask, maybe plead, for anyone who feels a different way about this decision, to not judge. For me, neither answer was the right one. I couldn't expect a baby whom I loved with everything in me, to have a life like his would be, but I also couldn't think of ending the pregnancy. I needed to talk to the counselor again.

I called her and asked about the chances. Genetics are genetics, but how much of what she told us involved a predictive element?

Were we talking 50% chance, 75%? No. She said that while some of the diagnosis had less than 99% surety, the severe, nonverbal retardation was as high as you could get on the genetic predictive scale. Maybe he'd be able to breathe on his own, or maybe he'd grow out of the feeding tube. Maybe he wouldn't have a seizure disorder, but the intellectual disability was not an "if". I did research, I looked at groups of other moms of 6Q deletion kids. Some were mobile. But when I read the level of deletion, theirs were exponentially smaller. There were no kids in any of the groups or any of the research I found with my baby's level of missing genetic material. The worst lottery in the world, indeed. The truth of it was that most babies like mine didn't make it this far in pregnancies. These were the types of babies that miscarried. My body didn't let go of any babies. My uterus wanted him just as much as I did.

We made the choice to let our little guy, Orion David, only experience a comfortable and loved existence in my womb. He would not experience the pain of what life outside of it would have meant. The worst lottery in the world begets the worst decisions in the world. I loved him so much. I was angry at being faced with this decision again. Why me? Why a mom who wanted nothing more than motherhood? Whose life goals had been motherhood and motherhood alone? I felt like with Phoenix the decision had been different, she couldn't survive outside my body and keeping her in my body was a risk to my own health and possibly my life. I had known what I had to do. And I still had some regrets about it. Sometimes I still wished I taken the chance of the extra few days and let nature take its course. Mostly I knew I had made the better choice, but out of two bad choices, there will always be questions. With Orion, it was different. Every consideration that popped into my head, every facet of deciding felt wrong.

I talked to Jessica. She told me that she was proud of me. She told me her fear had been that I wouldn't even consider this option. We cried together. I talked to my dad, who'd endured a life of physical differentness. He told me he didn't want to go out of the world the way this baby would come into the world. He said he'd decided long ago that he didn't want to be dependent on the supports that Orion would need to live. He said that wasn't life and he'd want me to make the same decision for him. He never told me what to do, he let me infer from the choice he'd want made for him. My tribe.

I called the genetic counselor back. I told her what we decided. It felt horrible to say it out loud. There were only a few places in the country where this was possible. Though I don't want to make any sort of political statement out of the choice, and the way I chose to love my baby, this type of procedure invokes protests and strong feeling. When you see protestors with signs that have pictures of partially formed babies, they are from moms like me. These procedures cannot be done without medical cause. There is no place in the country where an end of a pregnancy at 28 weeks is done by choice alone.

Once we made the choice, I wanted to make arrangements to get to the clinic and get it done as soon as we could. We had to take a trip to Boulder. We called the clinic, they got us an appointment, we'd have to be there for a week. I had a few days left with Orion before we left. We went for a run together out in the desert. I cradled my belly and talked to him and cried and ran out everything I could. I told him how much I loved him and that I was going to miss him. That I didn't want to say goodbye to him and that I wanted only to hold him. My little Cinco, my five percenter, my Orion. He moved like he understood, but I didn't know if he would. I didn't know if anyone would. I spent an hour on the trails and felt a modicum of something like acceptance come over me. It wasn't quite acceptance, it was definitely not peace, but I felt better than I had before I left. Thank you running, thank you Orion. I ran one final time with him on our last day in Mountain Home, just a thirty minute out and back down our street. I savored every step of that run and the feeling of having him there. God, how could I keep taking these steps forward? I was scared and hurt but resigned. One foot, then the other.

It was March of 2016. We drove to Boulder through a Wyoming white-out snowstorm. My appetite was gone, I was despondent. I didn't know how I could do this. Jeb kept us moving forward. I thought so many times on that drive about backing out. But on he drove. Going to the clinic the next day was horrible. They had told us there would be protestors and there were. They stood there with their Bibles and signs. Jeb had my arm as we walked through, he was a pillar of confidence, and forward motion. I was a mess. I couldn't stop crying. I read several books and pieces of writing afterwards about this experience because there are so many women who have to make these choices. Women who are pregnant with multiples and have too many risks to carry them all to term, women in all kinds of different situations where all the choices are bad. But I didn't read anything about how it actually happens because it was too much, but this is my attempt to tell it. This would be a good point to skip ahead if this part already feels uncomfortable.

They did an ultrasound that showed Orion hadn't grown at all from the last appointment. In fact, he'd gotten a little smaller, but his heart was still beating. I watched his heart and gave them his diagnosis on a printed piece of paper from my doctor. They reviewed the form and agreed that his condition was severe enough that they could perform the procedure. We'd return the next day and begin. As I said, this process takes a week. I didn't stop crying the entire time. The next day we went back, and it was time. They would inject something into Orion to stop his heart. That's what they do. I got into the room, it was me, the doctor, and a nurse. I was sobbing so hard that my body was shaking. The doctor told me I had to get myself under control or he couldn't do it. Eerily similar to Zeff's doctor who said he couldn't work with me if I kept being so loud. I thought even at that moment about leaving. The nurse was soothing, and the doctor had done this over 40,000 times. 40,000, that sunk in. Finally, I was still enough, quieter tears still rolling down my face. He told me that over the evening, I might feel the baby move a few more times and that it was normal, but by the time I came back the next day, his heart would no longer be beating. He did it. I felt Orion move one final time right there on the table and that was it. I didn't feel him anymore that night. Orion was gone. But his little body was still inside of me. Still, it gets worse.

Labor has to start. They insert something vaginally to begin dilation, so it can begin. It can take a few days. It's not comfortable. There's no way to describe what I felt. We tried to go for walks during the days, I'd be cramping and uncomfortable and so, so, deeply sad. Jeb held it together. We took some pictures in the hotel room with our hands on my belly as another goodbye. I've only looked at them once since then. Finally, the last day of the week, it was time to give birth. They gave me something else to get it going and let me lay down in a bed. They told me I may start feeling some fluid come out or may start bleeding a little and they'd be keeping tabs. I began to feel a warm, wetness, but I thought it was exactly what they had described. The nurse had come in to check a few times, nothing other than the wetness was happening. When the nurse came back in again, I told her that I didn't know if I had peed or the water had broken or exactly what was going on, but I still wasn't feeling contractions. She lifted the sheet to look, and I had been hemorrhaging severely, I had lost a ton of blood and tissue. They rushed me into the delivery room and it was an emergency. They had to get someone else out and have another person wait because I needed medical attention right then. They gave me something for the pain and I needed to push. Here's the even worse part. A baby who is alive participates in the birthing process, one who is not, cannot. So, the doctor has to be more invasive. Sometimes the baby doesn't come out in a way that would be viewable to the mom afterwards. My actual memories of being in that room feel like a nightmare, but they are dulled by how much blood I had lost and whatever they gave me for pain. But I do know, and I knew in that room, by the words they used to describe what was happening, that I would not be able to see Orion afterwards. Finally, it was over. I had to remind myself that he was already with his sister and that he hadn't been there for that part. I had been there though. My God, I had.

We'd had counseling throughout the week we were there to talk through making this choice out of love and I knew that was the reason, but it just felt like life had stopped. Although we couldn't see him, they did bring him to us wrapped up. They gave us a chance to say goodbye. It didn't feel like him, but I still didn't want to let him go. We decided to get him cremated. And we got a birth/death certificate with his hand and foot prints.

The doctor told me to take six weeks off from running to let my body heal, it had been very hard on me physically. I'd lost almost twice as much blood as a normal birth and I was very weak. He also told us not to drive home all in one day because of a risk of blood clots. He said I needed to take it easy. As soon as I could walk without passing out, we left. I'd had some juice and crackers that stayed down. I wasn't pregnant anymore.

We left the motel the next day to do a one-day drive back home. There was no way I was going to be apart from the boys any longer than I had to. I'd get out and walk frequently, but I was not breaking up this drive, not even because of a risk of blood clots. I have to give Jeb credit for being a rock during that time. He said the right things, took care of me, made me feel loved. Of all the times in our marriage so far, the trip there, the experience, and the aftermath, was probably the most he ever did to take care of me in the way that I needed to be cared for. He said to me on the drive back, that we weren't done. He said in a few years, we'd have two more little ones running around the backyard. He wanted to do exactly what we'd already done but be more present for it this time. We weren't done. That's what he said. It was exactly what I wanted to hear. I could picture it too, maybe a boy and a girl this time. I could be a good girl mom, it seemed like it might be so different from what it had been with my boys. I sat there, trundled in the car, feeling so much older and wiser than the first car trip he and I had taken together. I still loved this man beside me, taking care of me. I wanted that vision so deeply in my bones and through my being. To grow my family with this man, we could do this. Not easy, but we could do it.

I left them there, folded

The maternity clothes I had worn,

I hoped someone would be able to use them

And knew that I wouldn't again

I had arrived with them on,

Belly swollen but growing no more

I felt his last kick

Remembered and relished

And said a broken-hearted goodbye

Would someone find them and be thankful?

Would they know where I had been, what choice I
had made?

…They would never know how much I loved you,
that much I knew.

Does the pain stop there? Does the healing begin? No. Because moms lactate after giving birth. I came home from the hospital without a baby and with my breasts overflowing with milk. They were so full, and he wasn't there to drink. It was so painful, both physically and emotionally, I couldn't get into a comfortable sleeping position and I just had to endure. I could express a little milk in the shower to alleviate some of the pain, but I also didn't want to do anything to prolong the creation of it. So, I tried to tough it out. I didn't want to get out of bed.

On the first school day after we got back, Jeb went to work. I couldn't function without outbursts of tears. Everything made me think of everything, and on top of that, I was leaking milk all over the place. I couldn't figure out how to pass the time, how to get through minutes or hours. Thank the universe, Columbus didn't feel well that day, so he cuddled with me in bed for the first few hours of the morning. Success. I had made it through the first chunk of time. And I couldn't run. The one restorative thing, the one activity that could cut through all the emotion. And I couldn't do it. But I could walk. So, I started walking for hours every day. I'd put in headphones, bundle up for that cold March weather, and walk and cry. I did it every day that first week and on the last day, I finally cried less. My milk production had slowed down, my body was starting to feel like itself again and I found it was easier to get out of bed, though I was still spending a lot of time in it.

During this time, as during all the other rough times, I had my angels. My coworkers arranged for each of them to bring me dinner one night that week. Athena knew that I needed to see everyone before I came back and that everyone needed to see me not pregnant. She arranged it all. They came, they brought food and we cried together. The last night of the week was the hardest. One of the women had accidently gotten pregnant a few months after me. She already had three beautiful kids and wasn't planning on a fourth but she was blessed with an easy, healthy, surprise pregnancy. She brought me dinner and we cried together and embraced. How is it decided who gets to be a mom? This was a question too big for us, but we made it through the dinner drop off. Athena also invited me to her house that week for lunch and some time. I got to share all the horrors of what I'd just been through with someone who didn't judge me at all. It was the first time I said many of those things out loud. Somethings I couldn't talk about, but Athena would have listened no matter what. She was there, to take a sliver of the pain and help me keep moving my feet. I had been out of work for over two weeks, I was going to go back for a week and then the family was going to take a Spring Break trip to Texas to see Jessica and enjoy some warm weather and a break from everything else.

My first day back at work was a managers' meeting in Boise. I had sent an email to all the coworkers outside of my office who had known that I was pregnant to let them know that I was not anymore. At least I thought I had included everyone. I stepped into that meeting and the first person I saw was a friend who had just recently had a beautiful baby girl. I broke down immediately. My other friend Megan, saw me, grabbed my arm, and walked me to the bathroom. I had no business being at work yet, but I also couldn't stay home anymore. Megan brought me to the bathroom, and she gave me her room key. She told me that any time I needed to during the day, I could leave and go to her room for as long as I needed. She held my shoulders and looked at me and made sure I was going to be okay, that I could walk back out. I told her that

I'd seen a couple of people who didn't get the email and asked her to update them so they didn't come up to me and ask me how the baby was, or even how I was. When you lose a baby at 28 weeks and you see people who you don't see often, who don't know the details of how far along you are, etc., they just assume you had the baby. Megan did what I needed her to do. One of the people I'd forgotten to include was an older guy who'd been managing an office for almost thirty years, we'd always gotten along, and he was seated at the table behind me. We'd been at another meeting a couple years before and I'd told him how much I wanted another little one, of course I had shared my happy news with him when I'd found out I was pregnant. Megan had found him before he'd had a chance to interact with me. He looked at me and knew that I was falling apart. He knew not to say a single word; he must have been able to tell that I couldn't even accept his words of condolence. He just put his hand on my shoulder in a wordless move of solidarity, care, and love. I held it together. I got through the day. I even had to present at the end of the day, and I'm sure I did it well. My god, how we persevere. The rest of the week amongst my coworkers was manageable. It felt like being around family, it didn't feel like I was their boss and they reported to me, it felt like home. I was right where I needed to be.

As the week wound down and we got closer to the Texas trip, Jeb started getting stressed, he hadn't really shown that side of himself over the prior month when we'd been dealing with everything, so it was an unpleasant reminder of how difficult life in the dream house was feeling for him. He was going to leave on a work trip to Singapore about six weeks after we returned from Texas. He'd been putting off some house renovations that he really wanted to do and he had several in progress. One of which was that he'd torn out part of the bathroom downstairs that was adjoined to Zeff's room. He didn't want to go to Singapore with projects undone and the six weeks after our return from Texas would feel too crunched to get it all completed. He said he was thinking about not going to Texas because a full week of work on the house, uninterrupted, would be a huge advantage and might even be enough to relieve this stress burden he'd been feeling. I really wanted him to come with us. I thought now more than ever, we needed some family time. I needed him. He'd gone back to work as soon as we'd gotten back from Boulder. And he decided not to go to Texas.

The boys and I left and made it to the haven of Jessica's house with her two gorgeous, healthy twins, Alexandra and Connor. But, had things gotten easy for her? No. W had said that he had fallen out of love with Jessica while she was pregnant. In reality, he had fallen in love with someone else, spent their life savings on an online game, and had been living a lie for quite some time. He was still living in the house, but they were in the process of divorcing. Jessica had quit her job when she was pregnant and was planning to stay home. So, her life too was upside down. But you put two upside-down warriors together and sure as shit, they are going to end up right side up! The week was everything we needed. One foot in front of the other.

A couple of things happened while I was there. One was that I tried to call Jeb one night and couldn't reach him for hours. He finally called me back and said that he'd been in a bar. My heart dropped into my stomach and I immediately felt sick. He told me and I wanted to badly to believe that he didn't drink. He had gone there with a friend and was reminded of how that wasn't his lifestyle anymore and he wanted nothing to do with it. Some part of me knew he was lying, but I chose to believe through clenched stomach. I called him back an hour later, figuring that if he was drinking, he wouldn't stop, and if he answered there was a good chance he was telling the truth. He answered. I felt somewhat appeased. The second thing that happened was that I decided to run, I couldn't wait any longer. Jessica had a paved trail around a manmade lake by her house and I did some laps. It was hard, it was Texas humid hard, but I did it, and my uterus did not fall out. Immediately, I started to feel more like myself.

When the boys and I got home, none of the projects had been finished. In fact, they were worse. Jeb had decided to knock out another wall in addition to just doing the bathroom work. He was so stressed, he had so much to do, he hadn't done anything, but the one thing I knew he'd done, was go to a bar. The boys started baseball season and one of the mom's who'd been pregnant with me during wrestling was looking huge and ready to burst. Our due dates had been just two weeks apart. She'd looked big and had been moving slow when I wasn't even beginning to show. She complained about everything to do with her pregnancy. I had to avoid her. Through no fault of her own, except that she was a bit of a bitch, I was angry at her for complaining. She knew I'd been pregnant. I know she didn't think about how it might sound to me, she was just uncomfortable and pregnant, but in my state of pain, it felt very inconsiderate and direct. How could she complain about her gift of a healthy pregnancy?

Jeb volunteered to coach with another family we'd befriended, and it was one more thing added to his plate. He showed up late, he was angry when he got home because he couldn't do any of the projects, but at baseball, he looked like a happy all-American dad. Time kept moving. I was running and had added weights back into my routine, I was feeling more like myself all the time, but the pain was still very raw, anything unexpected could send me over the edge of emotion. I hadn't wanted to go back to the gym. Pre-pregnancy and during pregnancy, I had gone to the gym on my lunch breaks from work and I was avoiding the return. It was another group of people who had known I was pregnant. Finally, Athena made me go. She said I needed to jump back into all the normal things, putting it off any more was just making it worse. She was right. I went back. Over the next couple of months, four or five people asked me how the baby was. I teared up every time. They felt horribly awkward. What do you say to that? But in some ways, it felt good to be asked, it felt good for Orion to be remembered. And I was in the right place to be asked, a little faster on the treadmill, a little heavier on the weights, one foot in front of the other.

Jeb left for Singapore in May. I got the boys to their baseball practices and tournaments, I worked, I made it through the semester of school. That was actually my semester of the heaviest class load. I'd gotten a little behind when in Colorado, but I got caught back up. Jeb would be gone for Orion's due date and my birthday which were nearing. We were at a baseball tournament between those dates and there was a night I couldn't get in touch with him. It struck me as weird. We talked every day. Why couldn't I reach him? Why hadn't he let me know what was going on? He told me he'd worked a long day and had fallen into a deep sleep earlier than normal. He kept it vague and it didn't resonate with me. After that he moved hotels and there were more days he didn't want to, or couldn't, talk. His tone had changed. Something was different. And for me, I'd thought the due date wouldn't be too hard despite everyone warning me that it would. It was. My god, it was. I had finally gotten rid of the bassinet but wasn't quite ready to get rid of the few clothes that I had. I had to hang on to something. Orion's due date came, I held those tiny, folded clothes to my chest. I had his remains. I did not have him.

Towards the end of the season, the bitchy mom with the healthy baby, had her baby. A couple days after the birth, the dad showed up at practice with the baseball playing son. At the end of practice, a group of dads and me were standing around talking. Husband of bitchy mom kept the conversation going as the other dads started to leave, he wanted to stay and chat. He said he wanted a few more minutes away from the craziness at home. He needed a little normal. Something along those lines. I. Was. So. Angry. I wanted to so badly to yell in his face what I would have given to have that kind of crazy at home right at that very moment. Of course, he didn't know, of course a brief respite from a newborn made sense. Then though, it sat on me for days. I know it was just because I had one concrete thing to focus my anger on, but still. It seemed so callous.

So many things painful and yet progressive that summer. I must now introduce yet another hero in my life, Alejandra. She was my coworker and friend. She'd helped Athena organize the dinners for me and been there for me too without fail. I was hesitant to tell her the details of Orion because she was deeply Catholic, and I was afraid of judgement. When I did tell her, finally, much later, there was none. Alejandra, like any real friend, loved me for who I was. Our pregnant coworker, Marina, had her healthy baby girl that summer. I was still fully in my healing phase, most days good, some days rough. When Marina had her baby, and was still in the hospital, she invited all of us to come visit. For many reasons, I didn't want to go. It was so much easier to avoid pain. Alejandra made me. She told me that if I didn't go, I'd never be able to take it back and she'd be there with me. It was time to face babies again.

Even the babies of people I knew and loved.

We went to the hospital and the most perfect, beautiful baby girl possible greeted us. I could do nothing but cry. It was just a few tears at first, but there was nothing in my power to stop them. Here's the best part of this though. All the women (and Marina's husband) who were there, just let me. They let me have my moment. No one said one word. They let me feel all the things I needed to, while they experienced the joy and beauty of life. It is a very pure and refined human experience to feel such a depth of emotion and know that you are loved, that you are family, and that others around you will let you feel authentically without qualifying it or trying to make it better. There was no better. I was a mom who lost a baby I loved after years of wanting, almost a year of trying and seven months of carrying. Here was a mom who welcomed pregnancy while not trying and had been blessed with this beautiful gift. Ale was right, it was exactly what I needed. I needed to see that life goes on and that my story was my story and that everyone loved me and understood. I remember trying to staunch my tears and then just letting them go. It was one of the most meaningful friendship things I experienced around my pain.

The boys and I spent the 4th of July with the other baseball coach and his family and my dad. It was a fun night; four boys running around, good food, fireworks, and family. Jeb would be home soon. Even though I felt like something was off, I was so excited to have him back. Since we'd lost Orion, I hadn't gone back on birth control, and we hadn't really had much opportunity for intimacy after my body was finally ready and before Jeb left. . The night he got back, he was hesitant about intimacy and then put a condom on. We had used condoms in the past, but Jeb was not a big fan of using them, he preferred to depend on his own ability to control things. So, this was weird. Prior to his return, I'd told myself that if he used a condom that night, I'd know he had cheated. I asked why he was using one, he said that he had a sore that maybe it was an ingrown hair or something. He wasn't sure. These were my clues. But did I really believe that he had cheated on me? No. Which Malcom Gladwell book is it that describes how people will ignore everything in front of them until they absolutely can't anymore? Tipping Point? Yes, well that was me. I didn't have enough evidence yet to not believe him. I didn't know it, but he made an appointment to get checked out. We were going to take one last summer-family-trip to Yellowstone before the boys went back to school. We were surprising the boys, just telling them that we were going to Boise or something for the day and putting off their questions as long as we could until we had to tell them.

A day or two before we left, Jeb said he needed to talk to me. We were in the laundry room. He told me he'd gone to the doctor and gotten some test results back and that he had herpes. Fucking herpes. Yes, my husband had gotten herpes in Singapore and come back and had sex with me. But he used a condom, how nice of him. He did this while I was home with our kids very close to the due date of the baby I was mourning, oh and also close to my birthday. He told me this whole story about how he had been walking around looking for some food and some Irish or Scottish or English guys were watching soccer and asked him to come sit with them. They were all drinking and he'd had a hard week so they bought him a beer. And then another. He got drunk with them and they all left together. He had no memory of where they went next, he remembered a couple more flashes from the night, but the next thing he knew he woke up on the floor of his hotel room with his pants off. He said that was why he had to change hotels, he couldn't stand the thought that some people there had seen him come in and knew more about what happened that night than he did. He was remorseful, so remorseful. He postured that maybe someone had put something in his drink. How could he remember nothing? He felt taken advantage of. Yes, he said that. And through my anger, I may have even felt some sympathy for him. Yes. He begged me not to leave. He knew that the alcohol was the problem, he would never do it again, ever. never and ever are such loaded words.

I sunk to the ground. I felt like I couldn't breathe. How had this become my life? I told him to leave me alone. I sat in the laundry room and cried. And then I went for a drive. I told him I didn't know when I was coming back. But I couldn't leave the boys, not even for a night. I drove and cried for an hour and was so, so hurt and confused. Mostly though, I was still such a mess from everything else that I still wanted Jeb to protect me and take care of me. Here's that destructive pattern again, once hurt in a certain way, we go back to the inflictor. This was maybe my lowest point ever of personal strength. I had the strength to be a good mom to my boys, I had the strength to show up at work and do a good job, I had the strength to keep going with school. Sounded like strength, and looked like strength, but inside I was raw and broken and saw Jeb as my strength. He was my rock, a sharp rock with the edges that kept cutting me, but a rock, nonetheless.

On a phone call with Jessica after getting back from Colorado, I'd confessed something to her that felt a little scary. I'd told her that I realized that before Colorado, there'd still been a part of myself I'd been holding back from Jeb. My trust, myself, I hadn't put it all out there, I'd kept a little piece protected. After we got back though, I didn't have that piece anymore. I was all in. I told her that I'd been a little embarrassed to realize that I had still held something back, something in reserve that I could rely on to get me through if I ever needed it again. But I also said that I was also scared to not have it anymore. Now that I had given up my own, internal safety net, what if something happened? Could I go through it again? Jessica reassured me. To be married meant to be all in, it was okay to be at this point, yes, I could get through, yes, being all in was alright. Now here was this, I did not feel okay.

I went back to our bed that night. I wanted to be close to him. I didn't know what else to do. I was a mess. I don't even know how to accurately describe what that felt like. Such a deep and lonely pain, but some aching, hurt part just wanted the comfort of being close to another human. It's sad that, that's the thing I wanted most, or maybe sad that I only thought of Jeb to go to, to receive it. Oh, it hurt. We left to go to Yellowstone and I was angry, but in my halfway state. I rode in the passenger seat, looking out the window. I decided what music we were listening to (something I rarely did) and I pretended for the boys. Being the victim of a cheating partner is a strange thing. You go through the "enough"s. Was I enough? Was the sex good enough? Was it frequent enough? Adventurous enough? This question of enough is something that pops up unbidden. Our rational selves "know" that it isn't about us, but when you've loved a person for so long, it's not easy to not blame yourself, your enough-ness. I wanted to be everything my husband needed. And somehow, I wasn't. Even though he told me he couldn't remember and that he had blacked out, I kept picturing it. Or trying to and alternately trying not to. We stopped along the way and took some family pictures. Jeb setting up the camera, setting a timer and running to us to put his arms around us and get the perfect picture of our perfect family. When I looked at the picture later, I saw that my belly still protruded a little, I was a little over four months out from giving birth. It hadn't quite gone back to flat, it's all I could see in the picture. That round belly that didn't look like mine. I couldn't even look past it to see how empty my eyes were. I made him walk with me that first night in Jackson, Wyoming. Asking him about the details that didn't make sense. How did he find himself in the morning? How had he realized that he'd had sex? I knew these were answers I didn't want to know, and I also knew that he was lying. I knew it. I'd heard it so many fucking times before. His tone changed. But he wouldn't change the story. Some of the details changed and I pecked the hell out of them. To no avail. And of course, it would have made no difference. Maybe I thought I could be more punishing to him if I knew, but really it was just punishing myself. And yet, I wanted to be held. The old dichotomy, the bifurcated mind of the emotionally injured. Hold me all ye who would do me pain!

There was a big mountain that I could get to from our motel. I ran it. I almost ran to the top on the first day but didn't want to be gone too long. On the second morning, I made it to the top. I started the process of running out the pain again. Nothing like a mountain in Jackson, Wyoming to get that going! On the way back, we stopped in another favorite place. Lava Hot Springs. By this time in the trip, Columbus was getting on Jeb's nerves and we all knew Jeb needed a break. I took the boys to a park so he could rest. While we were there, a kid threw an apple which hit me square in the head. It hurt a little and I let some tears fall, I couldn't really stop them. I knew it had nothing to do with the apple and the kid, and parent of kid felt horrible. I cried. Cried for myself and the brokenness. And then I stopped, got it together, and walked the boys back to the motel. This time in my life was maybe the most exemplar example of my ability to keep putting one foot in front of the other, single-mindedly. The universe literally sent an apple careening into my head and I walked back to that motel room with that "resting" man. I wasn't ready to listen.

The boys started school. They were in fifth and seventh grade. Columbus's behavior problems had grown bigger. There were a couple times that year I had to go pick him up after banging his head on the wall or hitting his arms. We tried medication which would work only in initial bursts and then fade. I read all the books, I worked with him, I held him, I loved him. Jeb loved him too, of course, but would get so frustrated. He'd ground, he'd yell, he'd cross lines that I didn't think should have been crossed. I only remember one time in that house that he picked Columbus up off the ground and pushed his back into a wall, holding him by his neck against it, but there were other examples of physicality that hurt me to watch. I'd try to stop any extremes, but I felt like irreparable damage had already been done when I'd intervene. How can a mom undo the much-maligned Adverse Childhood Experiences? How does she stay married to the spouse who imparts them? And does she add to them too, by coddling the spouse, by trying to smooth the hurts, by accepting?

Jeb got Columbus a dog that Christmas. She had been abused and had a little bit of an odd personality, never quite remembering that she should only pee outside, but she was very food motivated. Columbus's love for her was immediate. One of her first days with us right after Christmas, she jumped up to get food out of Jeb's hand, he slapped her face so hard she skidded across the floor. Columbus let out a blood-curdling scream of "NO!" Watching her, whom he loved so deeply and so quickly, get that beating broke his heart in the most profound way. I got angry at Jeb for that too. One of the first times I ever felt, true, deep anger. She was an abused animal and he was abusing her further. And seeing and hearing Columbus's heartbreak made it all the more wrong. He was a kid. I watched him watch this scene unfold. It was there, imprinted now in his brain. I watched him unable to unsee what his father had just done. Who was this man?

Another time that late winter, I went to the gym. There weren't as many places to get good long runs, and my run group had long ago broken up. I was gone for probably a couple of hours. I knew that Jeb had wanted the whole family to do yardwork that weekend, but it was another one of those ice-rain days with heavy winds. I knew he wouldn't make the boys do the yardwork in that weather and felt some sense of relief because he wasn't very nice to them when we all did chores together. Nevertheless, I got home and saw the boys outside, not dressed appropriately, doing yardwork, wet and cold.

Things were getting bad. Jeb would go days without talking to me with the exception of a few words here and there. Then he'd tell us what work had to be done that weekend. And then he'd have a day that he'd apologize and tell me he was scared I'd leave him because of his anxiety and stress. He'd say he just needed more help, if we could all help, we could get him back to feeling normal. But what was normal anymore? Where were we really trying to get? I was losing sight of what I wanted the end point to be. The boys still had several more years of school and home life, but they'd never spent one-on-one time with their dad. He'd been absent through deployments for their formative years yet he'd never reintegrated. He didn't take them camping or dirt biking or out at all. I was the constant and he was absent for years of drinking and then when we were divorced the first time. Now he was unkind for long stretches with little bursts of relative kindness. Would there ever be a time when the bursts were his norm, our norm? We all tried to help to make him happy. Zeff worked his butt off. We'd come home and find him on the riding lawn mower. Taking care of the chickens. Trying. I'd try too. Only Columbus did his own things in his own way and we all tried to shield him. Maybe our common goal was to just keep it together for the sake of family. With Jeb, the good moments were so good. We all kept going. One foot in front of the other.

Chapter 24
Marching On

*"They say you learn a lot out there
How to scorch and burn
Gonna have to bury your friends
Then you'll find it gets worse"*

-Nathaniel Rateliff & The Night Sweats, And It's Still Alright

After losing Orion, I decided that I didn't need to stay in Mountain Home managing the office. When I'd been pregnant with him, I'd decided that even if it meant giving up career mobility, I wanted to keep working where I was, so I could be home as much as possible. A promotion would have meant working in Boise, almost an hour commute one way. I wanted none of that if it meant being away from a baby more than I had to be. Now though, I could apply for bigger jobs. I applied for an Operations Manager job in the Boise Central Office and got it. It was a huge promotion with a sizeable raise. THIS WAS HUGE! I think I'd either doubled my starting salary or had gotten pretty close in a little over five years. I was awed by my own success, but not in a self-aggrandizing way, just realizing, little by little, that I had power beyond my own belief. I was finally starting to understand my own potential. I'd wanted motherhood to be my career and I was good at it but working in the home provides a different feeling of contribution than a work-career. This was a different empowerment. I wasn't doing my job well because I related to the down-trodden anymore. I was doing my job well because I was good at it, was smart, was a hard worker who did hard things. I was an Operations Manager; I'd get to shape the way the Department of Labor did its' business. Crazy. Me. I did this.

My second week on the job, I needed to go on a work trip to San Francisco. It was a two-night trip, the absolute longest time I was comfortable being away. Well maybe not comfortable, but it felt important to be able to travel so that I could be successful in my new job, and two nights was my limit. I called Jeb after getting to the hotel the first night and he cried on the phone. He was not a crier, unless of course he was drinking. I had an uneasy feeling in the pit of my stomach, but I was still not using the overwhelming evidence in front of me to draw reasonable conclusions. I assumed he was having a rare fit of emotion and that he would not consider drinking when he was taking care of the boys. I tried to put my unease to rest and was marginally successfully.

And there was another amazing thing! I graduated with my bachelor's degree from BSU. In December of 2016, I walked that stage with more pride in my step than anyone could see. I barely believed it was real until after I had the mailed degree to me weeks after. I kept feeling like they'd figure out some reason I hadn't actually earned the degree, some credit falsely claimed, some grade that wasn't right. Something. I cannot adequately describe how it felt to have never had this huge thing and always been ashamed of it, and then to have it. There are some things that once done can be undone. Your status can change back. But not this; no one could ever take it. I was a college graduate; I'd never not be again. It was such a threshold to cross. As I promised myself, I started immediately in graduate school. No rest for the weary, I plowed ahead. An actual good use of my one foot in front of the other mentality.

The new job was awesome too. I could make some of the changes I had just ideated, I actually had control over the way things worked. It wasn't just some small office manager from Mountain Home with plans that would fade. I decided. I made things happen. People respected me. They respected my approach, the outcomes that came from my approach, and my intelligence. These things were getting more normal, but when I stopped to think about it, sometimes I was still just that faking it girl who showed up in the Mountain Home office with a bad resume and not enough confidence to even carry-on normal conversations. The new job meant, though, that I did have the dreaded commute to Boise. All together it took about an hour and forty-five minutes of my day to get to and from work. I had to take a thirty-minute lunch break so I could leave at 4:30pm to be home in just barely enough time to walk back out the door and get the boys to sports by six. I did absolutely all of it. I still made dinner every night, I did all the cleaning, all the laundry, all the homework. And still made Jeb breakfast on the weekends whenever he woke up.

I went to see Jessica for another weekend (my two-night maximum) and when I came back, I found a receipt for a bottle of alcohol in his truck, obvious, on the floor in the front seat. I couldn't believe he'd gotten drunk with the boys there, but he had. Still not using evidence to my advantage. He made some excuse, another bad choice, they didn't see it. They were sleeping. It still didn't feel like a pattern. It felt like a series of bad choices. He apologized and it always felt sincere. Was this something I had to adjust to? I didn't really know what to do. Was it still alcoholism if it was only a happening when I travelled? Could I deal with him occasionally drinking a bottle of Jack? I wasn't really asking myself those questions out loud, but some corner of my brain was already adjusting to these new increments. First when we got remarried, it had been an unequivocal promise of sobriety and now it wasn't. I wasn't leaving, so therefore, I was accepting. I had accepted that my alcoholic husband was drinking again. It didn't feel like it though. I guess I was denying it too.

And then there was my brother. His transient, addict lifestyle had continued. That spring, he'd gone to the doctor and found that his kidneys were failing. He was thirty. At first, he didn't want to live anymore. He wanted to be comfortable in hospice care and be done. And then a flicker. He did want to live, just a little more. Just a little more time to figure out if he wanted more after that. He decided to go back on methadone and dialysis. My mom went to visit, my dad went to visit, my sister went to visit. I didn't visit. I didn't want to leave my children with my husband, especially after the last drinking weekend, I was scared it would be worse. I told myself my beloved brother was getting better, he had his will to live back, there'd be plenty of time. Thirty-year-olds don't die, right? Even thirty-year-old addicts?

So, there I was, in March of 2017, on my way to work, my long commute. It was getting close to the one-year anniversary of losing Orion and a song came on the radio on my drive that made me think of it. I started crying (again), I stopped before I got to the office though, and felt okay going into work. The commute was time for thinking and feeling, once in the parking lot, I buttoned it up. A couple hours later, my dad called me during a meeting. He left a message to call him back right away. I listened to the message and heard some urgency in his voice. I hadn't heard that tone before. I called and he said, I remember exactly, "Your brother." He couldn't get any more words out. "Your brother…" I didn't know what he meant. My brother what? My little brother what??? This little boy who I loved, who taught me love, my little brother what???

My brother was dead. My brother was dead. They'd been having trouble with ports for the dialysis because his veins were so collapsed. They brought him in to make one last attempt for a port and he had an anxiety attack which led to a heart attack on the table in the hospital. There was nothing they could do to revive him, though they tried. His body was like that of someone decades older. I was in shock. I told one or two people on my way out of the building and I went to sit in my car and figure out what next. I called Jeb. He drove over from work and met me in the parking lot. I could not decide what I should do; what action does a person take when their brother dies? How does anything make sense?

Jeb drove me to get a coffee, I think. It's a little blurry. And then he took me back to the parking lot and asked if I was okay to drive home. He didn't want to leave a car there because it would have been complicated to come back and get it. Yes. I could make it. But I didn't want to make it. I wanted to curl into a ball on the front seat and be taken care of. I wanted my husband to drive me home, to plan dinner, to take care of the boys. To take me home and tuck me in and take fucking care of me. That's exactly what it was, I wanted for once, to be the one taken care of. I needed it. But I got into my car and drove home, and you bet your ass I showed up for my kids that night. Why? Because they needed someone to. I took another week off from work while I grieved. Grief was becoming familiar. I felt both lonely and hollow at the same time. I felt like I knew exactly how to go through the motions because I did. I knew going through those motions intimately.

Oh Jon, I missed him so much. The thing I wanted was just one more cup of coffee with him, in a café somewhere, on a street corner, on a patio. He'd spill it because he always did, his eyes might be glazy, but I wanted one more opportunity to look in them. They were such a deep, beautiful brown with a little amber mixed in for good measure. Jon. He was a boy still, but a man too. And he had hurt so much. We told ourselves, like you do, that he wasn't hurting anymore, that all the dysphoria wasn't a thing anymore that he'd have to wake up and face. We told ourselves that at least he didn't die on the street, we'd worried about it so much before, thinking at some point he'd OD and it might be a while before he was found and identified. Jon. Quick-witted, deep hearted, and big thinking. The rules he hated, no longer applied. Nothing did. He was gone. I wanted to still feel his presence, that's another thing I hoped for, to dream about him, to feel him on runs. It didn't happen. Sometimes I'd see a butterfly when I was thinking about him and feel a little glimmer, but mostly my brother was just gone. I deeply regretted not going to see him. And it doesn't matter how much you know that you can't save addict, it always feels like there could have been something more you could have done.

My sister and I talked so many times about the differences between his childhood and ours, how our mom was checked out in her depression. How he would ask her for money for a coke and come home drunk. How when we told her, she'd get upset with us. How she believed everything he said despite all the evidence to the contrary that he was lying and using. We remembered finding him drunk for the first time at the end of sixth grade, we remembered all the times that there was no parent there for him. And we came to hate the line, "We all just do the best we can with what we have." Because do we? And what if the consequences are fatal? What if our best is not even close to enough? I guess there's always something you can find to be angry at. And I guess there's always a continuum. Even if doing your best means you do show up, show up every fucking day and do the job, it might still not be enough. Ultimately, your best might still mean you lose a brother or a son. That's the truth. But, one thing I do know, is I'd rather show up and I'd rather try. I hope, I can always give that best. I hope I always have that much of myself available.

And there I was. Another miserable March. Have I mentioned that I don't like March? With all of its false promise, spring close, but so far away, cold, cold nights and days too short, ugh, March. I was trying to take stock of everything; where I was, who I was with, and what I wanted. I didn't want to meet my end like Jon and not be where I had tried to get. But that was maybe exactly where he tried to get. Jeb was getting restless. The house was too much, the chores were too much, the work was too much. He had never finished the bathroom project from the year before and now there were other house issues on top of it. We were making good money, but he didn't want to hire anyone to help with anything. Either he would do it, and do it right, or it wouldn't get done. I adjusted. Like always, to one less bathroom, peeling countertops, a dishwasher that didn't work well, a hit or miss washer. I didn't want to add to his list because it was so long, so I'd never push. For him, somehow that made it worse. He wanted me to be upset when things were broken and not accommodate them into my normal. Maybe some things he left broken to see what I could take, but mostly he just couldn't see the things through. And we all felt what must have been his frustration at himself directed outward. He'd tell me over and over that I needed to do more. I'd tell him that I'd be happy to, but that my way would be to hire someone and pay for it to be done, and that was the end of that. I didn't support him enough; I didn't recognize what was important. The boys didn't work enough, they had it too easy, they didn't understand the value of work. None of us did. So, we all kept working the way we did. Zeff in school and sports year-round, Col in school and sports and struggling with worsening anxiety. He had a full room of stuffed animals by this point to help, but the worries still ruled him. And I did everything else. Commuting almost two hours a day, getting the boys to all of their sports, all the shopping, cooking, and cleaning and graduate school along with it. I had no time to think about what I wanted to do with my time. Until something happened like losing a brother and then I had to think about it.

Jon had written a will, he wanted to be cremated and his ashes to be sprinkled in a river in Seattle, where he felt the most at home. He knew all the bums in Seattle, and they all knew El Jonno. In May, the whole family, my mom, my dad, Alycia, her daughter, and Alycia's boyfriend, all went to Seattle for our remembrance.

In the interim between Jon's death and the service, Jeb had gotten a new job. Same title, different company. With the other job, he felt that they didn't understand him or the right way to do things and they didn't take care of their people right. This new place was a "grass is greener" choice. I couldn't believe he was leaving the old employer after what seemed to me to be a short period of time when they had done so much to bring him on board. I felt like it was an affront to loyalty and I didn't understand why he couldn't make it work. Of course, I supported his choice fully. He was to start at the new place the Monday after Jon's remembrance. We spread the word on social media about where we'd be meeting for our get together. It was All City Coffee in Georgetown. My family and my parents got to the hotel Friday night. It had been a long drive, Jeb was agitated, but we made it.

I woke up before everyone else and ran on the hotel treadmill, I had to keep something normal. We all made it to breakfast before my mom. It was heart-breaking to see her walk to the table. She had a smile affixed to her face and her eyes were empty. She dressed like a combination of going to church and how she used to dress as a teacher. She dressed up. To say goodbye to her only son, the boy she'd loved more than us, or at least in a different way. I don't say that in a "she loved him more" way, just in an acknowledgment that she was always different with Jon. He was her boy. He was mine too, though. I couldn't stand to watch her cover up her pain with a fake smile. I couldn't look in her eyes. I couldn't watch the swish of her church skirt. She was still doing the best she could.

We checked out a little of Seattle and then met up with Alycia and her family for lunch at a place Jon liked for their milkshakes. We ate. I guess. I don't remember eating, but I know that I did. And then we walked around the corner to All City Coffee. We brought all the pictures and photo albums we had between us and set up a big table. I looked at all the homeless encampments around where we were and knew that Jon had been happy there. That's where he had been at home. It was hard to synthesize. But it was beautiful to me too, I finally understood something about him that I hadn't quite gotten before. These were his terms. He'd been to my house, stayed in my shed, understood my traditional terms. I didn't understand his. I got it more than I had before, though, and that seemed significant. We hoped one or two people that knew him would show up, but no one did. It was just us. He'd known so many people, but none of them showed up on that final day. Alycia and I cried and cried. We looked at his baby smiles and laughs, we looked at him with the puppy he loved, we looked at him as a child. Me carrying him around in a cloth shopping bag, school pictures, family pictures. His life. My mom got a little teary, but not really. My dad cried too, he seemed lost and confused about how his boy had been taken, but also resolved to never ask why. He knew there wasn't an answer. He had to accept. We drank coffee, the kids had hot chocolate. We reminisced, we laughed, and we cried.

After a couple of hours, we packed up and left his coffee shop. His will indicated that he wanted to be in the Duwamish River. So that's where we drove. Coordinating all the vehicles to get to a mostly industrial river in Seattle was not easy. But we finally found a spot. There was a parking area and river access. We found a sign that said, "Private Ramp/ No Trespassing/ For Marina Use Only." Exactly where Jon would want to be. We traipsed down that ramp with his ashes in hand and we got to the end. What do you do at the end of the ramp by the river where your brother wants to be dumped? How do you let go? You're there, you know his wishes, you know what's right. But these little, tiny granules are all you have left. They cannot be dumped. This cannot be that goodbye. I wanted coffee with him.

We read some things that others had said about him, we played a song, and we dumped his ashes. They spread like slow, gray, mud. It didn't look like a brother. It didn't look like goodbye. I heard my dad's heart break. We had to walk away. We had to go back up the ramp and we had to keep going.

I think it's important to take a brief hiatus here and talk about the power of motion. It was 2017. Parts of me were so empty and broken and parts of me were full. My boys brought me joy every day. Zeff was thirteen, turning fourteen that December, and Columbus was ten turning eleven in August. I felt the privilege of being their mom foremost amongst all the other things. But I was so deeply hurt. The pains we go through as an adult can be ameliorated and muted by the simple fact of having our children. There is always something to do for them and in the doing, we keep going. The doing keeps us in motion and the motion is restorative. But it's also sometimes easy to ignore the parts that aren't healed by motion and time. So that sometimes, seeing a guy hitchhiking on the side of the road with the eyes of my brother could bring me to tears in an instant, so that seeing a beautiful, round, pregnant woman could cause me to avert my eyes and feel the question "why" screaming in my head. My boys kept me alive, they gave me back the life that I gave them. I could think enough, but not too much, and I kept going. I was back to runs leaving tears mixed with sweat on the trails if I even got out to run. This was maybe the time of the least running of my adulthood. I'd gotten a treadmill but had so little extra time that sometimes I'd get two quick miles in the morning and two more after everyone was in bed and their homework and mine was done. Every moment from six or earlier until 10:30 or later was full. And thank goodness for that.

Jeb's tension continued to build. He'd drawn in, he'd take it out, he'd be the most loving guy ever for a day or two and we'd start it over again. We never knew what we'd get but we all loved his happy moments, he could be so fun, until he wasn't.

At the beginning of July that year, he came home and was particularly upset. He told me he hated this life. He hated coming home to this house and having so much to do that he could never get it done. He'd add three things to the list every time one thing came off, even though nothing really came off. He was done. He used the word hate. I was shocked. Was there anything else that could shock me? The boys were supposed to start school in Mountain Home in about six weeks, he told me we'd sell our house, move to Boise and be there before school started. There was no question. That was what we were doing.

And so we did. We had a friend of a friend look at our house that weekend and make an offer. That same weekend, we found a house in Boise. We moved out of the huge house on the land, where "we" wanted to have babies running around, and into a house in a perfect neighborhood in Boise in one month. We were there with two weeks to spare before the start of school. Columbus was starting sixth grade and Zeff was starting eighth. I got them enrolled and life changed again. I got my two commute hours back. That was the most amazing thing ever. Our new house was adjacent some to trails. I could literally be on a trail in less than two minutes. A trail. Across the street. That in and of itself reoriented the way I felt about life. I had come to realize that for the most part I can be happy anywhere. Give me the ones I love, and I'll make the other pieces fit around it. But give me two hours of my day back and trails across the street, and m quality of life grew exponentially. I had more of what made me, me. More time to reflect and ultimately more time to think about what wasn't working for me. I had just turned thirty-nine. Thirty-nine felt fake, I exuded youth, what did thirty-nine even mean? It seemed unreal. The time between subsisting, raising babies, and being almost "middle aged" was a series of long, slow, interminable phases and then they were gone. Time had been both a marathon and sprint; I didn't know if I'd caught all that I was supposed to, what had I missed in the whirlwind, and what was I still holding on to?

We had come to Boise for a day trip before we moved. We rented bikes and rode ten miles on the greenbelt together. We ate lunch downtown. Jeb said this was what he wanted. Weekends like this. No worry about chores and land and fences and chickens and rebuilding bathrooms. I had believed him. But we had not a single weekend of rented bikes and riding together after we moved. Life got weird. The chores didn't go away, they just changed. Jeb started sending me lists at work of what I would need to accomplish on the weekends and the time he estimated it would take me. His stress remained, he'd refrain from speech with me for days, I'd try to joke and cajole or even be serious, I'd make him extra anything to try to make him feel better. And then it would break, and he'd ask me to never leave him for his anxiety. I assured him that wasn't a reason a wife leaves a husband.

I was still chipping away at my master's degree and was on track to finish in December of 2019. My career at the Department of Labor was going great. I was shaping how we managed our workforce grants and contributing my vision. It felt good. I got selected to go to a conference in Washington DC and I was going to be able to present on a project that Idaho was working on. It was my first time presenting at a national conference. I couldn't believe it; it was still hard to believe my success until I was confronted with big evidence of it. My dad, still living in North Carolina, was going to meet me in DC. It was late evening when I landed and took a shuttle to the hotel where we were meeting. I hadn't eaten and my dad and his girlfriend sat with me while I ordered and ate a small meal in the hotel restaurant. It was good to see them, and my dad looked happy. And then Zeff called. He was scared. His dad was drunk and falling down the stairs and he didn't know what to do. He didn't know if Col was going to be okay or what Jeb might do. He had been angry, but now was emotional and he was incoherent. My fourteen-year-old called me crying because his dad was drunk, incoherent, and couldn't stand up. I told Zeff to take care of his brother and I'd get there as soon as I could. I asked him to try to get Col to school in the morning and get himself there too. I had packed lunches and made food before I left, so I knew they had that basic need met. I told him to try to take care of the other things and if he thought he wasn't safe or anything else happened to call me back immediately. I'd be there as soon as I could, but I had to fly across the country.

I finally confessed to my dad. I confessed how Jeb had gotten drunk and gotten herpes in Singapore, how I'd suspected he'd been drinking on my other work trips, how I'd found a receipt for alcohol after another trip. I sobbed and told him everything. He listened. He loved me and he told me I'd know the right thing for the big questions, but that I was right in the moment, I needed to go home. I changed my tickets and flew home the next day. It was the only thing to do.

When I got home, my boy, my little Zeff had lost something. He was in eighth grade, Columbus in sixth. Zeff was never a crier, tending to hold things in. When I got home, he cried too. I assured him it was okay and that I was home. I told him that he'd done the right thing. His answer: But I shouldn't have had to. He was right of course. He shouldn't have had to. This is what staying does, though. Ultimately, it puts our kids in places they shouldn't be. It forces them to grow up in ways they shouldn't have to. It forces them to be more adult or to learn how to self-protect. That night, he'd protected his brother from his father's "condition" and the potential for harm, he'd checked to make sure his dad passed out in the right place, that he was okay, he'd kept it together. And he did it without me at home. My boy wasn't so little anymore.

A couple months earlier at work, I'd been on the hiring committee for someone new. He was incredibly handsome, smart, and very fit. We hit it off immediately. He was a dad to two boys, both adults, and had some of the same work interests as me. He was one of the few people in my life I was so physically attracted to upon my first meeting that I felt the blushing, butterfly, say-stupid-things type of reaction. It was movie worthy. The timing, as always, was interesting. Here I had this crush at a time relatively shortly after my husband had cheated, he had betrayed me in so many ways including my trust in his ability to care for our children, and I was feeling increasingly lonely. Cheating would have been easy, and probably seems like the direction this is going. But it wasn't. We had some work lunches together, during which I found myself so flustered I almost couldn't chew. Looking back, it's fair to say the attraction was mutual. In the moment though, I felt like I was not worthy of such attraction and therefore it couldn't be real. He'd had a girlfriend when we first met and at some point, they broke up. After I came back from DC, he wondered at my early return. I explained the situation and he looked at me a little incredulously, like why are you there. The same question I would ask myself. During one walk together, he said something like, "I can't wait forever" and I had no idea what that meant. No part of me could comprehend how that might relate to my life and my romantic situation. Sometime shortly thereafter he met a beautiful woman whom he ended up marrying. I assume they are still happily wed.

The value in this lesson was twofold. First, despite having a monster crush, I stayed true to my marriage. I would have forgiven myself for not staying true, but it didn't feel like me. My second lesson was the smallest inkling of a hint that there was more available to me than what I had. The process of rebuilding self-esteem and building an identity as a woman with a career and an education while still in an abusive relationship is a strange dichotomy. While my confidence had grown exponentially in so many ways, I was still unformed. I had regained my belief that I was smart and capable, but not, to my core, that I was lovable.

Chapter 25
Rock Bottom-Not Yet

*"I recall a time, you were mine
All the time you bared your teeth
It was always just a smile for me"*

- Nathaniel Rateliff & The Night Sweats, Mavis

Predictably, I keep trying. And trying and trying. Trying to keep the family together, trying to keep Jeb happy, trying to give everything that I had in me to something that wasn't working. The lengths of time that Jeb wouldn't talk to the family got longer. He'd have to leave the dinner table if conversation was too loud, if Columbus's behavior wasn't perfect. I'd chase him, I'd reason with him. I'd try to explain that it's dinner, it's our one time of the day together, can we try again? I'd plead with Columbus to change whatever behavior didn't match his dad's needs. Some things would be taken out on me, and they were never predictable. There was too much dog hair on the floor; he couldn't stand to look at it. Which was really, you didn't clean enough. The house needed curtains; he couldn't stand the living room anymore. Which was really, why can't you decorate like normal people? The boys were lazy and didn't understand the value of work. Which was really, you've parented poorly and created these soft boys who will never be men. It was always subtly, or not so subtly, directed at me. Every problem seemed to have one root cause and I kept trying to fix it. When I could only get one-word answers for days, I'd try intimacy and be told no or pushed away. But then on the weekend, however much later he woke beyond the rest of us, intimacy would be what he wanted. Oh, and a massage and breakfast. I'd be so happy to get the attention that I'd happily agree. He'd ask so sweetly and pull me to him like there'd never been a problem. He loved me so much, why couldn't it always be just like this? I understood, didn't I? He was so stressed at work, he had so many projects at home, it would all get better soon. Just rub his back a few more minutes.

In March of that year, we went to Moab for one of my favorite races. This was my second running of it. It coincided with the boys' spring break. We were supposed to pick them up early from school on Friday and head out for the eight-ish hour drive. The race was Saturday morning. I had planned everything, made our reservations, packed everything for everyone and was ready to go. Jeb got off work later than planned and we didn't get the boys picked up before the school day was over. We headed out close to four with Jeb stressed and unhappy, but ready to get out of town. We didn't get into Moab until after midnight and I had to be up bright and early for the 30k race. No big, who sleeps before a race anyway? I got what sleep I could and was up early for some coffee and a light breakfast. Jeb dropped me off at the race and went back to get some more sleep. He got more rest, got the boys up, they had a nice breakfast and came back to meet me for the finish.

Now, this Behind the Rocks Ultra may have been a 30k, but it felt like a full marathon. The course was tough, on challenging terrain, but so fun and the pervasive red rock beauty is magical. I finished, exhausted, and found my men waiting for me. I loved those finishing moments with all three of them there. Columbus jogged in the finish with me, my slow pace holding him back. I was overwhelmed with love. We headed back to the hotel, and I showered and felt the exhaustion of the drive, the limited sleep, and the four hours of race time hitting me. Apparently, it hit Jeb too. He needed to nap immediately. We all tried to be quiet enough in the small hotel room for him to get his sleep. Unfortunately, silence is not one of Columbus's many gifts. Jeb couldn't handle it and, as usual, I couldn't handle his not handling it, and wanted to keep us all out of the wrath. Zeff was quiet and wanted to stay in the room, but Col just couldn't manage. I took him out for an hour walk, trying to make a game out of it and keep him interested and not wanting to go back to the room, I'm sure he was tired too. We walked the strip in Moab, went into some stores, picked up snacks in the Dollar General, and did some more walking. I kept looking at the time, hoping enough had passed that we could go back without interrupting any slumber. I was tired though. This I didn't understand. It wasn't that I wanted to be the one who got a nap, I wanted a partner who would tough out being tired with me while we wrangled the kids, who would be by my side, rather than making sure his needs were met. That was it, I didn't have a partner and I wanted one.

I had one more race planned that year. Unfortunately, it was only a couple weeks after the Moab trip. Weiser 50-k was another one of my favorites and also being run for a second time. The first time I'd run it, it had been my first ultra. I knew since it was just two weeks after our trip, it would be inconvenient for Jeb to dedicate another chunk of a weekend day to my racing. I told him he didn't have to come. Exasperated, he said that he would, but I'd drive myself there and he'd meet me so that he didn't miss as much of the day. I left the house in the dark and got to the start about ten minutes before gun time. He told me he'd be at all the aid stations after the first one. That way he could sleep in, get Columbus ready and get there; Zeff was spending the day with a friend. I got through the first aid station, thinking maybe they'd have left early and would surprise me. No. Second aid station, yay, family time. No. Third aid station, about halfway through the race. I was ready for a glimpse of their faces and whatever extras they might have brought for me. No. Not there. I got a little worried but figured that they were probably just running late. Fourth aid station, they'd be there. No. I was sad. I was dehydrated, this race was much harder than it had been the first time. The final aid station, I had six miles to go, finally there they were, Jeb and Columbus. Jeb barely said a word to me, Columbus ran to me. I was kind of a mess. Moving slow and I hadn't taken in enough calories or fluid. It had gotten warm; I was feeling dizzy. I looked at Columbus and he said they hadn't brought anything for me. (Not even water!!?!) Columbus had his own water bottle which had a few sips left in it. I looked at him, feeling strange. I was so happy to see him. I said, "I might need you to run a little bit with me." He said, "That's what I'm here for."

That's what he was there for. That's all he said, and we took off. He walked when I needed it, he carried the water bottle for me, he talked to me, and that boy ran six miles while I finished. Those six miles, some of the best miles in my life. At the end, I was a full hour longer than I had been the first time, I had to sit. I lowered myself to the ground with my railroad spike finisher's prize and had a bottle of water. No time for more, Jeb was ready to go. He wouldn't speak to me in the car, he drove me the thirty-one miles back to my car, let Col and I get out, and he drove away. Okay, so maybe he didn't always take the actions needed to meet his needs. Clearly, he shouldn't have come. I wanted him to be there. I wanted him to want to be there. And it was these little punishments that broke me down in ways that would take a long time to heal. I couldn't and shouldn't have taken this time. I couldn't and shouldn't have taken him away from a day that he could have been working on the house. I wasn't there to help him. I took him away from his preference and he made me feel it. It felt horrible. I sat there with Col a minute, bathing in the light of his presence. I wrapped my head around the sore drive home, and we took off. My sweet boy. "That's what I'm here for." Yes, love, that's right. That's what you were there for. And thank you.

We limped through the rest of the school year. The weather started to get warmer and then one May evening I came home to see that Jeb had the grill going. I sensed something was off. I looked at him and his eyes met mine. They were drunk eyes.

My universe cracked open. The crescendo, the buildup that had been coming, it was here. My heart was pounding uncontrollably, and my stomach immediately seized up. I went upstairs to put my stuff down. He followed me up. He said three words. Three words I will never forget barring a cognitive lapse. "I bought beer."

"I bought beer." It echoed; it rang. It was a serrated edge sawing through my heart down through my intestines. I tried to answer. "How much?" He answered, "Does that fucking matter?" It did to me. I needed to know what I was getting into; what kind of night I was going back to. You know those stories of how people in abusive situations will serially return to the same situations because they know exactly what to expect and there's comfort in that. That's what I needed to know. How to gird myself, how to get through the night. I had to take stock. So, yes, it mattered how much he bought. Spoiler alert: it was a lot. He told me he wanted to be able to drink on weekend nights. He said he was fine, he deserved to relax. Well, there was no way I was relaxing after that.

I went for a run the next day and I knew. I knew for a brief moment everything that was coming. It felt like time travel; I saw the past, I saw it was the future, and I felt it all there in the present of that moment. I cried, I railed on the universe. I knew better than to ask "Why?", but the question still hung. And then I started bargaining. I knew I couldn't go through what I'd gone through before. Of course, I knew that, but what would it take? Could he drink on the weekends? What was too much? And was there less than that? I'd had my moment of clarity, but even then, I wasn't quite ready to accept it.

Within weeks, he was back up to his pre-sobriety amounts of drinking and sometimes he was mixing hard alcohol in. Those nights were bad. His anger got crazy, the vitriol behind it spitting and leaving us reeling. Zeff's room was dirty, he yelled in Zeff's face that he lived like a "Fucking Crack Whore." This to our eighth grader. Zeff, no fear, got right back in his face. I had to intervene. Columbus got slammed into his bed so hard that the frame broke, he wouldn't let me hold him afterwards. I hid the broken frame. I taped it up. I knew Jeb wouldn't remember it or believe that it was his force that had broken it, so I hid it. I facilitated the situation. I didn't protect my babies like I should have. I was trying to protect some fucked-up notion of being a family and I wronged the ones I loved the most. I know, I know, I did the best I could with what I had. But just then, it wasn't enough.

Jeb thought this time was better. He wasn't drinking and driving this time, he was being responsible about his drinking and the choices he was making. So, he started asking me for rides. At nine or ten at night on a Friday night, he'd ask me to take him to a pool hall. One night, I remember leaving the boys at home. There was a horrible storm and I could hardly see. I never feel scared driving, but that night I did. The pressure of the wind pushed the car around the interstate. We got to the pool hall. I asked him to please come back home with me. "No." I asked him to please keep his phone on. "I will." Are you calling for a ride? "Yes. It won't be long. Maybe a couple hours. I just need to play some pool. I had a long week." He jumped out of the car, slammed the door, and ran through the pouring rain to the front door of the bar. I couldn't believe that my husband whose protection I desired, had had me drop him off at 10pm at a pool hall in a storm and I was driving back to the kids alone while he blew off the steam from his week. No steam blowing on my behalf, not even the smallest bit of concern, he slammed the door. He called me that night or rather the next morning to pick him up too. I went. He was sitting drunk on a grassy knoll across the street from the bar. So drunk. I hated the drunk smell on him, but part of me felt like I was doing the right thing being there for him. Part of me, of course, knew that this wasn't the right thing, but I wasn't all the way there yet.

As a Christmas present for the family that year, I'd gotten a trip to the Dominican Republic. It was our first out of country trip since we'd moved to Idaho and it was going to be in June, to coincide with my fortieth birthday. Jeb, on the other hand, had done something different for Christmas. Christmas was pre-return to drinking. He'd spent some time before Christmas putting a photo montage together and setting it to music. He didn't finish before Christmas, so Christmas morning after he slept in, he went back to the computer to finish it. My mom was there, and the boys and I were waiting to see what he'd done. We all sat there and watched the memories of our family, from pre-Zeff until now, splayed across the screen. He got down on his knee and vowed one thing for each of us. For Zeff, a promise to go dirt biking with him. They would fix Zeff's dirt bike together and start going on weekends. Zeff was elated. For Columbus, a promise to learn to skateboard at least enough to skate with him and to take him to skate parks. Columbus was in awe. It was the perfect present. For me, for his wife, he apologized for all of his absence from me. He said in front of all of us that the pictures were the life he wanted. ALL that he wanted. We were it. I was it. He wanted to rededicate himself to our marriage. He got me a new ring. He asked me to forgive him and take him and his promises. A couple years before, or even right after losing Orion, I would have melted into a puddle of acceptance at his feet. This year, I did cry, I shed some tears, but part of me was reserved. I wanted to see it. I needed to feel the change. He told me we'd go on a date every month. He'd plan it. He just wanted me and us back. Okay, I had told him. Okay, I was still his, it wasn't too late.

We did go on two, maybe three, dates. He never fixed the dirt bike and he never learned to skate. I think that might have been the first time I felt like there was an element of a show to what he said. Like he had thought about how he'd look on one knee professing re-found love for his family, it was just a little performative. By June, the vacation dates approached and the drinking worsened. I was taking the boys on vacation no matter what. Jeb vacillated. He couldn't go, he had too much to do. The only time to do it was that week. He couldn't take a week off. Finally, at the last minute, he agreed to come with the family. He also, in his change of heart, decided not to smoke or drink the week we were going to be there. He said it was not what he wanted. Is it silly that I hoped? I knew, but still I hoped. Hope takes a long time to extinguish. It splutters and sparks, but it hangs around, persistent.

On my fortieth birthday, I started the day out with a run. I felt so powerful and strong. I flew over the trails by my house, amazed at where I was in life. How was this forty? I had a beautiful house, two healthy kids, a good job, and I was almost done with my master's degree. I had made progress. Fifteen years earlier, I was couch surfing with a baby, our belongings portable. Not everything was right, but the direction was. I was on the verge. The gathering was getting closer. Strength was afoot. Quite literally, as I came home from my run and got ready to head to the airport.

The trip was amazing. Tropical and humid with beaches, bathing suits, good food, and family. I watched the boys take in the poverty of the people, listened to their desires to help. Watched them try new things and for a little bit just to be, without all of the ups and downs we'd all been experiencing. And the coffee was amazing. I would start the day out with a workout, go wake up the family for breakfast, and sit and sip coffee in an open-air dining area. Breathing in the fullness of my very humid break. Heavy air filled my lungs and my soul differently than the desert did. I liked the fullness of that breath and the way it has its own weight as it infuses and cleanses your whole body with sweat. We were away, we were taking vacation. I could forget Orion and Jon and Jeb and just breathe that full, heavy air, sweet with tropical flowers. Of course, Jeb was there, but I could forget what we were going through. I treated it like our last vacation as a whole family. And we had a good time, Jeb was happy for most of it. He brought nicotine gum and stuck to his plan. Even with the free alcohol, he abstained. He had even spoken a couple times about how he was over drinking and smoking. He said it just didn't feel like him and the vacation was cementing that. He felt free from the feeling of need that he had before he left. He finally felt better. We spent the nights in bed together, enjoying the time, the boys a floor below us. He got angry only a few times the whole trip, mostly if there were clothes or sand on the floor. But mostly it was just vacation, it was just fun. Five days of being out of routine. It was just what I needed.

It was late when we got home, I got the boys in bed and got myself upstairs ready to fall into bed. Jeb wasn't quite ready for sleep, he wanted to check the outside of the house and make sure everything was okay, that there were no signs anyone had been there or that anything was wrong. Tonight? In the dark? Yes, it'll be quick. I had the bathroom window open, and I could hear the gravel crunching as he made his walk around. And then I heard it, the flick of his lighter and the crack open of a beer can. He had warm beer that had been stashed in the garage when we'd been gone. He had a couple and came in. Was my hope completely gone? There were some embers hanging around, but I knew. I told a friend that it was our last vacation together and that I was sad. I said it out loud. The last vacation. But I still wasn't all the way ready to let go.

Things got worse. Or, stated better, I let things get worse. Jeb was going out every weekend again, he was talking to other people, he'd fall asleep when he got home with a message from his high school ex-girlfriend flashing on his home screen. He passed out in the bathtub, his underwear hand washed and hanging by the tub. Giving up another night of sleep, I'd check every so often to make sure he was okay and not slipping into the water, sure that the cold would wake him.

Writing from the time from after a social event:

I looked around at the other women.

Two mending broken hearts, one fighting a
rebellious body

And thought of being a woman

My daughter in a Kindergraben in Germany with
the other babies

Who passed before their births,

Of my son's ashes on the sill,

The tiniest vase for the tiniest death,

My brother's ashes,

The little vial that I meant to send to his ex-wife
and then just couldn't let it go

Of growing and feeding our babies to slowly let
them go

Of doing it all and showing up

At work, at games, at home

Of dinners and treats at schools

At showing up and making it all work

With our quiet storms raging

And breaking hurts, known only to ourselves

All while we smile and open our arms

We love and we lose and we love again

And no one told us and maybe it's better that way

No one told us the cycle doesn't stop

Chapter 26
Salmon Marathon

"It was cold outside when I hit the ground
Said, I could sleep here, forget all the fear
It will take time to grow
Maybe I don't know"

-Nathaniel Rateliff & The Night Sweats, And It's Still Alright

In August that year, 2018, my sister was coming to Idaho to run her first marathon in the small town of Salmon. She'd done the work and was ready to go. Like the DR trip, Jeb wasn't sure if he wanted to go, he might have to work, he couldn't be away from all the house chores that he had to do, it was an inconvenience. The race was a Saturday morning and finally, on Friday afternoon when I was leaving work early and ready to go, he texted that he was coming too. I was excited. Columbus was joining us and Zeff was going to spend his first weekend alone. We'd have to leave later than I planned, but I was happy to wait. The drive to Salmon is a long, windy and picturesque; I couldn't wait to have this time on the road. Alycia, her boyfriend, and her daughter had rented a vehicle and left earlier to get there in plenty of time for a good dinner and solid rest. We weren't going to be getting there until at least ten and that didn't include time for a dinner stop. We took off, I assumed we'd stop somewhere for food. But Jeb didn't want to, he wanted to get a little further and then a little further, and then there wasn't going to be anywhere to stop. I was running a marathon in the morning, but I didn't insist that we stop. I didn't really believe that he wouldn't stop and make sure I had something. Of course, I could have packed a dinner, but I hadn't. There were all these moments when I could have done more to advocate for myself and it's not that I didn't know it then. True, I wasn't in the habit, but also, I wanted him to make it a priority to take care of me. I could ask myself, why it would it have been a priority for him if it wasn't for me. But I wanted to be what he put first in his head. Not all the time, but sometimes, like the night before a marathon. He wasn't sure if he wanted to come, he decided, and I waited for him. I put the evening on hold to let him decide and then he didn't even care if I ate dinner or not. Such a strange mix of deciding which things were important and which to ignore. Well, I had some Chex mix when we got to the Airbnb that night and called it good. Alycia's pace and my pace weren't the same, but I promised to run the whole thing with her no matter what. We all went to bed soon after we got there and were up early to take the bus to the start. The bus broke down, but somehow, we made it. The gun went off and we started at the back of the very small pack. And there we stayed. Just under fifteen minute miles the entire time. Her pace never faltered, even a little bit. We kept them up, one after another, 14:45, 14:50, 14:40, 14:55, the miles ticked off. Jeb expected that we'd be faster so by the end he was sure that something bad had happened and was upset that I hadn't communicated the potential time difference to him. Alycia finished so strong, her first marathon, and I got to be there for every step. She committed to this big thing and did it. Despite Jeb's discomfort at the end, it was one of the coolest running experiences of my life. Columbus was there at the end too, happy to see me as always. Jeb decided he couldn't stay, he needed to get back. He might have to work on Sunday, blah, blah.... He took off. He just left. Zeff hadn't liked being home alone, so he'd ended up at a friend's house and was going to stay the night there again. Jeb went home and would be there alone. I tried to call him later that night and couldn't reach him. When I got home Sunday, the bed hadn't been slept in. I knew because I'd left hangers and the remnants of packing on the bed, and it was all there. All in the same spots. I decided I could ask about this. So, I did. Instead of some other, more believable reason, like he'd fallen asleep on the couch, he told me that he had, in fact, slept in bed and just hadn't disturbed anything on top of it. Right. I didn't argue. It's hard to argue with a bold-faced lie to your face. What do you say? I know you didn't sleep there? How did I know? I wasn't there. So, I let it go.

Finally, I started seeing a counselor, Coby. Sometimes the people who change your direction, or show you the path, emerge out of the haze and sometimes you have to seek them out. I made the choice to see a counselor and it was at first subtle in its power to change my direction and then it was everything. I talked about the drinking. I talked about the distance between Jeb and me. I talked about not having any boundaries and how they changed every time I thought I had found one. Coby would suggest that I ask a question or suggest a way to frame a conversation. Sometimes I would be able to try and sometimes I wouldn't. Jeb was beginning to tell me often now how I wasn't enough for him and never had been, how he'd spent the whole marriage catering to my desires, and I'd never had the courtesy to care about any of his. He'd wanted to play pool on weekends the whole time we'd been together, and he'd never even been able to share it because he knew I'd dismiss it. He knew it wouldn't be important enough to spend Friday nights in pool halls watching him play. I'd reason with him, tell him all the ways I'd showed up for him, car races and rallies, encouraging his long-distance motorcycle rides, all the things I could think of, never realizing that it was pointless to argue. There was always another thing I hadn't done. Always. And then he'd change his mind completely. He'd tell me Wednesday and Thursday that on Friday night, he and I were going out and that he couldn't wait to spend time with me. It would be perfect. Friday morning would come, he'd leave for work, and tell me to be ready for the evening. But he'd get home, have a drink or four, and tell me he changed his mind. He never wanted that anyway, he needed some time to himself, to be himself, maybe we'd go out another night, but what the fuck was I thinking, I knew he needed Friday nights to let loose. I'd stand by the window and watch an Uber come pick him up. I'd go sit with Columbus and try to pay attention to whatever it was he was doing or watching. I'd hold back my tears. When you're on the roller coaster, you can't always see that there's a spot to get off. You just keep going, despite getting sick all over your life. It's weird to be told I was "loved" and then rejected simultaneously. When you've felt that the expression of love was genuine, it feels like there must have been something, some action, some lack of action that you've done to change it. And you want, with everything in you, to make the love stay.

I planned a day trip for his birthday. I'd made reservations, it would take from ten in the morning until the evening, but we could do it in a day and the boys were old enough to stay home alone. He went out the night before with promises to be home early, be up "early", and be ready for our celebratory day. He'd told me over and over again that he wanted to celebrate more. We'd come so far, but we never took time to celebrate it. He got home in the wee hours of the morning. At 9:30, he slept. I tried to wake him up, already packed up and ready for the day. He wouldn't budge. At 10 I tried and 10:30 and then at 11. And then it was too late. I called to cancel. Sometime after noon he got up, angry, I'd let him sleep. I made him breakfast and told him it was okay. When I told the counselor about this, he asked how it made me feel. Was I disappointed in Jeb, did I feel resentful, or did I never really expect him to go anyway, is that why my reaction was so minimal? I think he was really asking why wasn't I angry? The answer sucks, it's that anger didn't occur to me. Every molecule of my being hoped that he'd get up by ten and we could have this day of just us, just time, just connection. Was I surprised that he slept through it? No. But I was so accustomed to this type of behavior that it was always mine to accept and move forward. I believed, fully and deeply ingrained, that to show unconditional love meant that I had to accept all the behaviors, words, and deeds that this man could throw at me and move forward. I felt good when I was able to do this. I felt that despite what was happening, I was embodying love. I never thought to ask whether I should have been treated that way to start with. Never. It was my job to love unconditionally. It was my job to wait this out, wait until he was ready to feel what I was exuding. I would wait with open arms for him to be ready. I knew, I KNEW, that in twenty years we'd be looking back on this moment on a front porch swing and remembering this hard time we got through. Of course, I also knew that we'd had our last family vacation. There must have been discordance to have known both things so fully, so completely, and that's probably where Coby helped. He treaded the line of discordance and asked the questions that made reality the louder voice in my head. How did I feel when I experienced this rejection? I felt like making him eggs and toast and Cream of Wheat. I felt like rubbing his back and waking him up with kisses. I felt like showing him that nothing could push me away. But something, some tiny piece was ready to love myself too.

Towards the end of September, the drinking was constant and the anger insurmountable. He'd started being mean again and had been including hard alcohol which made for not fun nights. I wanted him to leave to avoid what would happen, but I also wanted him to stay so he wasn't out when he was acting like that. Coby and I had talked a lot about boundaries; what would work for me, what was reasonable for the family. I'd started suggesting some to Jeb, not ready to enforce, but ready to discuss even if I retracted. Finally, Jeb decided to stay with a friend. He said that he needed to go and get his head right so that he didn't lose all of us, so that he didn't lose me. He needed to go. He'd also told me that he didn't think family life had ever been the right fit for him. He felt like he'd been faking it our whole lives together. Was he being honest or was he drunk? When I told Coby about one of these conversations, he looked at me strangely. He said something to the effect of it not mattering whether or not Jeb felt like family was the right choice for him. Coby pointed out that he'd already made that choice. He had a family. He couldn't opt out of a having a family. He could opt out of being there for the family, but the choice had been made. I hadn't thought about it like that but here it was. It didn't matter if Jeb wanted us or not, he had us. He was married, he had kids. He was trying to distance himself from that part of his identity while living in the same house with us. Talk about discordance. So, he decided to go, to remember that he wanted to fix this, he said. To be able to figure it out and be there for us again. He left again. I watched him go, again. And I went back to my life, to my kids. To all the things that I didn't have a choice to opt of, that I didn't want a choice to opt out of.

After this first separation, a counseling idea was to tell Jeb he was welcome to come home if he wanted to stay sober. Anytime he wanted, my house, my heart was open to him, if he was willing to choose to be sober. This was a boundary. This was me letting Jeb choose to come home anytime he wanted because I still loved him and wanted him there. To Jeb, it was me having rules for him, me making rules for him to live in his house. Of course, we were both right. It was that. He didn't see it as a choice for him to be there at all, but he agreed. Our house in Mountain Home that we'd kept as a rental was now open, the tenant having given notice that she was leaving before October 15th. She was out a few days before. On October 15th, Jeb moved into our rental house. More time, he just needed a little more time.

It was temporary. Just some time to get adjusted correctly. He could come home anytime, he just had to be sober in the house. We talked, we texted. He was drinking every night; I could hear it in his voice. He was angry and he'd yell about work, about life, about the military, and that no one had been there for him. I'd remind him, softly, that I was there, that I was still, inexorably, there. That's not what he meant, he'd insist. Not what he needed. He didn't have a father figure, his dad had drunken himself into not being there for him, it wasn't fair.

His dad had passed away the year prior, from drinking. He'd held out for all of his kids to get there to say goodbye. He'd said he was sorry. Jeb's mom had bought beer while her husband was dying in the hospital, to make sure that the fridge was full of his only sustenance when he got home. He didn't come home though, he died. She fought to get cirrhosis taken off the death certificate. He'd never been diagnosed prior to his death and it sure as shit wasn't going to be on the death certificate. They took it off. Jeb watched his dad die from alcoholism. He didn't even know if he wanted to say goodbye, but when he was there, everything had fallen away. He held his dad's hand and they said all they needed to, most of it non-verbally, before his dad left. I imagine it was "son, don't be me and I'm sorry I missed so much" and Jeb, "dad, I love you anyway." Now, a year later, here was Jeb, drinking himself down the same path. None of it made sense. What is this power of addiction? Who was it to steal these men away from me? It had chewed up my brother and spit him out broken until it swallowed him completely. And now, my husband was jumping into its embrace. I tried to will that future porch swing into existence. I wished for a point where Jeb could rebuild what he'd lost with the boys. Where we could all sit around a big Christmas dinner and all these men would laugh at how long it had taken them to get to this point of closeness. They'd look at me, they'd know I held that line, I kept us on this path. We'd toast some sparkling cider, and my eyes would be shiny with tears. But no, that's not how it would go. Addiction wasn't done wreaking havoc. Not even close.

Jeb took his wedding ring off. I left mine on. I wasn't quite sure how to go about being done. I read Byron Katie's book, *I Need Your Love – Is that True?* It helped in a slow way. At first a reminder that it was okay to be where I was, and that still having love for Jeb was a good thing too. My interpretation of the book was that I didn't have to decide before I was ready, if I could accept where I was, then when I needed to know, I would know. It took some of the pressure off. I could do this. What did I know in this moment? What decisions could I make? I decided that I needed to do some things for myself. I did three things: I reached to a mom of one of Zeff's friends who I'd seen running, I asked her if she would want to start running with me. I reached out to Jamie, still in Mountain Home and asked her about the powerlifting group she was a part of, she invited me to come. She told me she'd always just wanted me to be happy. And the third thing was something for Columbus. He was struggling and needed a thing to do. We found fencing. I signed him up for an intro class.

Reconnecting with Jamie was nice. It was a reminder of the primary friendship that I'd had as I gained my first bout of strength. It was a reminder of platonic love, we'd both grown and changed so much. It was good to reconnect but living further apart and still having kids and jobs and all the stuff made the reconnection difficult. I think Jamie and I knew that we always have each other if we need it. Perhaps there was something to do with the seasonality of friendship or perhaps not, I don't really know. But I knew that I loved Jamie and she me, and our friendship catalyzed something for us both. It was good.

The new running friend was a breath of fresh air. We started running two mornings a week, early, before work. We talked and we ran. She was about a year out of a horrible relationship;

a relationship that had been borderline abusive to her son and had caused them both some serious heartache. As soon as she'd gotten out of that relationship though, she'd met the woman who changed her life and with whom she was madly in love. She'd literally closed one door, and another had opened. Jeb had been officially moved out for about four weeks and I was starting to feel better but still confused overall with what I wanted to do. Counseling was helping, connection was helping, and my running friend suggested that I may want to just try having coffee with a guy or find something to remind myself that there would be life after.

At running friend's request, I decided to be a little more open to what might be out there. I took my wedding ring off. Literally, the next day, I met a guy. Zeff was playing high school football and I was at a game spectating. One of the parents struck up a conversation with me and we hit it off. He was handsome and funny. His son was on the opposing team and the game flew by, we talked the whole time. Towards the end, he asked if I was dating anyone and I told him no. I told him I was still married, had only recently taken off my ring, and that though my husband wasn't living with me, I was not ready to date. He said that he'd been through a similar situation with his ex-wife and would be a good listener if I did want to talk, even if it wasn't dating.

I didn't want to date too soon, but when I told running friend, she assured me that coffee wouldn't be a big deal and it might just help me get my head a little straighter. After about a week, I sent him a message saying that I thought coffee would be okay. He was all over it. We decided to meet in the afternoon, I'd leave work early and we'd have that coffee. As the time approached, he suggested a drink instead since it was later in the day, so that's what we did. We had the same easy conversation, but it felt so weird to me to be talking to, and flirting with, someone other than Jeb. I was nervous and very unaccustomed to drinking, so I was feeling the glass of wine very strongly. He had two drinks while I had one which felt a little like a red flag, but mostly I was just feeling good to be out and talking and not thinking too much about anything with the weight of a life changing decision. We went for a walk around downtown Boise after the drink, and he immediately held my hand. I was uncomfortable because I worked downtown and my coworkers all knew I was still married and it just felt too soon, I unclasped my hand a couple times but still he reached for it. He tried to kiss me too, but I was not having that. I hadn't thought about the hand-holding limit, but I knew that kissing was past my limit.

We began texting frequently and talking on the phone in the evenings, he wasn't a big sleeper, so he'd want to talk later than I would and for long stretches. I was still enjoying the conversation, but I felt like he was already past where I was by a long shot. The conversations got increasingly flirty, him asking all kinds of sexual questions that I definitely didn't want to answer. Part of me liked the raw attraction that he was showing, but it was also complete disregard for what I was ready for. We went on one more date, a lunch date, this time. I was not feeling great, not sick, but not my normal healthy self and was mentally exhausted. He told me to ditch work, meet him for lunch and then we'd go for a drive. A chill afternoon. Okay, I needed a chill afternoon. Lunch was good, he spoke with easy familiarity to people everywhere we went, I don't know if he knew everyone, or if he was just that much of a people person that it seemed that way.

We went for a drive to a small, hidden town somewhere about forty-five minutes outside of Boise and my unease returned. I didn't want to be this far away from my boys, from everything, with this person I barely knew. On the way back, we stopped by the side of the road for him to show me something cool. He was a tall guy and he tried to pick me up so that I could get a better view. Yes, he tried to pick me up. And he couldn't budge me. He exhorted, "You're much heavier than you look!" Who gets picked up? Small children, pets, I don't know. Not me. A message to any men considering physically picking up women, in most cases, please don't. If for some reason, you do feel like you need to pick a woman up, I wouldn't suggest following up your failure to do so with a phrase about her weight, probably isn't going to win her over.

I continued talking to this "gentleman" for a couple weeks longer. He got more graphic in the detail of sexual acts he wanted to perform and needier with my time. He began telling me that I needed to "loosen up." I told him that I wasn't uptight, this was just who I was. Back to the ol' suggestion that I "loosen up" again. I am NOT uptight; he was just making me uncomfortable and trying to push me right back into not being what I wanted. This, however, was the first time that I recognized being told to "loosen up" as someone telling me to be different. This may seem small, but it was a pretty big shift, like tectonic plate shifting, shift. Jeb had ingrained in me for so long the things he wanted to change about me and I always tried to be what I thought he needed. Here, I was, unwilling. I wasn't changing for pick-me-up-guy. I liked the way I was. The picker-upper continued to let me know he'd be able to loosen me up. Yes. These conversations happened. Additionally, he'd been having a years' long relationship with a married woman. They had a mutual understanding that it was just sexual, however, when he started talking to me, he told her he wanted to cut it off. And she tried to end her life. I quickly realized that this was way too much crazy for me. I told him I didn't want to talk to him anymore. He tried a couple more times, maybe several, but eventually stopped. What a situation. The picker-upper taught me a couple things: that there were other people out there, which was a reminder that I needed, and that I was a lot more comfortable with who I was than I had been in the past. I was still very sensitive to what Jeb's needs were and was trying to avoid making him angry, but as for me, I was who I was.

I kept going to Coby for counseling and even though the shifts that he guided me towards were small, they were helping immensely. I was sticking to the limit that Jeb could come home when he was sober. He still wasn't wearing his ring and he was talking to other women, but he would still tell me that he wanted me sometimes and that he was still working on us. He was working on his drinking, he was working on the rental house, he was working, working, working, but not much was happening, and nothing was changing. Sometimes he would tell me he was ready to come home. But then Friday night would come, and he'd need to go to the rental for something. He'd tell me that he'd come over later. But then he'd go to the rental and drink and then not show up. He'd sleep in until Saturday afternoon and then come over. He'd show up bleary-eyed and with stale alcohol on his breath and seeping out of his pores. It was sad. I wanted to be there for him when I saw him like that. Saturday at two, his resolve would be fresh, he'd want to hang out on the couch, have the family around. He would have packed stuff for a couple nights and he'd stay on Saturday. But then Sunday would come and he'd make it until the middle of the afternoon when anxiety would come over him like a wave. He'd get mad, he'd accuse me of controlling him, he'd say the boys were stressing him out, and he just couldn't do it. He told me I didn't understand how hard I was making it for him, forcing him to be in and out of the house like this. He'd work himself up until the only option was to leave. And he would leave, and it would hurt all over again. Every time he left it was a fresh wound, shallower but just as sore. Having him choose alcohol and going through the blame cycle time after time, was exhausting. Nevertheless, I persisted. I kept taking care of the boys, kept getting them to all their activities, didn't miss any work, and I kept working on my master's degree. The finish line for that was almost on the horizon, just a little over a year away. And of course, I kept running. It was the one foot in front of the other approach, every day, day in, day out, keep forward motion.

One weekend that fall, Jeb invited the boys and I over to his house. Jeb had told me he'd be sober. He wanted to show me all the progress he'd made. He'd let me know over and over again that I'd made him start over, that he'd left everything with me and had had to start from scratch. Zeff was busy, but Col and I agreed that we'd try it. We went over on a Friday night and Jeb had ordered a pizza and rented a movie. We sat down to eat, and I noticed that Jeb was carrying a cup around everywhere he went. I also noticed his eyes. They were not sober eyes. At first, I suspended my limits. He invited us, it was his house, and I didn't want to drive the forty-five minutes home, I could stay and just see how this would go. We ate, he was drunk, and it wasn't beer. This drunk started out with niceness, but the edge was there. We started the movie after dinner and Jeb spent most of the time either in the garage or in the kitchen, he only sat with us for a few minutes. And then the anger came. Columbus was made to go to bed and fortunately for him, he fell asleep quickly.

A note about this house: It was still the first house we'd bought, still full of those first house memories, back when thrift stores were my friend, and my boys were babies. Where sandboxes and mud pits gave way to treehouses and bike jumps which gave way to pizza parties and movies with friends. It was where I moved back in to after having been apart from Jeb the first time. And it was where we'd built an extra room.

When I was pregnant with Orion, before we'd bought the dream house, we did a little remodel and put in a fourth bedroom. A nursery. New carpet and paint and cute little closet, we built it for him. Every time I went back there, I wanted to sit in his room, and I also wanted to run from it. And there I was, Columbus sleeping on a mattress on the floor of that room and Jeb drunk and angry. He was angry that I hadn't talked to him enough that night, though he'd been outside most of the evening, that I'd seemed like something was "off." Angry that I'd made him be there. And whatever else could be snowballed in. It was strange to be back in that house where all of his verbal garbage had begun. Where I'd sat, huddled and crying, while names were called and threats were made, where holes had been punched and so many, many things. Now here I was. My younger son sleeping, my husband from whom I was separated drinking and yelling. I didn't want to be here. I told Jeb I wanted to leave, but without much resolve. I went to bed, thinking that if I just went to sleep, it would work itself out. But it felt wrong. I started to feel that rumble of something I just couldn't quite stomach, I knew this wasn't the right thing. I told Jeb I was leaving, he told me how wrong it was, what a poor parent I was to wake Columbus up to take him home. But I didn't listen this time. I woke Columbus and packed him into the car. We left. I left. I left the drunkenness and the anger, the accusation. I took my son, my car, and my newfound strength. I left Orion's room, left that house, left those painful memories. I took me. I drove through some tears and some feeling I wasn't familiar with, in the chest and around the heart. It's a solid pressure with some electricity to it. It's what strengthening feels like it.

I thought back to a time in Panama City Beach when I worked at Harco Drugs. Van had left a couple of hickeys on my face to show that I was not single. Why hickeys on the face, I have no idea. It was probably the act of holding me down and doing something that should have been act of physical intimacy through force, that made her feel like it would be an obvious display of being taken. Her territory had been marked, the fight was out of me, I was probably laying dejectedly when it happened. They faded to nasty bruise-looking marks. Some handsome, young, navy guys who were regulars, noticed them. They said to each other and a little to me, something about they might have been worried, but they could tell I wasn't the type to be hit. But anyone can get hit. We get held down while marks are put upon us, we get called cunt and bitch and whore, we get told if we didn't think we were better than everyone else this wouldn't be happening. We can all be the type because there is no type.

That night, for truly what felt like the first time in my life, I left an abusive situation. It was horrible and liberating. Jeb called the next day to apologize, he knew he shouldn't have acted that way, that I was right and he overreacted. He shouldn't have been drinking when I got there. A little of the back and forth continued, but mostly he stayed at the other house. He called many nights, always drinking, sometimes yelling, sometimes apologizing. I stayed on the roller coaster, talking it through with Coby, setting new limits where it made sense. Being not married was feeling like a more and more real outcome, it was going from ideation to reality. I wanted to be sure I'd get the boys, though, and that was something we couldn't agree on. Jeb said when we talked about it, he wanted them half the time. I couldn't imagine not having them home, I honestly couldn't imagine being home alone for any stretches of time. It wasn't how I defined myself or how I felt like myself. Talking to Coby, it gave me instant feelings of panic to think of evenings in my big house all by myself. The feeling was similar to when I had suspected Jeb had been drinking while travelling for the past several years, clenching and gnawing. But that's what divorce meant. It meant that I might not have my boys with me all the time. I hated the thought.

Chapter 27
The Final Straw

"Standing out on the ledge
With no way to get down
You start praying for wings to grow
Oh, baby, just let go"

-Nathaniel Rateliff & The Night Sweats, And It's Still Alright

We invited Jeb over for Thanksgiving. The boys and I wanted to get out of town, though. It had been a crazy fall for us, so many ups and downs. They also never knew if their dad would be around or not. He'd missed all of Zeff's freshman football season, he'd missed so much. Jeb was going to be there "early," but he missed that too. He arrived mid-afternoon, wearing sunglasses, lethargic and with a headache. He ambled up the stairs to the door and went to the couch while I finished cooking a small, simple dinner. We always said what we were thankful for and that year, I don't remember what mine was, I'm pretty sure Jeb's had something to do with family. I talked to Zeff about our trip out of town, he didn't want his dad to join us. I didn't quite have it in me to tell Jeb that no, we didn't want him to come, but Zeff did. This boy's strength and resolve left me in awe. I knew that it wasn't from me, or maybe it was. But if it was, it was from a part of me I couldn't yet regularly tap into.

Jeb said that he understood; I was excited to get out of town. We picked up one of Zeff's friends and headed out for the four-hour trip to Salt Lake City. We had an Airbnb and no agenda. We got hamburgers that night and just relaxed. My soul was breathing. Jeb called that night and his understanding had evaporated. He was so upset that we'd taken a trip without him, how could we, how could I plan a holiday trip and exclude him? I tried to explain it away, explain it as more than what it really was. The truth was that I needed to be away from him and I had every fucking right to travel wherever I wanted to, but that's not what I said. I placated. I did not have Zeff's strength of conviction. The next morning, I went for a run with a light snow falling on my face. It was the most refreshing hour I'd had in a long time. Towards the end of the run, though, I got that panic thing again. I'd left the boys in a strange place, it was snowing, what if something happened? What if I'd taken them on this trip and left them while I ran, only for this strange house to catch fire or have a break in? This panic thing was far from my natural state, and it was something that started happening more regularly as the separation and impending divorce from Jeb got more real. I was scared to mess up. I was scared to make a solo choice that might harm the boys. I was scared to let them do the things that Jeb would have said no to knowing there was a possibility they might get hurt, they might not be safe. Before, imperfect though it was, I had him to say no whenever I wasn't sure about a parenting decision. Even if I'd try to convince him, his no was always final. Not anymore and it scared me. I guess my own power scared me.

I got back from the run, and we spent a couple hours meandering around the Natural History Museum. It was just what I needed to contemplate my place in the Universe with all the tumult going on. How big and how small my worries. We drove back to Boise that day, family. Zeff, his friend, Col, and me, against the world.

We had a month until Christmas, Columbus was still fencing, Zeff was wrestling, I was schooling and working, and we were making it. Jeb would show up once in a while, not when he said, and we'd adjust. A couple times, he showed up drunk at night telling me I was all he wanted and all he would ever want. He knew family was the most important thing and I'd put up with so much already, if I could just hang on a little more, he had so much left to give me. Please work it out with him. And sometimes he'd show up cold and upset to get something he'd left and barely look at or speak to me. And I'd want him to. I wanted the intensity of that love to be showered down, even when the other side hurt so bad.

Coby talked to me about that, about how a relationship might feel if it didn't have such intensity. At the time I didn't know what he meant. That's what love felt like to me. We talked about the what if's of Jeb moving on. What it would be like when he was with someone else, and they picked up the boys together. What it would be like if he had a baby with someone else, when I'd wanted one so badly. I could imagine the pain of it. But I did not understand the question about love feeling different.

The in between time was weird. There was more of all of it; name calling, yelling, crying, and being left. There was another incident when Columbus was slammed against a wall by his neck. He went for a walk after that and didn't immediately come home. I was worried sick, but still some part of me tried to assuage Jeb. I went for a run looking for Col, calling his phone, calling Zeff to ask if he knew what was happening. Col was in the backyard. He needed some time. My strong little boy, I'm sorry I didn't do more on that day. I'm so sorry that I let your dad stay after he did that. My sweet boy, with so much happening in your head, every moment. I didn't do enough for you. You deserved better.

And then it was Christmas and yet another new resolve. Jeb said he was done drinking, again. He came over Christmas Eve or maybe even the day before. And he didn't drink, he was true to his word. We made it through Christmas and the days between Christmas and New Year's Eve. There were still some anger-tinged moments, but mostly he was just there. None of us knew how to take it. I didn't trust it, but hope still peeked through. On New Year's Eve, Jeb went to drop one of Zeff's friends off and it took a little longer than what I thought it would. Col and I were going to make homemade pizza that night and Zeff was having a couple of friends over. Jeb went to the garage and came back up with those eyes. I didn't know it yet then, but it was a two bottle of Jack night. He was acting weird with the boys, standing behind Col to help him cut veggies for the pizza, being loud and rough housing with Zeff. I could see where it was going, and I did not like it. This night was not going to be good. More time away, a few minutes here and there and every time he came in, it was worse. And then he had his gun with him. The hanging-out-with-the-boys sentiment was gone, anger had replaced it. He yelled at Col, following him to his room, I followed too, getting him to leave Col alone and getting scared for myself. Zeff's friends didn't know what was happening, I tried to keep it that way. Finally, in a rage, Jeb left drunk in his truck to go shooting. He drove away drunk on New Year's Eve to go shoot. I called a cop friend and asked what to do. I didn't know where he was going, not even the direction, but I didn't want him out there on the road. As I talked through it, and decided to call the police, Jeb came home. Even drunker. He still had the gun, I suspected it was loaded since he'd just been shooting. He was acting like he couldn't hear out of one ear, and I didn't know if it was true or not. Zeff's friends thought it was hilarious to see him drunk stumbling around and saying "What?" after everything. I got the boys downstairs and asked them to stay there, and Jeb followed me up to our bedroom. I asked him if he'd give me the gun or at least take it off in the house, he shook his head slowly. He said he felt like he needed in the house that night. He pulled it out of his waistband and aimed it at the floor, also at my feet. Enough at my feet that the threat was there. Enough for fear, but not enough to stop me from trying to reason with him. Then with it aimed at my feet/floor, he cocked his gun. And that was it. I told him to leave. I said that he had to leave. It was not an option to stay. He said I couldn't kick him out of his house, it was his house too. I said that I'd take the boys and go, but we were not all staying. I told him I'd pay for his Uber back to the Mountain Home house; he wasn't driving, and he wasn't staying. He kept the gun loaded, grabbed his keys, and left. It was fear I think, but I still didn't call the cops. I remember only relief that he was gone. And that was my rock bottom.

He came back the next morning; he'd slept in his truck not far from the house. I wanted to take the boys to a mountain bike park that day despite the fact that it was freezing. He told me no, we couldn't use the truck, but ended up relenting. I didn't want to have to ask him for anything and I realized that what advantages there were of any semblance of togetherness, were about to be gone. I used the time that afternoon to run while the boys biked and to think about the path forward. Always forward.

When I went in for my appointment with Coby the next week, he listened to the New Year's story. He looked somewhat somber while I was describing how Jeb had been with the boys and how he'd been with the gun. He said to me, "You know that's what we call a domestic incident." He told me that I could have gotten a restraining order and although he didn't say I "should" have called the cops, it was implicit in his words. A domestic incident. I hadn't thought of it that way. He told me that whether or not I'd felt seriously in danger, those were just the kinds of situations that resulted in far more serious consequences than what the boys and I had experienced. Two bottles of Jack, a gun, anger, and a wife from whom you're separated. It felt like a crazy story that had happened to me, not that I was a part of. Maybe my brain was protecting itself, maybe because I knew it could have been worse. Either way, I didn't feel traumatized by it. It turned out to be the thing I needed, to know what to do. It's sad that that's what it took. I guess I was addicted too. I needed that thing, the thing I had called love, so deeply and so intensely, that I kept coming back despite what it did to me. But I got my rock bottom too. And I was done.

Rock bottom, final straw (the one that breaks the poor camel's back), the moment of absolute clarity…all the terms we use to describe the things that catalyze change. I thought back to my mom's break; when I had been called that straw and she broke. She broke down and there was no going back. I broke through, no going back for me either. Maybe I'd been making up for her breakdown for a long time, maybe it was atonement that from then until my break, I didn't ever take care of myself first. Or maybe, especially as a mom, I believed that to take care of others was the highest good and lost myself in the shuffle. Standing in my bedroom though, the room in which I had loved the man holding the gun, I experienced the straw breaking the camel's back in a whole different way. It had come full circle. Yes, it broke me, but I broke free, I did not break down.

Jeb didn't want to go back to the Mountain Home house after that. He told me our house was his house too and he was right. I told him if he insisted on staying either he or I could sleep on the couch until one or the other of us found another place. I wasn't taking the boys and myself to Mountain Home to live and I wasn't leaving, but I wasn't living with him as a couple. The blame game began again, all the ways it was my fault, all the ways it was unreasonable. I told him I was willing to be the one to sleep on the couch, but he told me he would. I think he did for maybe one night. It was miserable for me, but he was right, I didn't feel like it was within my power to kick him out. He chose to go, though, back to the Mountain Home house, leaving us in the mix of tumult and peace that remained in his wake. It was a lot; I was reeling without really knowing. I felt like I'd stood my ground, but I don't even think I could find the ground.

So many things about that time are blurry and dull. I remember looking at Jeb and thinking there was no way I'd ever not love him; no way I wouldn't still be deeply attracted to him. I felt like I was choosing not to be with the person I loved because I couldn't, for myself and for the kids, not that maybe this wasn't really what it felt like to love someone, or to be loved. There were moments I still felt like we were giving up a future that had potential. Like I was giving it up.

About a month before this end, he had shared something with me. Jeb had literally made a list of the things about me he wasn't happy enough with. A physical list of the ways I wasn't enough. He referenced it one night and then another in his anger and I almost didn't believe it existed. He had made it at work. It wasn't a drunken deluge of words, strung together with a loosened tongue. It was thought out and added to over time. It included things such as: that I didn't care about the same things he did, that I wasn't materialistic enough and didn't want to keep upping the quality of our lives through the acquisition of better stuff. Also that I was always okay with what we had. He thought I didn't want to get better. Apparently keeping up with the Joneses wasn't my thing and that had really impacted him. It was pages long and very hurtful to have him read it to me. There was more, of course, but those were the things that stuck. It's funny when you've perhaps felt that you aren't enough for a person and heard it in different subtler ways and then when you hear it out loud, the confirmation feels not quite like what you expected. Validating in some ways, to know that there were actual words and concrete things that hadn't met his standard. I'd wanted to be accepted for who I was, we all do, but here was this big other thing. I didn't buy curtains at your first suggestion, now I understood how serious you thought that was. You wanted a curtained house, you wanted me to buy them, I didn't. To me this was nothing, but you added it to the growing list. On some deep-down level, it was freeing. It wasn't me who wasn't enough after all, it was some sort of strange expectations that I didn't live up to and that list confirmed that I was *exactly* who I wanted to be. I was still me. After all of that. Still running, still paying attention to the foods I put in body, still basing my life on the love of the people in it, and not how they were adorned. Here we were, upper-middle class. I wasn't carrying around a backpack on my back and a baby carrier on my front while sleeping on people's beds or couches. I wasn't down to seventeen dollars in my account to take care of three people for a week. Financially, we were comfortable, and things had shifted. But my strength gathering had taken shape, my force was there unscathed. That list was my liberation. Thank God I wasn't enough for him, and that I was for me.

After our domestic incident, I had moments of doubt. It didn't shut off like a switch. It was still hard to know if this was best for the boys. Divorce is not little thing; would they think it was silly that I had done it twice? Jeb kept the rollercoaster going full speed. Some days he'd text me and ask if we could just forget everything that was happening and remember us. Remember being together. We'd hug sometimes and it still felt like home. In those moments I felt weak, I wanted the comfort of what I'd known, but I wanted the strength to walk away from it. I don't generally use the word abuse, even though I know that's the description for what my children and I experienced. However, I do know that abused bodies and minds find comfort in familiarity. Being with what you know is easy. And you will pick it many times. A harmless hug, a comforting hug, can be enough to start the cycle again. It's surprising how little it takes. But this time was different for me. Something essential had shifted. He wanted to go on a date. I said no. It got incrementally easier. By degrees, always by degrees, but this time the direction was right.

He went to a couple AA meetings, drinking in between them with no serious attempt at sobriety, and wrote me a couple of apology letters. The letters were nice, but felt insincere because I knew he hadn't done the work. He knew the deeds to apologize for and he knew the words to use, but there was no change of behavior. It was, it finally was, over.

I had so, so, so much work to do. There were pieces so broken and pieces so strong, griefs I hadn't grieved, and my children whom I'd wronged. I was still there for them; I showed them love every day, cooked all their food, spectated all their sports, helped with homework, and was plainly present, but I could have done better. It's hard too, to know that you can't undo childhood. There are no take backs. This is woven. I hope it has woven threads of strength. I hope they are threads of steel. I hope, my sweet boys have learned who they do and do not want to be.

Chapter 28
Still Gathering

"I believe the truth is around us all the time. The anonymous angels, the butterflies, the answers, are always right there, but we don't always identify, grasp, hear, see or access them — because we're not in the right place to."

-Matthew McConaughey, Greenlights

Significant things continued to happen, little nudges, little proofs from the Universe that yes, finally, I was learning to listen. First and foremost, whether ready or not, I met someone, or got to know better someone whom I had met a few months prior. He asked me out on a date. It would have been his first in a while, I said no, I said that I wasn't ready. But then I changed my mind. I told him yes, that I did want to go on a date. We were both a little rusty on the dating thing, despite my very recent experience with the picker-upper. Maybe we were rusty at normal dating, that sounds about right. Of course, this wasn't quite normal either because I wasn't yet legally divorced which neither of us felt great about. The nice things were manifold; emotional maturity, honesty and a very, very slow pace. We saw each other once or twice a week while I worked towards a legal end of my marriage. He listened to me. He held me and gave me respite, he assuaged my doubts without trying. It was, so calm. He did things for me because they were things that I liked, no agenda, nothing for him. All of these things may sound like small building blocks of a normal, healthy relationship to those who have experienced them, to me it was revolutionary.

Coby had asked how I might adjust to a relationship that didn't have the intense ups and downs and I hadn't known what he meant. Now I did. Calm. It was so calm. He was the same all the time, every day, day in and day out. Revelatory. It took some adjusting; Coby had been right. It didn't feel the same. I had mistaken intensity for love so long that I had to relearn. I had so much learning to do, and I had the space to do so.

Jeb and I filed for divorce together. We agreed on the terms. I put 50/50 custody in the agreement knowing it would never happen, but that he'd agree to it that way. Otherwise, he told me, he'd fight. I still felt sad the day we filed, it made me sick to my stomach. I drank a glass of champagne, putting it into an already cramping stomach and threw it up a few hours later. Finally, I felt better. One last expulsion to get Jeb out of my system.

He had told me, told the boys, that I couldn't afford the house on my own. In our divorce agreement, we agreed that he'd get the house in Mountain Home, all of the money he'd put into stock and all the nicer vehicles (which were all his anyway) and I'd get the Boise house. It was expensive enough to make me house poor, but I could do it. Barely, but I could. I told the boys I'd keep as much the same for them as I could. They'd been through enough. So, I kept the house that would again make the checks tight and that I had never really felt at home in. They got to stay in their rooms. To me, that was important.

So much changed. All things that had been tense, were no longer stressful. Dinner was just dinner and I even stopped cooking it some nights. A strange effect, perhaps, but after all the years of all the cooking, sometimes we just wanted to fend for ourselves, and we did. Sometimes I let them eat in their rooms. I didn't know if that was the right thing or not, but it felt like the pendulum had to swing back from forced family time that left us all uncomfortable, to being together by choice. Even when they didn't always choose it. I chose to give them more freedom than they'd ever had and began parenting in a new way. I let them choose. I decided that I wanted them to learn to make choices now, so they weren't bombarded with the opportunity after they left home. We were all adjusting.

Zeff spent a lot of time in his room that first year. It hurt my heart, but he needed the space, and I gave it to him. He was so strong, and I could see it. He told me one day in the car, early on, that he didn't want Jeb and I to get divorced. Jeb had been out of the house for months when we had the discussion. I asked him what he meant and he told me that his dad had told him we'd have to move soon. I told him we wouldn't. I asked if he wanted his dad to move back in. NO! That wasn't what he wanted at all. He wanted us to stay separated, but not to move. He wanted things to be the same. Divorce felt like another change. He said like he did as a small kid, I don't want you to get in a divorce. I loved that phrase. It made it seem as if divorce were an accident, something that might befall you. But I was getting a divorce, not getting in one. I gathered and I chose.

Columbus, sweet Columbus, the first year was hard on him too. At first, he spent a lot of time with me and had some anger towards Jeb and at some point, it shifted, and I got it full force. I didn't know how it would end and for a time I felt like I had lost him. I spent nights crying, scared that our relationship would never be the same. I loved him so deeply.

I wrote:

To Col,

I love more than the word love could ever put
bounds on.

To name it one thing would be a vast
understatement.

Your heart, your eyes, your smile

With such depth, I wish I had done, and could do
more to protect you from pain, because you feel it
differently

I see it seep through you and wish I could hug
it away, like when you were little, curled into my
arms.

I see you striving towards independence when I
still feel your needs so keenly, feeling that I should
be but can't be, doing more

So I'll spend more time

Maybe saying yes to watching you play video
games a little too often

Maybe clinging a little too tightly in a hug

Maybe putting aside my own tiredness when you
ask me to stay up a few more minutes

Maybe, maybe, I can hope, it will insulate, envelope,
and keep you safe just a little bit more

And to no one in particular I wrote:

But have you really wondered, thought about, how
we have become these versions of ourselves?

Older because we age

Wiser because we have hurt

But a self that is different from a younger version

Or is it?

What is it that pain does?

Not embitter, at least not always, but does it
temper?

Taking something, something essential, and
carefree and attaching tethers.

Answering what-ifs with blows to something
simple, pure, and believing

How can I remember with joy,

Living in a motel, a baby attached to my breast?

Hours and hours pounding the pavement in a
cheap running stroller

You had only socks, no shoes

Your tiny feet shuddering slightly as you slept

Everything seemed bright and shiny and perfect

The cliché of love being enough, seems somehow
puerile and expectedly naïve

In the sixteen summers since then…

Even the taste of love has changed

And then there was:

I felt the weight of loss today,

Like holes where parts used to be

Phoenix, a little hole, but deep, somewhere around
my shoulder

Orion a gaping spot on top of my right lung,
sometimes sucking in the beat of my heart

Jeb, a massive chunk around my abdomen

A big spot where hope and promises fell in,

Where trust disappeared

I try to fill them up, from inside

But I don't always want to,

I like the sharp edges, the missing-ness

But what comes next?

Do they, like scars, turn pink and small

With puckered edges?

Do they get patched?

Does love patch them more quickly, or do they
stay on their own timeline, slugging along, until
they are muted

I was working through a lot, to say the least. It would take years.
I had less than a year left of graduate school. I kept stepping
one foot in front of the other. In those first months, Jeb saw the
boys sporadically, if at all. I kept dating and I remembered what
smiling and laughing without any strings felt like. I kept running,
whenever I could fit it in. Some of my running was happening early

mornings on the treadmill while the boys slept. I started watching videos on ultrarunning. I had run a couple of 50ks, but I wanted to go longer. I wanted the feeling of pushing my limits. I'd had limits imposed upon me in so many ways, it was time to figure out a few edges on my own. It's strange to think of the ways I limited myself to prevent others from imposing the limits they would. Running ultras, though, was a way that I could transcend, and it just felt right for my soul. There is so much freedom in locomotion.

I set my sights on the 50-mile distance. A day on the trails, I could do this. No one could tell me that I couldn't. I was living in the same house, I had my boys, I had my job, I had my education, and I had my running shoes. I didn't have a spouse and had never really had a partner. Not all that much had changed, but also everything had changed. I was different. What was it that was so different this time? For so long, I'd gone back to situations of poor treatment, I'd never really extricated myself. Now, though, I knew with finality that it was final. I was out.

Chapter 29
Scout Mountain

"It was then that I realized, I wasn't being pushed around by a force.
I was the force."

-Me

I decided to run Scout Mountain Ultra in Pocatello on June 1st of 2019. Scout Mountain was a fifty-four-mile race, the first thirty miles of which had some serious elevation shifts, followed by ten-ish miles uphill to Scout Mountain, and ten-ish miles downhill to the Start/Finish. Alycia was going to run the twenty-mile event, which was the last twenty miles of my course. My dad was coming too.

June 1st, 2019, I was still forty years old, it was a couple of weeks before I turned forty-one. I felt like I was in some of the best shape of my life, but it was more than just physical. I was getting strong in a new way. It was early still, but I was starting to feel like someone different. The version of myself that had cried, huddled and alone, had wanted to be held after revelations of cheating, and had gone back again and again, she was slipping away. It was time to say goodbye to her. But like divorce, even when we should, it's still hard. She had been me, been with me, for so long. She'd pop up every now and again, I'd feel the pull of a weaker version of myself for a moment, a version that I didn't need anymore. It took so long to gather the courage to say goodbye, but that's where I was running to. Oh yeah, and to the top of Scout Mountain.

Early in the morning on June 1ˢᵗ, my dad took me to the Start. My dad, there for all of it. Like he'd dropped me off at the airport when I was eighteen, to say goodbye not knowing if I would ever come back to him. I did come back after that goodbye, forever changed. And in all the years since, had he ached, had he hurt, had he been unsure how to be there? Maybe, but he always showed up. Always. He dropped me off at the Start, he waited until the runners took off, and he drove away, but he'd be back. Of course he would.

I had no idea what I was getting into. I had a theoretical idea, but I hadn't run longer than thirty-one miles, this was almost a marathon longer than that. I stood at the Start with the other runners, I had my vest and my headlamp on. Ready. Not sure what was coming, but ready. I took off on some single track that was slow going, the pack dense at the start. The sun started to come up and beauty was abundant, it infiltrated every part of me. The sun had risen. It was beautiful…yes, die Sonne Scheint. It was shining on me. I ran those first thirty miles, some of which was so steep I had to scrabble hand over hand the ground in front of me. My goodness, this was hard. "Did anyone tell you this was going to be easy??" No, no they didn't.

And then the last twenty miles started. Up, up, ever up. The three miles at the top of Scout had snowpack. At the very top, there was section of snowpack so deep and thick we had to slide on our butts to get down it. There was no other way. I wanted to quit, but I couldn't. I had to get down, I had to keep going. I slid off track a little; for a moment I wasn't even sure where the course was, but I figured it out and got back on and I just kept moving.

The best part of the race was the end. Columbus had been waiting for me for hours. It had taken so much longer than I had predicted, my family worried briefly whether I had gotten lost. Finally, seventeen hours after I began, I was coming in, and there was Columbus to finish up with me. I was so happy and so emotional to see him there. We finished up that last little bit together and there were my dad and my sister at the line. It was perfect. I had come so far, from showing up in Keds my freshman year of high school, finishing my first 5k, my first marathon, my college cross country, and my 1000-mile pregnancy. It had led up to this. This perfect moment. The race director was waiting for me. I was one of the last to finish. He hugged me. It was a great hug. I told him this was my first 50-miler. He said, "You picked a hell of a first." Yeah, that I did. Easy. No. But I guess the easy route was never really my thing.

Epilogue

"Grow roses from the poop."

-Tiffany Haddish, The Last Black Unicorn

That is, as you may suspect, not a true end, but a beginning. It has been over two years since that run and there was so much more right on the horizon. I got my graduate degree that December. I was able to keep my boys and myself in our house with financial stability. I got a new job. I watched my boys and felt pride. But there were moments too that weren't great, days that I cried, nights that I questioned my direction. I took the occasional step backwards and said hello to past selves, but I never stepped too far back. The lessons learned are manifold. We are all collections of our best and worst selves, I can strive every day to feel and be my best version, but sometimes it's healthy to remember and to feel the other sides too. Why? Because, Proustian, though it may be, that great, heart-breaking suffering has brought me here. It's brought these versions together at this perfect moment and that moment always exists.

I can be for a moment, back on the high school cross country trails in Germany. Crispy leaves swirling around as I forged intervals through the so-familiar routes. I can be in my first apartment in Florida, borrowing ten dollars that would come out of my next check from the Blimpie register, to make it through the week. I can be walking down the halls of Gulf Coast State College, followed by my girlfriend as she whispered insults about what I wanted to do, to whom. I can be running at Florida State, shrinking myself down while realizing my division one dreams. I can experience again the ache of loneliness I felt in Germany watching my mother's depression steal her away. And then there was the rest of my life. Jeb and Zeff, coming into my life so close together in whole scheme of things. Ah, finally, a family of my own. Seeing Phoenix give me a thumbs up on the ultrasound screen. She was telling me she was okay, but not the okay that I thought, not the okay that meant I'd get to hold her at my breast. It was okay, I would be okay, and hold her little, tiny translucent body one and only one time. My Columbus, scaring me so deeply before you were even born. I could always count on your intensity. Idaho. Eeek. How dare you? The first long, slow goodbye to Jeb. Walking down the aisle with a sober Jeb, my dad giving me away. Sure, so sure, that that was it. That was it. Orion and Jon, you left me almost together. This sloughing away of what felt like the most essential elements. Worn down to the nub but prepared, I guess, to say goodbye again. One more goodbye, another big one. It took everything, all the strength. All the words I didn't say, the thoughts I wrapped up, the repressed moments of strength, they were all still there. A huge rubber band ball in my core, building and building, until they could bounce out together, a cohesive unit of strength. Done. Free. Free to run fifty miles, free to grow. Free to not be stuck. The gathering and the letting go of everything I wanted to hold the most.

I have thought about so much as I've gotten these words down and in this form. Back to that bathtub splash when my water broke and all the life and loss that has happened between then and now. It's been a lot, that's for sure and I wonder about the balance of the way I've represented it all. Is it too dark? Do I miss the light parts or gloss over them too much? Because they were there too, even in the darkest moments, they are always there. The trick, of course, isn't to avoid the darkness, it's to always be finding the light. Your pupils will adjust, but don't get to the point that you can only see in the dark, that the dark feels like home. It did feel like my home for a time, but I had light at my fingertips, through my boys, through my friends and tribe, through my running shoes. The writing has allowed me to let some of the residual darkness out of my soul. I hope that I have learned to love, even from a distance, all of those of whom I have written. For they've had their own battles too and it's only because our battles were joint battles, that I've had the gift of being able to commit to paper, where those battles intersected. Our ending points might be different, they are different, but for a while at least we fought together. I hope that I've found forgiveness, I feel most of the time that I have, but it's a hard thing. Something that I will keep working on, as I remember that Die Sonne Scheint. And that it doesn't have to be easy for it to be amazing.

I've also considered how it will be for my boys to read this. I want them to be proud of me, like I am of them, but parts of this may not make them feel that way. I questioned at first whether they might be mad at their dad for some parts or mad at me for writing it down. Maybe one or both of those things will be true, but I hope not. I hope they understand better, but my main worry is that they won't. That they might read these words and think, mom, why did you stay? Why did you keep going back? Why couldn't you be as strong as you want us to be? I worry that they might be disappointed that it took me so long and that they might realize how unfair it was to them that I stayed when I did. To that, I would tell them only that I know they would do better, and I hope, above all hopes, that their babies and future partners always see the strong, loving men I have raised them into.

I would also like to, I need to, apologize to them. It still feels bad to write, the truth of it is weighty. I'm okay saying what comes next because of who I am now, because of the healing that we've all done. The easy route would be to say that I "did the best I could with what I had", but it's more important to me to recognize that, "there my loves, at that moment, I could have done better." And that's really what it is. It doesn't matter if it was the best that I could do then because the truth is, I'm sorry that their childhood exposed them to some of the things I hoped it wouldn't. I'm sorry that I acted like it was okay and I'm really sorry that sometimes I picked their dad over them. That's the hardest to write and the truest thing. I never should have comforted him before them after an outburst. But I did. I did that. And it wasn't my best.

Boys, please do and be better. I loved you before I loved myself and that will always be true. And although the fact may be obvious that I gave you life, simply by being the vessel through which you greeted the earth, the real truth is that you gave it to me. From the moment, the very first fraction of a second, of knowing that my

Zeff was on his way, you have made me better. For that, my boys, I am grateful. Your hearts grew in me, they coursed first my blood, but then and now, it is the watching of them as you learn to love and protect them on your own, that makes mine beat. My boys, my life. You are me, you made me.

I'd also like to take the space to apologize to myself. I'd like to apologize for not knowing how to put myself first when I needed to. There are many places in the writing of this missive that I felt compelled to go back to the girl I was. And sometimes, I want to hold that past self and comfort her and tell her she will be okay. But I recognize, there was a point in this book that I didn't need to have that wish anymore. At some point, it changed from a dirge to a melody, a melody about gathering, even if it didn't sound like a song.   Like the water pulling back from the shore before a powerful wave is summoned and released. There was a point that that girl switched from giving to gathering. Grains of strength, had become pebbles. One blow, another, and another, and she withstood. She gathered. She was getting ready. As I read books now by powerful women who have overcome pasts, I recognize this gathering in all of them. There was a time of stuck, a time when all the evidence pointed to a different eventuality than where they ended up, a time when the message was fuzzy or they didn't know how to listen. But once that crescendo builds, when it reaches that critical mass, you may want to move out of the way, out of *her* way.

And a few epiphanies realized in the writing of it:

On the nature of love: I thought that if I could accept apology for every egregious act, then I had shown unconditional love. Accepting every apology and every bad behavior meant that my love was true. I NEVER asked myself, not a single time, if he should stop acting in a way that required apology. If that was how he should have loved me. *Love isn't shown by a capacity to accept.*

On the nature of the Universe: 1) The voice of the Universe is always there if you are ready to listen, but if you ignore her enough times, she might just say fuck it, try it your way and let's see how it goes. 2) There is always, always a door at the end of every dead end. 3) The Universe respects the blind courage to fake it until you make it. 4) The big one, if you put on your shoes and move forward, you don't have to stay stuck, but you have to choose some small motion. It doesn't matter how small, but has to be intentional and it has to come from within.

"Move, you got this" – the Universe

I went to a graduation party this past summer for the daughter of Athena. She was the oldest of our kids and the first to finish high school. Athena's husband told me that I looked taller. "Didn't she get taller?" he asked a couple times.

Taller, no. I am not taller, but I have let go of the yoke. I am not crouching down under the weight of stuckness anymore. Do I look taller? You know, maybe I am. Maybe it's because I'm breathing deep, maybe you can see all that I have gathered to me. I breathed deeply and like iron ore to a magnet, my size has expanded. I am just more me. No longer whittled down, no longer concerned with being the smallest version of myself. This is me, writ large.

So, what's next Universe? I have gathered my strength and I am ready.

Acknowledgements

There are so many people who were a part of this manuscript and, for one reason or another, their part in getting me here was minimized or excluded.

Foremost among the undermentioned is my sister, Alycia. She is not as fully represented in these words as she should be, because she knows better than anyone all of these struggles, but she has her own story of them. To have assumed her perspective or her experience of it because I knew what mine was, would have been unfair. But she has been, and is always, there for me. She is there in the undercurrent of many of these stories. To Alycia, thank you for loving me, for accepting me, and for being my sister. Whether it was driving me to Aberdeen and leaving me at that motel against your better judgement or running the streets and trails of Portland as I told you about Orion, you've been there. My ride or die. My sister.

To Jeb, you gave me the best gift of my life in our boys, for that I will always be grateful. And you made me test my wings when I finally got out there to the ledge. I wish for you healing.

To the Kinderbloom women, my first coworkers at the daycare, you gave me the first building blocks that set this whole thing in motion. You fed my spirit those first few bites.

My IDOL family, you were just that, my family. Without you, I never could have kept going.

Ray Cotton, your words, your encouragement, at once paternal and full of care. You let me cry at your desk and reminded me that I was okay, that it would be okay. You were the first to tell me that you saw something special in me when I needed to hear it most.

You kept me on the path.

To Athena (Idaho Jessica), you were my symbol of strength.

To Jamie, we transformed together and held hands through some of the hardest times for both of us.

To Alejandra, you taught and continue to teach me how to set standards for yourself and stick to them.

To Vicki P., the miles we walked, the things we shared, you kept me going with the constant reminder that life keeps on, you were a friend who mothered me, and you always had tissues.

To Jessica, the friend of my life. You know all the secrets of my heart and have loved me through every single one. You continue to remind me that trust is real, and that people can be true. You give me the comfort of knowing that in this life, I will never be alone.

To Andy, thank you for the time and the space to heal, for giving comfort to my soul.

To my boys, you make me want to do and be more. You make me want to keep fighting. I will always show up for you. Thank you for keeping me going. Thank you for being my reason for one foot in front of the other when I couldn't find it in myself.

To my running shoes, thirty years so far, let's keep this thing going.

I'd also like to extend a thank you to Leah, my editor, without whom this book would have been a record but not a story. And a thank you to Emma, for finding a mistake the rest of us missed.

And to all the others, thank you for the pieces and the parts, the smiles, the words, the pushes, all of it. To all of the angels who were there at exactly the right moment, reminding me, sometimes softly, sometimes loudly, that you have to ask if you are to receive. Thank you.

9 798985 744811